SMART SCHOOLS

BETTER THINKING AND
LEARNING FOR EVERY CHILD

David Perkins

THE FREE PRESS

Riverside Community College
JUL 07 Library
4800 Magnolia Avenue
Riverside, CA 92506

LB 1590.3 .P473 1995

Perkins, David N.

Smart schools

Copyright © 1992 by David Perkins

All rights reserved. No part of this book may be reproduced or transmitted in any form or by any means, electronic or mechanical, including photo-copying, recording, or by any information storage and retrieval system, without permission in writing from the Publisher.

The Free Press
A Division of Simon & Schuster Inc.
1230 Avenue of the Americas
New York, N.Y. 10020

First Free Press Paperback Edition 1995

Printed in the United States of America

printing number
                    10

Library of Congress Cataloging-in-Publication Data

Perkins, David N.
    Smart schools: Better Thinking and Learning for Every Child/
David Perkins.
        p. cm.
    Includes bibliographical references (p.   ) and index.
    ISBN 0–02–874018–1
    1. Thought and thinking—Study and teaching—United States.
2. Learning, Psychology of. 3. Comprehension. I. Title.
LB1590.3.P473   1992
370.15′2—dc20   92-13763
                                                              CIP

To my schoolchildren:
Ted, Alice, and Tom

CONTENTS

ACKNOWLEDGMENTS

Some of the ideas expressed in *Smart Schools* were developed under grants from the MacArthur Foundation for integrative work on the teaching of thinking, from the Spencer Foundation for research toward a pedagogy of understanding, and from the Pew Foundation and the MacArthur Foundation for research and development work on project-based learning and after-school programs. The help of these foundations is very much appreciated. Of course, the ideas expressed here are my own and do not necessarily relect their positions or policies.

Several colleagues were kind enough to comment on an earlier draft of this book. My thanks to Phillip Cousins, Howard Gardner, Peter Kugel, Jack Lochhead, Jerry Murphy, Steven Rhodes, John Thurner, Shari Tishman, and Chris Unger. Their counsel was very useful, sparking a number of important changes. I am particularly grateful to Susan Arellano, my editor at The Free Press; her thoughtful counsel made this a better book in a number of ways.

Special thanks go to Diane Downs, who both found many sources and managed the production of the manuscript, and to Tina Blythe, Joyce Conkling, and Noel White, who provided invaluable help in locating sources, making corrections in the text, and otherwise facilitating the production of this book. Their systematic and assiduous efforts made the preparation of the book much easier than it would otherwise have been.

Finally, *Smart Schools* also benefits from my close work with a number of individuals in addition to the above over the past several years. They are many, and I will not try to list them here. But I am grateful. The intricate and exciting challenge of good educational practice is nothing to be pondered solo!

SCHOOLS

CHAPTER 1

SMART SCHOOLS

The Hanging Gardens of Babylon counted as one of the seven wonders of the ancient world, alongside the Colossus of Rhodes, the pyramids of Egypt, and the Temple of Artemis at Ephesus. Word comes down to us of a terraced wonderland of fountains, trees, and flowers, rising up from the banks of the Euphrates. King Nebuchadnezzar II constructed this sumptuous adjunct to the royal palace more than half a millennium before the birth of Christ.

Of these ancient wonders only the pyramids remain. Today great physical constructions play second fiddle to the wonders of everyday life—for instance, the transistor, which packs little boxes with great powers of voice, image, and computation; or, more humble yet, the light bulb. How hard it is to imagine life without light available at the flick of a forefinger!

And another invention: schools. Yes, schools. A wonder, really. A very new thing, if we mean public schools, schools for everyone, schools as part of a massive committed mission to bring to virtually all of a population with its multifarious ambitions, misgivings, talents, and quirks basic knowledge,

1

skills, and insights. Schools are wonders in the same way that light bulbs are—too much a part of everyday life to amaze us, but, from a historical perspective, quite novel and exotic in their ambitions and accomplishments.

Not, it must be said, that schools always seem to function in as wondrous a way as we would like. Not that we are so happy with how schools work and what they achieve. Not that society gives over to schools and teachers the resources and the honors they deserve. But with all that, still a wonder indeed. Gripe how we will about what schools are *not* doing these days, they are already doing things undreamt of a couple of centuries ago, much less in Nebuchadnezzar's day.

USING WHAT WE KNOW

Dreams are where the dilemma starts. Although schools already achieve things undreamt of earlier, we have more ambitious dreams today. We want schools to deliver a great deal of knowledge and understanding to a great many people of greatly differing talents with a great range of interests and a great variety of cultural and family backgrounds. Quite a challenge—and why aren't we doing better at it?

Some say, "We don't know enough. We don't know how learning really works. We don't know how teachers really think about their craft. We don't know how to cope with cultural diversity. We don't know how schools can work better as institutions. We just don't know enough."

I think they're wrong. Of course, we want to know and understand more about all those things. But we know enough now to do a much better job of education. We know because we have made an effort to find out. Over the past quarter century, psychologists have come to understand more deeply how learning works and how to motivate learning. Sociologists have studied how classrooms and schools as institutions work, what makes them resistant to change, and how to foster change. Innovations in various educational settings around the world allow us to compare experiences across contexts and cultures. We know a lot about how to educate well. In the later chapters of this book, I'll do my best to prove this.

The problem comes down to this: We are not putting to work what we know. In the school down the street, in the school across the river, students are learning and teachers are teaching in much the same way they did twenty or even fifty years ago. In the age of CDs and VCRs, communications satellites and laptop computers, education remains by and large a traditional craft.

Of course, the educational landscape sparkles with isolated innovative programs. Some individual teachers are ardent experimenters, trying worthwhile things. Some initiatives score important successes here and there. But most are limited. Most do not put to work in any full and rounded way what we know about teaching and learning. We do not have a knowledge gap—we have a monumental *use-of-knowledge* gap.

To close this gap, we need schools that put to work, day in and day out, what we know about how to educate well. We can call such schools "smart schools"—schools wide awake to the opportunities of better teaching and learning. We can think of smart schools as exhibiting three characteristics:

Informed. Administrators, teachers, and indeed students in the smart school know a lot about human thinking and learning and how it works best. And they know a lot about school structure and collaboration and how that works best.

Energetic. The smart school requires spirit as much as information. In the smart school, measures are taken to cultivate positive energy in the structure of the school, the style of administration, and the treatment of teachers and students.

Thoughtful. Smart schools are thoughtful places, in the double sense of caring and mindful. First of all, people are sensitive to one another's needs and treat others thoughtfully. Second, both the teaching/learning process and school decision-making processes are *thinking centered*. As we shall soon see, putting thinking at the center of all that happens is crucial.

Informed, energetic, and thoughtful—three broad characteristics for the smart school. These characteristics are not revolutionary. They are common sense by and large. But they are not common practice. In most schools, faculty and students are not well informed about how teaching, learning, thinking, collaboration, and other such elements of schooling work best. In all too many schools, energy levels are low; students, teachers, and administrators fight a thousand frustrations. And most schools do not put thinking at the center of the learning process or at the center of working together with one another.

In this book, I want to describe in broad stroke the contemporary science of teaching and learning that can inform teachers, students, and administrators about how learning works best. I want to touch on factors that create positive energy in a school setting. And I want to focus particularly on the role of *thoughtfulness* in the teaching/learning process, the key to genuine learning that serves students well. My hope is that this book, along with other publications and events, will help communities everywhere to work toward smart schools.

The goals of education are a good place to start.

GOALS: TOWARD GENERATIVE KNOWLEDGE

What do we want of education? This is the key question for the entire enterprise. Unless we know what we want and pursue it with ingenuity and commitment, we are not very likely to get it.

Of course, in a broad sense, we know all too well what we want. It can be put in a single word: *everything.* In *Popular Education and Its Discontents,* Lawrence Cremin, late historian of education at Columbia University, especially emphasized how we bedevil education with agendas. We try to solve all our problems by assigning them to educators—not only knowledge but citizenship, moral rectitude, comfortable social relations, a more able work force, and so on.*

It is easy to like the sound of all of these goals. Most of us would be happy to see public education working away at them insofar as it can. But we should also wonder whether the educational enterprise has a core.

One reason to worry about a core is that the "everything" agenda for schools is an energy vampire. It drains teachers, students, and administrators. Think how crucial an energetic spirit is to any institution you want to thrive. Nothing drains energy more than having too many things to do and too little

---

*For the sake of flow, citations for ideas and sources mentioned in the text appear in the Notes organized by chapter and section at the end of the book. The full references appear in the References section that follows the Notes.

time to do any of them anywhere near well. I certainly am not saying that schools should focus very narrowly on reading, 'riting, and 'rithmetic, for example. But I am saying, in common voice with many others these days, that some focus is imperative.

So even though we want everything, what do we want *most?* Without apology, let me attempt an answer. Here at a minimum is what we want, three general goals that stick close to the narrower endeavor of education. These are goals almost no one would argue with:

- Retention of knowledge
- Understanding of knowledge
- Active use of knowledge

A summary phrase for the goals taken together might be "generative knowledge"—knowledge that does not just sit there but functions richly in people's lives to help them understand and deal with the world.

No futuristic agenda this! These goals are not meant to sound exotic. They do not reach for anything very new. They follow directly from the core function of education, passing knowledge from one generation to the next. Whatever else a school is doing, if a school is not serving these goals well, it hardly deserves the name of school.

Lest these goals sound altogether too narrow, let me emphasize how broadly I mean "knowledge." While the term sounds somewhat circumscribed, the English language seems to offer no perfect word to cover the many kinds of learning. So let it be knowledge, emphasizing that this includes factual knowledge, skills, know-how, reflectiveness, familiarity with puzzlements as well as solutions, good questions to ask as well as good answers to give, and so on. As to its content, think in terms of typical subject matters, if you like—reading, writing, mathematics, science, history, and so on. They will do for the present.

We need to pursue every one of these three goals to achieve generative knowledge—knowledge that serves people well in later academic and nonacademic pursuits, knowledge that empowers the new generation to build even further.

Take, for example, goal number one, retention. Having knowledge for the Friday quiz does learners little good unless they still have it when they need it months or years later. Or take goal number two, understanding. There is little point in having knowledge that is not understood. Of course, not everything has to be understood completely. But, for example, if you do not understand when to use the arithmetic or algebra you know, it cannot do you much good. If you do not understand why history unfolds as it does, you will be ill equipped to grasp current events, vote wisely, or steer your own life with an eye on historical forces.

As to active use, the third goal, there is little gain in simply having knowledge and even understanding it for the quiz if that same knowledge does not get put to work on more worldly occasions: puzzling over a public issue, shopping in the supermarket, deciding for whom to vote, understanding why political turmoil persists at home and abroad, dealing with an on-the-job human-relations problem, and so on.

Retention, understanding, and the active use of knowledge . . . three goals of education hardly anyone can argue with. Of course, one can have other sets of fundamental hard-to-argue-with goals for education besides these. In his 1982 book *The Paideia Proposal: An Educational Manifesto,* Mortimer Adler advocates the trio of (1) the acquisition of organized knowledge; (2) development of intellectual skills; (3) enlarged understanding of ideas and values. I like Adler's goals. Retention, understanding, and the active use of knowledge include them, when we remember that knowledge has a broad interpretation that includes skills.

However, I like my terms better, because they describe not only what the learner gets but what the learner is supposed to be able to do with it afterwards. In particular, retention and active use point toward action. Not stopping at acquisition, they declare that the learner can go on to do things. Understanding too points toward action. As we shall see in chapter 4, understanding involves what we will call "understanding performances."

MEANS: THOUGHTFUL LEARNING

They seem innocuous, the three goals proposed here. They do not ask for any more than what we have always been asking for. They do not sound like much of a wake-up call for schools.

But I will let you in on a secret: These goals by themselves are enough to lead us to an ambitious vision of smart schools. Simple and agreeable though they are, they demand a great deal of schooling. Contemporary educational practice in the United States and in many other settings comes nowhere near achieving reasonable versions of these goals.

Nowadays, students emerge from primary, secondary, and even college education with remarkable gaps in basic background knowledge about the world they live in. A case in point: Most seventeen-year-olds cannot identify the date of the U.S. Civil War within half a century. In addition, students do not understand much of what they are taught. After education that directly treats important and accessible principles of physics, biology, and mathematics, many people persist in fundamental misconceptions about the world around them. And further, people do not use what they know. At home or in business, people fail to muster basics of writing, reading, and relating to others that have been prominent in their educational experiences. Chapter 2 says much more about all this.

The bottom line is that we are not getting the retention, understanding, and active use of knowledge that we want. If what we are doing is not working, what do we do instead? What do these shortfalls argue for?

The research and experience of educators, psychologists, and sociologists over a number of years offer a clear answer, the harvest of what might be called an emerging new science of teaching and learning. It is not a completely original answer. Many thoughtful people from Socrates on have expressed the same spirit. But the contemporary understanding of human thinking and learning has buttressed their insights with an array of careful evidence that makes the conclusion difficult to challenge.

The answer is this: We need *thoughtful learning*. We need schools that are full of thought, schools that focus not just on schooling memories but on schooling minds. We want what policy analyst Rexford Brown in a recent study of schools called "a literacy of thoughtfulness." We need educational settings with thinking-centered learning, where students learn by thinking through what they are learning about.

While the chapters to come will revisit this theme again and again, that in a nutshell is the message of extensive research on the nature of human thinking and learning. The rationale can be boiled down to a single sentence: *Learning is a consequence of thinking.* Retention, understanding, and the active use of knowledge can be brought about only by learning experiences in which learners think about and think with what they are learning.

Notice how this single sentence turns topsy-turvy the conventional pattern of schooling. The conventional pattern says that, first, students acquire knowledge. Only then do they think with and about the knowledge that they have absorbed. But it's just the opposite: Far from thinking coming after knowledge, knowledge comes on the coattails of thinking. As we think about and with the content that we are learning, we truly learn it.

Indeed, this even holds for the simplest kind of learning, straight memorization. Over and over again, studies have demonstrated that we memorize best when we analyze what we are learning, find patterns in it, and relate it to knowledge we already have. In other words, when we think about it. As early as 1888, the renowned American psychologist William James expressed the point eloquently this way:

> . . . the art of remembering is the art of *thinking;* . . . when we wish to fix a new thing in either our own mind or a pupil's, our conscious effort should not be so much to *impress* and *retain* it as to *connect* it with something else already there. The connecting *is* the thinking; and if we attend clearly to the connection, the connected thing will certainly be likely to remain within recall. [Italics are James's.]

Therefore, instead of knowledge-centered schools, we need thinking-centered schools. This is no luxury, no utopian vision of an erudite and elitist education. These are hard facts about the way learning works.

PRECEDENTS: SWINGS OF THE PENDULUM

The idea of informed, energetic schools focused on thoughtful learning is hardly new. Indeed, it has figured centrally in the history of education in the United States. Sometimes it has been seen as a mainstay of the educational process, sometimes as an elitist enterprise, neither possible nor needed for the majority of students. The pendulum swings back and forth.

During the first half of this century, one of the persistent champions of thoughtful learning in the United States was the seminal educational philosopher John Dewey, a founder of the progressive education movement. Dewey had this to say about the essential role of thoughtfulness in schooling:

> Of course, intellectual learning includes the amassing and retention of information. But information is an undigested burden unless it is understood . . . And understanding, comprehension, means that the various parts of the information acquired are grasped in their relations to one another—a result that is attained only when acquisition is accompanied by constant reflection upon the meaning of what is studied.

Dewey and other advocates of progressivism envisioned a child-centered education that took account of children's interests and abilities and built on that foundation. Education, Dewey maintained, should take as its foundation what the child knew and build from there toward intellectual insight into and appreciation of the landmarks of culture and science—the wisdom of Shakespeare, Newton, and others.

But progressivism took an odd turn, one quite contrary to Dewey's picture of it. In the child-centered spirit, others began to see schooling as practical preparation for everyday life, serving students who by and large lacked the intellectual ability to aspire to more. In the mid 1940s, "life adjustment education" became the watchword, and subjects like business English and business arithmetic became the paragons of the educational enterprise. For a while, most folks seemed satisfied with a less ambitious model of education. The pendulum had swung away from Dewey.

Then, in October 1957, Russia preempted American ambitions in space and challenged the image of the United States as the premier technological power with the launching of Sputnik, the first space satellite. Concerns over the intellectual quality of the nation rekindled visions of a more ambitious kind of education.

Through the 1960s and early 1970s, a spirit of innovation held sway, and new curricula, conceived in universities, came into the classrooms to run the reality gauntlet of teachers and students. Those were the days of the controversial "new math," which urged students studying elementary arithmetic to learn the logical foundations of the subject matter—set theory, the distinction between a number and a numeral, number systems with bases other than 10. Those also were the days of *Man: A Course of Study*, an innovative social studies program developed by Jerome Bruner and his colleagues that asked schoolchildren to open their eyes to a broader view of the human condition. Children learned how evolution worked, compared baboon and human societies, and became acquainted with the ingenious survival strategies and the spiritual dimensions of Netsilik Eskimos. Also in that period, *Project Physics* was developed, a serious and thoughtful effort to humanize physics by providing a curriculum and materials rich not only in concepts but in the historical, social, and biographical roots of the science.

The great moral of that era was that most of these programs did not fare well in practice. It was not that they did not achieve their instructional aims when well implemented. But committed, thoughtful implementations were few and far between. And there was an energy problem. It was so much easier to do something else, to stick to more conventional texts and aspirations.

Those years were the previous time around for a concerted wide-scale effort to create something like smart schools. But the pendulum swung away from that for a while. In the late 1970s it was back to the basics. Sound foundational skills of reading, 'riting, and 'rithmetic became the educational priority in the face of sorry performance by an alarming percentage of the nation's youth. But bit by bit, the educational community became aware that "back to the basics" did not provide the hoped-for payoffs. The problems highlighted in the previous section and reviewed in more detail in chapters to come began to emerge. Youngsters did not know what it seemed they should. Youngsters did not understand what they were learning. They could not solve problems with the knowledge they had gained.

This inspired the contemporary effort to rethink and reform educational practice, much of it in the general direction of thoughtful learning. The current zeal to restructure schools generally brings with it an emphasis on students' thoughtful engagement with content. Mortimer Adler's *Paideia Proposal,* mentioned earlier, envisions schools with high academic standards and an emphasis on discussion of and thinking about great works and ideas. Theodore Sizer of Brown University has become the philosophical leader of a number of "essential schools," high schools which reduce the number of subject matters for the sake of more deeply pursuing core subject matters and emphasize the idea of "authentic work," where students engage in genuine intellectual inquiry. The "whole language" movement urges involving students in a rich range of writing and other language-oriented activities across subject matters. New standards for the learning of mathematics proposed by the National Council of Teachers of Mathematics underscore the importance of problem solving and mathematical inquiry.

And so here we are again today, involved in the quest for a thoughtful, energetic kind of education that serves well those three key hard-to-argue-with goals celebrated earlier: retention, understanding, and the active use of knowledge.

PROSPECTS: PUTTING WHAT WE KNOW TO WORK

This time around in the quest for the smart school, do we have any hope of doing better? After all, during the previous swings of the pendulum, efforts to make education more informed, energetic, and thoughtful drew on some of the most ingenious figures of the era along with ample government support. What makes us think that today, when we are no smarter and government commitment to education is sparser, we can do better?

Knowledge. The answer is knowledge. Because of the last quarter century of research and experience, stimulated in good part by the not-quite-successful initiatives of the late 1960s and early 1970s, we know far more about the quest for effective schools than ever before. A new science of teaching and learning is emerging. We can put that knowledge to work.

I have already said that current reforms do not take full advantage of this knowledge. On the contrary, different movements and programs typically have distinctive historical and philosophical roots. They generally proceed with little awareness of other knowledge resources that might help them advance their missions. Indeed, an aim of this book is to put in one place a number of broad principles reflecting the new understanding of teaching and learning emerging from research and experience, so that anyone can put them to work wherever they seem helpful.

So what is this knowledge? What does it say to us about the problems? And how does it point to possible solutions? The following chapters try to put the pieces of the puzzle together, building a better picture of the smart school. A preview is in order.

2. *The Alarm Bells.* Researchers have taken a careful look at just what students are achieving. The shortfalls in retention, understanding, and the active use of knowledge are well documented, and severe consequences for economic development seem likely. All this underlines the need for the smart school.

3. *Teaching and Learning: Theory One and Beyond.* If students are to learn with good retention, understanding, and active use of knowledge, some very basic and well-established principles of teaching and learning have to get much more attention than they typically do, even in innovative settings. Theory One spells these principles out. Beyond Theory One, other instructional methods such as cooperative learning offer further leverage.

4. *Content: Toward a Pedagogy of Understanding.* What is it to understand something? Contemporary psychology is building an understanding of understanding. Even current reforms often do not recognize how much learning for understanding demands in the way of artful instruction. This chapter explores what understanding is and how to build learners' understandings.

5. *Curriculum: Creating the Metacurriculum.* In the past several years, how people think and how they can learn to think better have been major areas of inquiry for psychologists and philosophers. Effective learning turns out to involve much more than just acquiring the facts. Students must not just *know* the content but *think* with it. This recommends supplementing the content-oriented curriculum with something missing in most current efforts to restructure schools—a "metacurriculum" that pays attention to higher-order thinking and learning.

6. *Classrooms: The Role of Distributed Intelligence.* Schools tend to treat students as solo learners who do most of the real intellectual work of learning in their heads. But a revisionary view of

intelligence recognizes that people inherently think with one another cooperatively and with the help of artifacts from paper and pencil to computers. This calls for a basic reorganization of what usually happens in classrooms.

7. *Motivation: The Cognitive Economy of Schooling.* Many schools are wastelands of undermotivated students and teachers. But to what extent do even innovative school settings give students and teachers good reason to invest themselves? This chapter points up how the gains and costs of classroom life—the ''cognitive economy'' of classrooms—often inadequately reward students and teachers for serious intellectual investment. It examines how current efforts toward school restructuring and alternative methods of assessment can help to build a cognitive economy supportive of thoughtful teaching and learning.

8. *Victory Gardens for Revitalized Education.* The previous five chapters highlight five key dimensions of educational change—instruction, content, the curriculum, classroom organization, and motivation. But what do texts and programs that score well on these dimensions look like? While examples have been given all the way along, this chapter puts in one place several case studies, viewing them from the perspectives of all five dimensions and toward building a clearer image of schooling minds.

9. *The Challenge of Wide–Scale Change.* While wonderful educational achievements can be seen on a small scale in many schools and school systems, wide-scale innovation remains a daunting challenge. A large part of the challenge rests in helping teachers to develop new knowledge and skills and helping educational institutions to change in fundamental ways that make room for thoughtful teaching and learning. Fortunately, sociologists and educators have learned much about the process of teacher and institutional change in recent years. This knowledge, put to work, promises wide-scale progress toward more effective education.

The nine chapters build a vision of the smart school, the school that, informed about teaching, learning, collaboration, and other keys to effective education, fosters an energetic culture of thoughtful teaching and learning. Taken together, the chapters underscore a central point: A culture of thoughtfulness is not a simple thing. It is not just a matter of attitude or style or skill. It is not just a matter of longer class periods for greater depth or more writing in all subject matters. Like any culture, a school culture of thoughtful teaching and learning is a complex construction, built only with commitment, insight, and knowledge. Because we understand better today what such a culture requires, we are in a better position to create smart schools.

CONNECTIONS: SOME ISSUES SEEN ANEW

The idea of thoughtful learning does not stand apart from other contemporary themes in education. It overlaps and illuminates a number of the issues that figure in the lively discourse around education these days. For instance:

Slow Learners. Traditionally, schools have addressed slow learners with tracking and remedial programs that assume they need to focus almost exclusively on routine basics. In such classrooms, rote learning and drill-and-practice dominate even more than in ordinary classrooms.

It's a mistake. Thoughtful learning is the way learning works best. Thoughtful learning is just as important for slow learners as anyone else, honoring rather than demoralizing slow learners, motivating them more, and helping them to achieve more. Remember the energetic character a smart school needs. Let's face it: Slow learners are typically bored by what schools ask them to do. And no wonder! So thoughtful learning is for everyone, not just the gifted or the regular student.

At-Risk Students. "At risk" has become a broad and somewhat vague label for youngsters whose economic and family background forecasts poor performance in school and a high dropout rate. Many such students are slow learners, but not so much because of any lack of raw ability as of attitudes and skills ill-tuned to the academic expectations of school. The fact is that some economic and family backgrounds leave children much less prepared for school than do others.

Thoughtful learning is for at-risk students as much as it is for slow learners. At-risk students need the energy, involvement, and learning-to-learn that comes with thoughtful learning. While today's schools tend to widen cultural gaps rather than bridge them, it doesn't have to be like that. The smart school can create a safe, protected atmosphere and help to build the curiosity, confidence, and skills of at-risk students.

Assessment.   It's widely recognized among today's educators that conventional multiple-choice, knowledge-oriented testing does not serve the cause of education well. Such testing drives teachers and students toward rote styles of instruction that may help with retention of knowledge but have little hope of building understanding or the active use of knowledge. The smart school requires the new concepts of assessment discussed in chapter 7.

School Governance.   Traditionally, the principal leads the school much as the captain of a ship commands the crew. Contemporary lessons from the business and school communities alike suggest that a strongly hierarchical, nonparticipatory process of governance misses opportunities. Significant teacher, parent, and indeed student participation in school governance can boost motivation and involvement and harvest everyone's intelligence toward the good of the enterprise. This does not mean that principals should have no authority. Of course they should. It means that the smart school needs to foster a thoughtful involvement not just for students in their classrooms but for the adults committed to the school as well.

School Choice.   The basic idea of school choice says that parents and students should be able to select the school to attend within a region. A marketplace metaphor figures here: Schools not doing a good job will fail to draw students and, if they can't get their acts together, go out of business. Other, more effective schools will take their place.

School choice is a complex issue, and an unrestricted market economy should be viewed with caution (remember how far from *laissez faire* economics the real world of business has come). However, the idea of parents and students energetic about school choice, informed about the options, and choosing thoughtfully the kind of school that would serve them best certainly resonates with the idea of the smart school. Moreover, if school choice plans are to succeed, it's essential that parents and students have *good* choices. The notion of the smart school can help society to create such choices.

School Restructuring.   Innovators concerned with school re-structuring locate the malaise of education in organizational features of the school that drastically lower energy and make thoughtful learning difficult. Dull and ineffective patterns of education stay locked in place by short class periods, too many subject matters, conventional testing, command-style leadership, and so on. Thoughtful teaching and learning cannot take hold and thrive in such settings. Efforts to restructure schools typically emphasize fundamental changes in patterns of governance, class periods, curriculum, and testing in order to liberate and energize teachers and learners to get on better with the business of education. Most definitely then, some degree of restructuring is fundamental to the smart school.

Preservice and In-Service Teacher Education.   To achieve substantially better education, society must invest seriously in renovated preservice education and expanded in-service educa-tion. Parents and school boards are notoriously grudging about in-service time: "The teachers should be teaching our kids!" But such attitudes fail to recognize the rapid pace of development of new ideas about teaching and fail to honor how much teachers can learn from both one another and outside sources. Teachers cannot be informed, energetic, and thoughtful in settings, pre-service or in-service, that fail to inform them and shrink from providing them the time and encouragement to build energy and reflect deeply on educational practice. Schools need restructuring not just to foster students' thoughtful learning but teachers'— and administrators'—thoughtful learning as well. Chapters 7 and 9 look at some aspects of this challenge.

MISSION: SMART SCHOOLS

No book can attempt everything. This is not a how-to-do-it book. Teachers will not find formulas for teaching here (nor would they want them). It is not a technical review of research. Those looking for research summaries will discover that many other sources do a far more detailed job of that. It is not a meticulous blueprint for school change. Parents, principals, and members of school boards will find many useful notions but not a stepwise plan. Nor does this book deal much with the special problems of particular populations—poverty, ethnic differences, drugs. Nor with the organizational dilemmas of parent participation, teacher empowerment, and so on.

Instead, this book is a wake-up call. Whatever can be done about the particular woes of particular populations and the overall organization of schools and schooling, education ultimately depends on what happens in classrooms around subject matters between teachers and learners. That is fundamental. We know a great deal about it today. We need to put to work what we know toward making informed, energetic, and thoughtful schools.

What will you discover here? Most of all, information and ideas that can help to inform and energize schools and foster thoughtful learning. These pages offer an overview of the new science of teaching and learning. Although it cannot be complete, it will, I hope, be provocative and empowering.

I hope that parents will take to heart the risks of a diffuse education that tries to serve all agendas and find a common ground in the key goals of retention, understanding, and the active use of knowledge. I hope that business people will recognize the harm done by a routine, rote education that yields uninformed and disillusioned graduates and lend their ingenuity to furthering informed, energetic, and thoughtful teaching and learning.

I hope that teachers will discover an optimism and direction to combat the energy-draining pressures and frustrations of most educational settings, finding affirmation of many of their insightful practices, as well as new ways of thinking about teaching and learning. I hope that school administrators will come upon useful justifications for innovation in the face of discouraged and wary communities.

I hope that citizens will awake to a new interest in the power of public education and lend their views, voices, and votes to creating smart schools. I hope that politicians will recognize that ineffective education weighs a society down, sapping its potential, and appreciate how crucial a change toward thoughtful learning can be for intellectual and economic vitality.

The time is right. Expounding on the theme of education as a social invention, Jerome Bruner, one of the founding fathers of cognitive psychology and an innovative educator, wrote, ''For it is psychology more than any other discipline that has the tools for exploring the limits of man's perfectibility." Thanks to advances in cognitive psychology over the last decades, we have a better, albeit far from complete, understanding of human thinking and learning—its mechanisms, proclivities, and opportunities. Thanks to the vigorous work of scholars studying the school milieu, we have a better understanding of teacher and institutional change. Thanks to diverse advances and innovations in education around the world, we have a better opportunity to compare and draw conclusions.

But the use-of-knowledge gap remains a plain reality. If we can only get those fundamentals into focus and widely appreciated, we can create smart schools in every community. We can make schools even more ingenious inventions than they already are: wonders of the world indeed.

SCHOOLS

CHAPTER 2

THE ALARM BELLS

Sometimes a memory catches us by surprise, in the midst of something else entirely, telling us that there are connections we have not sought out and perhaps do not even welcome. So it was when I sat down a few weeks ago to draft the first lines of the essay that unexpectedly turned into this book. I discovered myself thinking of a poem I had not read for many years, a poem that nearly every schoolchild encounters, one of the most doggedly onomatopoeic poems in the English language, Edgar Allan Poe's "The Bells."

So I found a copy of the poem to remind myself what it said. Here are a few of its lines:

> Hear the loud alarum bells—
> Brazen bells!
> What a tale of terror, now their turbulency tells!
> In the startled ear of night
> How they scream out their affright!
> Too much horrified to speak,

> They can only shriek, shriek,
> Out of tune

In the process, I puzzled out what brought "The Bells" to mind. It was, of course, the troubles of education. They seem to be sounding from every direction—the woes of teachers, the unease of parents, the infighting of school boards, the restiveness of students, the discouraging findings of various investigative committees. Truly we hear resounding throughout the land Poe's "alarum bells" concerning the educational enterprise.

Poe's bells reminded me of another image of chaos. In *Popular Education and Its Discontents*, Lawrence Cremin committed a chapter to what he terms "The Cacophony of Teaching." By this, Cremin alludes specifically to the many helter-skelter ways that we in the United States seek to educate—through the public schools, television, museums, preschool programs, special education, and so on, each with its own goals, philosophies of education, economic structures, and hidden curricula, and so on. A *mot juste* if ever there was one, "cacophony" (although, Cremin emphasizes, not necessarily an unproductive cacophony) underscores the dilemma of making sense of education in a context of conflicts and crosscurrents.

With these images of turmoil so powerfully asserting themselves, there seems no better course than to listen to the bells, the cacophony, the assault of sound and fury, and try to discern the pattern of "alarum."

For a preview, we hear at least two broad shortfalls in educational achievement: *fragile knowledge*, which means that students do not remember, understand, or use actively much of what they have supposedly learned; and *poor thinking*, which means that students do not think very well with what they know. Searching for causes, we can discover at least two very pervasive contributing factors: a Trivial Pursuit theory of learning, which pervades educational practice and says that learning is a matter of accumulating facts and routines; and an Ability-Counts-Most theory of achievement, which says that what a person learns depends mostly on how smart the person is, not on how hard the person tries. Wondering about consequences, we can find at least one of great concern: a kind of *economic erosion*, where the rich get richer while the poor get poorer, and both economic productivity and the average standard of living fall behind those of many other nations. Research suggests that educational problems are a principal cause!

So let's look at the details.

A SHORTFALL: FRAGILE KNOWLEDGE

It's at least irritating and to many dismaying that many youngsters do not know bits of information they *ought* to know. For example, as mentioned earlier, a recent survey disclosed that some two thirds of seventeen-year-old schoolchildren in the United States cannot place the U.S. Civil War to within a half century. Eighty percent do not know what Reconstruction is. Two students in three think that Jim Crow laws actually helped black Americans. Half do not know that Stalin led the Soviet Union during World War II. Almost half do not know that the attack on Pearl Harbor occurred during the period between 1939 and 1943. Three in five do not know about the internment of Japanese Americans. A similar number misdefine the Holocaust. Thirty-six percent date Watergate before 1950, and one in five before 1900. Forty-five percent classify Israel as one of the nations occupied by the Soviet Union after World War II. One in three cannot locate France when given a map of Europe. Two in three cannot pick out Walt Whitman as the poet who wrote "Leaves of Grass."

Missing knowledge, we could call it. Missing from the minds of students who have been exposed to it and might have remembered it. Certainly it is reasonable to expect students to emerge from their education with a fund of basic knowledge that orients them to the world around them and equips them to understand its unfolding events and ideas—what is happening where and when and why.

At the same time, people too often see this missing knowledge as the principal shortfall of education. If only kids remembered the facts and skills they've been taught, everything would be fine!

Unfortunately, it's not that simple. Schooling minds is more than schooling memories. Missing knowledge is too crude a diagnosis of the malady. Research shows that there are many more problems of knowledge than just plain not having it. Three such are *inert knowledge, naive knowledge,* and *ritual knowledge.*

Inert Knowledge.   Startlingly often, students have knowledge that they remember when directly quizzed, but do not use otherwise. It doesn't come to mind in more authentically open-ended situations of need, such as writing an essay, pondering the morning's headlines, considering alternative professions, selecting a new stereo, or for that matter, studying another subject. Knowledge of this sort is called inert. As the phrase suggests, inert knowledge is the knowledge equivalent of a couch potato: It's there, but it doesn't move around or do anything.

Conventional instruction—reading textbooks and listening to lectures—tends to produce inert knowledge. For example, cognitive psychologist John Bransford and his colleagues conducted an experiment in which some students read items of information about nutrition, water as a standard of density, solar-powered airplanes, and other matters in the usual textbookish way, with the intent to remember. Other students read the same items of information in the context of thinking about the challenges of a journey through a South American jungle. For instance, the students read about the density of water in the context of how much water the travelers would have to carry.

Later, both groups of students were given the task of planning a desert expedition. The students who had studied the information in the conventional way made hardly any use of it. But the students who had studied the same information in the problem-solving context of the jungle journey made rich and extensive use of the information, pondering the kinds of foods that would sustain people the best, worrying about the weight of water, and so on.

For another example, research that colleagues and I conducted on students' computer programming abilities disclosed an often startling gap between knowledge that high school students could remember and knowledge that they used actively. One student, for instance, was struggling with a problem that required a FOR-NEXT command to solve, one of the most fundamental commands in the BASIC programming language. The student didn't recognize what to do. Had the student forgotten about the FOR-NEXT command altogether? An investigator sitting with the student asked whether a FOR-NEXT would help. Oh yes! The student immediately and effectively used the command to solve the problem.

Notice what this shows. The student retained the knowledge in question and even knew how to use it effectively. But the student *did not think to use it!* Unusual? Not at all. These students often knew and understood relevant programming commands that they did not think to employ in the midst of writing a program. When reminded of particular commands but not their details, many students slotted the commands into place and solved the programming problems.

The same appears to happen in all subject matters. Students retain knowledge they often cannot use actively for problem solving and other activities.

Naive Knowledge.   One of the discomforting disclosures of the past two decades has been students' fragile grasp of many key concepts in science and mathematics. Students commonly display naive ideas about things even after considerable instruction.

For instance, youngsters in the first half of elementary school often believe the world is flat. This is reasonable to start with—after all, the world *looks* flat as you gaze from a height out to the horizon. However, many youngsters, even after receiving some instruction with globes, still believe that the world is flat! Often, they have come to think it is flat in a fancier way, like a hemisphere: rounded on the bottom but flat on top, or like a disk, with a round periphery but flat on top and bottom.

"Well, they're young yet," we could say. "There's no hurry. Few students end up believing that the world is flat in the long run." All this is true as far as it goes. But the same thing happens at much more advanced levels, where students are unlikely ever to get it straight later.

As part of a project directed by astrophysicist Irwin Shapiro of Harvard University, Matthew Schneps and Phillip Sadler organized the making of a short film called *A Private Universe* that has won some attention in educational circles recently. In the film, graduating students of Harvard University were asked a very basic question about the world around them: Why is it hot in the summer and cold in the winter? All the students had studied this at one time or another. Almost everyone does in high school. But many students revealed a fundamentally mistaken conception, suggesting that summers are hotter because the Earth is closer to the sun in the summer.

This is not the right explanation. This is not the explanation they supposedly learned. Moreover, it does not even make sense in terms of other facts people often know. Most of us can recall hearing that when it's summer in the Northern hemisphere, it's winter in the Southern hemisphere, and vice versa. Well, if the Earth is closer to the sun in the summer, it should be summer in both Northern and Southern hemispheres at once. The "closer to the sun" theory is not only mistaken but does not make sense in terms of other information.

Over the past two decades, researchers have looked for students' naive theories in science and mathematics at all levels of education—elementary, secondary, and college. And they have found such theories in abundance. The point is not that students have naive theories before instruction, but that they still have them *after* instruction, often immediately after. To be sure, when students are asked to repeat facts or apply formulas, they are very often right. But when they are asked to explain or interpret, students often reveal the old naive theory intact.

While the persistence of naive knowledge has been most studied in mathematics and the sciences, it appears to have equivalents in the humanistic subject matters. In his recent book, *The Unschooled Mind*, Howard Gardner has pointed out that stereotypes are in effect naive theories that students harbor. We would like to think that the teaching of history and literature do much to alter religious, racial, and ethnic stereotypes. Certainly, in many places today, the emphasis falls on multiculturalism, with religious, racial, and ethnic groups of all sorts represented in what students study. Nonetheless, like students' naive theories in science and mathematics, stereotypes seem to survive and even thrive.

How can this happen? How can students seem to learn something new and yet preserve their naive theories? The answer seems to lie in recognizing yet another kind of knowledge.

Ritual Knowledge. Rather than coming to a new full understanding of something like the world's roundness or how other people are very like ourselves, learners often seem to acquire what might be called ritual knowledge. They learn the school game. They learn how you are supposed to talk about the world—you use the word *round*. They learn the routines of problem solving with equations. They learn about important black or Hispanic figures in U.S. history.

Unfortunately, these schoolish performances make little connection to their intuitions about the way things are. When asked to explain something or ponder a situation or express a view, they reveal the old naive theories, as much alive as ever.

Sometimes, these rituals can even be articulated point-blank by the learners. Here is a marvelous and rather famous example collected by researchers a number of years ago. A good performer in math had this to say about her strategy:

> I know what to do by looking at the examples. If there are only two numbers I subtract. If there are lots of numbers I add. If there are just two numbers and one is smaller than the other it is a hard problem. I divide to see if it comes out even and if it doesn't I multiply.

It is not that these students by and large are resisting what they have been taught, displaying thoughtful or even thoughtless skepticism. It is rather that they have not really gotten straight what they have been taught. So they substitute rituals that, like the one above for solving arithmetic problems, work rather well in the artificial world of the typical classroom.

Meanwhile, their naive theories survive unaltered or only partly altered. So, just as "Sunday Christians" do not connect up their daily moral lives with what happens in the church on Sunday, school learners do not connect up the phenomena around them with what gets said from the pulpit at the front of the classroom.

The Fragile Knowledge Syndrome

The summary lesson here is that the problem of knowledge is much more than a problem of missing knowledge, although that is part of it. To put a name to the overall malady, one might speak of fragile knowledge. Students' knowledge is generally quite fragile in several different and significant ways.

- *Missing knowledge.* Sometimes important pieces of knowledge are just plain missing.
- *Inert knowledge.* Sometimes present, but inert. So it lets the student pass the quiz but does not help otherwise.
- *Naive knowledge.* Sometimes the knowledge takes the form of naive theories and stereotypes, even after considerable instruction designed to provide better theories and combat stereotypes.
- *Ritual knowledge.* The knowledge that students acquire often has a ritual character, useful for schoolish tasks but not much else.

Notice how these four problems with knowledge run contrary to the goals of education underscored in the introduction—retention, understanding, and the active use of knowledge. Just plain missing knowledge is, of course, not retained. Naive and ritual knowledge do not constitute true understandings. And inert knowledge does not see active use, even though there for the test.

The problems of missing, inert, naive, and ritual knowledge combine in a learner to display a distinctive cluster of behaviors, the fragile knowledge syndrome. Imagine what this is like. Suppose, for example, that you are looking over the shoulder of Brian, who is tackling some fraction computation problems. For the simplest problems, Brian proceeds nicely. Encountering a mixed number, Brian has no idea what to do with it—a knowledge gap. On another problem, Brian obtains an answer that needs reducing but forgets to reduce it, even though he knows how. On an addition problem, Brian cancels a 3 in the numerator of one term against a 3 in the denominator of the other, mistakenly believing that cancellation works for sums as well as products. However, on a similar problem, he does not happen to try canceling and solves the problem correctly.

In short, you see an odd mix of competence and shortfall. Certainly, Brian and other students know a good deal about what they are doing. Yet the entire performance is fragile, troubled with knowledge gaps, inert knowledge, naive knowledge, and ritual knowledge. In consequence, performance is sometimes correct and sometimes incorrect on very similar problems, and problems with any peculiarity tend to throw the student off.

The fragile knowledge syndrome is not something to worry about only in elementary school because high school and college students manage fine, nor is it a matter of concern only for science and mathematics because the humanities fare better, nor a matter of more versus less "practical" subject studies. Dorothy, in the midst of her college-level course on American poetry of the twentieth century, may forget who wrote "Ars Poetica" (missing knowledge). She may not think to mention T. S. Eliot's notion of the objective correlative for an essay question the professor designed to elicit the idea (inert knowledge). She may persist in the belief that "good is what I like" despite the professor's efforts to build finer discrimination (naive knowledge, a tacit theory of aesthetics). Despite all this, Dorothy may score some points with the professor by dutifully defining and advocating structuralist literary criticism (ritual knowledge).

Not only is the fragile knowledge syndrome all too real, and all too present, but for weaker students it is all too painful. Many lower-ability students continue week after week, month after month, dealing with knowledge that is very fragile for them, full of gaps, confusions, and so on.

Even good students have had some experiences like that. We all have considerable fragile knowledge—missing, inert, naive, ritual. Remember a time when you were studying something that came hard and others were doing better? Remember how confused and disoriented you felt, how hard it was to keep wading along? Now imagine a learner for whom most subject matters are like that on most days. No wonder students get discouraged and drop out. Fragile knowledge hurts!

A SHORTFALL: POOR THINKING

Gary Larson, the notable and notorious cartoonist, displays admirable sensitivity to one of the most fundamental fears of students. In a telling cartoon by Larson entitled "Hell's Library," we see the licking flames of the inferno surrounding a tall bookcase. And what books! The titles read like this: *Story*

Problems, More Story Problems, Even More Story Problems, Big Book of Story Problems, and so on.

Students (including ourselves at one time or another) are right to be fearful, because investigations show that students have enormous difficulty with story problems in mathematics, far more so than with the numerical operations they have practiced so assiduously. They know more or less how to add, subtract, multiply, and even divide. More advanced students know the manipulative rules of algebra and even the calculus. But often they cannot puzzle out just what the problem is asking for. "Should I add, subtract, multiply, or divide? Should I set up simultaneous questions? Should I integrate by parts?" They know how to do any of these things. But they're not sure what to pick. So they resort to *ad hoc* strategies. They cannot think with what they know.

Thinking with what you learn is of course one of the goals of education. In fact, it's part of the third major goal of education expounded in the introduction: the active use of knowledge. Now and again, there are opportunities to use knowledge actively without a lot of thought, as when you check a bill in a restaurant to be sure it's totaled correctly. By and large, however, using knowledge actively means thinking with it—to solve problems, make inferences, generate plans, and so on. So what signs do we see that students are learning to do this? Few enough signs in the area of solving story problems in mathematics!

What about other kinds of thinking? One common, thought-demanding task arises in reading, when students are asked to read, interpret, and explain. Many reading tests ask youngsters to make elementary inferences from what they read. If, for example, Senator Fitzmorrison supported the antipornography bill but worked against the gun-control bill, what generalization could you tentatively make about his political leanings?

Unfortunately, students prove to be remarkably poor at reading between the lines and drawing appropriate generalizations and extrapolations from what they read. The National Assessment of Educational Progress offers a discouraging quote about students' standing here:

Students seem satisfied with their initial interpretations of what they have read and seem genuinely puzzled at requests to explain or defend their points of view. As a result, responses to assessment items requiring explanations of criteria, analysis of text or defense of a judgment or point of view were in general disappointing. Few students could provide more than superficial responses to such tasks, and even the "better" responses showed little evidence of well-developed problem-solving or critical-thinking skills.

To turn to another cognitively demanding activity, students are no more astute about what they write. According to research conducted by cognitive psychologists Carl Bereiter and Marlene Scardamalia at the Ontario Institute for Studies in Education, most students write using a tacit "knowledge-telling strategy." If spelled out in so many words, this strategy basically says, "Write down something you know about the topic. Then write down something else you know. Then write down something else. And when you have enough, write down something that sounds like an ending and hand it in."

The original work of Bereiter and Scardamalia concerned precollege students. However, many college professors, hearing a profile of the knowledge-telling strategy, react with a shock of recognition: "Yes—that's what many of my students' papers are like!"

With the knowledge-telling strategy as their mainstay, students generally do not organize their knowledge into thoughtful theses and arguments. Moreover, they are not even terribly good at tapping the knowledge they have—inert knowledge again! Bereiter and Scardamalia report an experiment where before writing, students were asked simply to think of key words that they might use in an essay. The students who did this simple exercise had considerably more to say in their essays than those who didn't. Apparently, students do not necessarily know how to stir the mental pot. So they have less to say than they might, even in the straight knowledge-telling mode.

Even plain old rote memory points up many students' sluggish thinking. As mentioned in the introduction, extensive research shows that if your goal is simply knowledge retention, your best approach is strategic and thought demanding. Students learn facts much better if they organize them, actively relate them to prior knowledge, use visual associations, quiz themselves, elaborate and extrapolate what they are reading or hearing. Many students, unfortunately, opt for a straight rehearsal model of memorizing—read it over and over, say it over and over. While repetition is some aid to memory, it helps much less than strategies that involve more elaborate processing of the information in question.

But perhaps all this sorry thinking is the fallout of a general disaffinity with schooling. Youngsters might think a lot better about something closer to their minds and hearts. Maybe. Rexford Brown, who recently wrote about a number of efforts to foster more thoughtful education in *Schools of Thought*, is skeptical. He writes of watching a teacher leading a discussion around a music video by Paul Simon, "Boy in the Bubble." The teacher tends to lapse into a didactic style. But the students too seem off the wavelength. Brown reflects as follows:

I realize that I have just been assuming that students would love to talk about a rock video, because they watch them so often; but what this episode tells me is that teenagers are as inexperienced in looking critically at videos as they are in looking critically at texts. They don't know how to look critically at anything. Distancing themselves from an event or an experience, analyzing its parts and their relationships, and elaborating its various meanings for themselves and others—these are not things that many teenagers do naturally, even with events or experiences that mean a great deal to them.

The bottom line? Thinking is in trouble too, not just knowledge. At a recent conference, codirector Lauren Resnick of the University of Pittsburgh Learning Research and Development Center emphasized that so-called "higher order thinking isn't higher order." Higher-order thinking refers to reasoning, argument, problem solving, and so on. Resnick urged that thinking should not be seen as an esoteric add-on to good solid knowledge and routine skills. On the contrary, the most basic and seemingly elementary performances require active strategic thinking. If students do not learn to think with the knowledge they are stockpiling, they might as well not have it.

A DEEP CAUSE: THE TRIVIAL PURSUIT THEORY

It is a neat intellectual move to look for subtle unities in the fabric of a civilization and an era. The Renaissance, for example, held deep currents that came to the surface in wellsprings of art, science, politics, commerce, and everyday dress.

In that spirit, let me suggest that "trivial pursuit" may be one of the submarine torrents of the American character. First and foremost, it refers to the popular game wherein each player advances by displaying his or her breadth of knowledge in various categories. But underneath the fun, I wonder whether the soaring enthusiasm for this game signals a naive love for the idea of wisdom as knowledge and knowledge as facts and routines. We are speaking here of generations that, now enthusiastic about "Trivial Pursuit," were breast-fed on the golden age of quiz shows, with such extravaganzas as "The $64,000 Question."

Deep currents or not, trivial pursuit makes a metaphor for many features of contemporary education. To this point, I have emphasized shortfalls in educational outcomes—achievements of knowledge and thinking. But what are the causes? The answer is inevitably complex, and the story will continue to unfold throughout this book. But here it is worth highlighting two broad attitudes toward teaching and learning that contribute to the malaise on many levels and in many ways. In fact, remembering the earlier discussion of naive theories, both are naive theories. Naive theories held not just by many students but by many educators as well. Here is the first:

Learning is a matter of accumulating a large repertoire of facts and routines.

Notice how this contrasts with the fundamental principle stressed in the introduction, learning is a consequence of thinking. That principle votes for a much more active, thoughtful kind of learning than accumulating facts and routines.

What does naive theory #1 say in slightly more expanded form? I can do no better than to quote a few fine lines from the beginning of my colleague Vito Perrone's recent *Letter to Teachers*. He writes:

There is, it seems, more concern about whether children learn the mechanics of reading and writing than grow to love reading and writing; learn *about* democratic practice rather than have practice in democracy; hear about knowledge . . . rather than gain experience in personally constructing knowledge; . . . see the world narrowly, simple and ordered, rather than broad, complex, and uncertain.

But wait a minute! Who really believes this naive theory about accumulating facts and routines? Do I know anyone who espouses it? Do you? No, probably not. But many educators and other people behave as though they believe it. That's what we mean by a tacit theory. Educators do not argue that education is about accumulating large repertoires of facts and routines. But this is overwhelmingly what happens in classrooms, where, as in other settings, actions speak louder than words.

One measure of the trivial pursuit model of education simply asks how often classroom events depart from it. For example, John Goodlad reports in *A Place Called School* that only 5 percent of class time is spent on average in discussion. Ernest Boyer mentions in *High School* an investigation revealing that fewer than 1 percent of teachers' questions to students invite them to respond in a richer way than answering a factual question or displaying a routine procedure.

Similar points can be made about textbooks. The educator-psychologist David Olson and his colleague Janet Astington at the Ontario Institute for Studies in Education have systematically surveyed junior-high science textbooks for their use of what Olson calls "mental state verbs," which make reference to such important elements of thinking as "hypothesize," "explain," and so on. They found that such references occur rarely, demonstrating a systematic squeezing out of this "language of thinking" from textbooks.

The tests that in many ways drive the educational system are another testimony to the deep reality of the trivial pursuit model. By and large, those tests press for fact upon fact, procedure upon procedure, emphasizing multiple-choice responding rather than thoughtful performance on complex, open-ended tasks.

The emphasis on coverage, all too familiar to those who work in schools, also points to the problem. The common teacher concern when trying out an innovation is "But I have to be sure to cover my text." A school administrator I know dramatized how entrenched the coverage philosophy was by relating how teachers she supervised would tell her, "But I have to cover my material." "Who told you that?" she would ask. They could not answer. Indeed, the school system in question explicitly did *not* make coverage a priority. But the coverage mentality is so much a part of the current culture of teaching that it was assumed. Now coverage is not pointless, of course. On the positive side, teachers who react this way are displaying a laudable dedication to acquainting their students with as much knowledge as possible. However, on the negative side, the result is a constant trading of depth for breadth.

Moreover, the conspiracy for coverage extends well beyond the classroom into the textbook industry. Over the past two decades, science texts have grown fat with superficial and disconnected information about every facet of science imaginable, with virtually no prospect of students' really understanding or retaining much of so vast a compendium. The same thing tends to occur in many other subject matters as special interest groups and scholars and others push for this or that point to be added. Everything, it seems, is important. And again, no one individual or group in this pandemonium of knowledge pushing is acting foolishly. Many, many ideas and perspectives are important in many contexts, and choosing is an intellectually difficult and even politically risky task. But the alternative is the familiar political compromise: By serving all agendas, we serve none of them well. Worse, we serve most of them downright poorly.

But the trivial pursuit model lives on. The case for this trivial pursuit has even had its popular champions, most notably E.D. Hirsch. In his wide-selling *Cultural Literacy*, Hirsch argued that American education should work assiduously to ensure that students gain a broad base of superficial acquaintance with a large number of concepts from different disciplines. Hirsch went so far as to offer a list of concepts people should be acquainted with, including, for example, Atomic Weight, Cleopatra, Pearl Harbor, Relativity, and The Three Little Pigs.

Hirsch's position should certainly not be seen as a naive trivial pursuit model. But neither, in my view, should it be seen as particularly enlightened. I agree with Hirsch that broad superficial acquaintance with a large number of ideas is one important outcome of a good general education. However, it is an outcome hard to strive for directly. Here's why.

The vision projected by Hirsch, although carefully hedged, is that schools can somehow "go through" the fund of needed superficial knowledge and kids will end up culturally literate. Well, it won't work. Remember the core precept that learning is a consequence of thinking. Without a thoughtful process of learning, "going through" will not even yield well-retained knowledge, much less understood and actively used knowledge.

We can have what Hirsch wants, but not by teaching youngsters point-blank what's on Hirsch's list. To be retained, understood, and used actively, that knowledge needs to be accumulated over many years as a consequence of thinking: the good learning that occurs when students engage school content thoughtfully.

A DEEP CAUSE: THE ABILITY-COUNTS-MOST THEORY

While the trivial pursuit model of education underlies much of educational malpractice, there is another major cause, nicely pointed up by comparing American and Japanese attitudes toward mathematics education. Japanese achievements in this subject matter as well as others have aroused admiration, envy, and not a little puzzlement as investigators have sought to understand the key ingredients.

One of those ingredients has to do with who or what gets the credit for learning and the blame for failure to learn. Ask a Japanese parent why a child isn't learning mathematics successfully, and you get a very clear answer: The child isn't trying hard enough. Ask an American parent, and as a rule, you get a very different reply: Math is a tough subject, or sometimes: The child isn't up to math.

What is true of mathematics is true of other subjects as well. It marks a contrast not only between American and Japanese attitudes but between American attitudes and those of several other nations with more successful educational systems. Predominant in American culture is an "abilities" theory of success and failure. In fact, it is another one of those naive theories. Let's write it down that way:

Success in learning depends on ability much more than effort.

If you learn something, it's because of your inherent innate ability to catch on to that something, given modest exposure. If you don't, it's because you lack the ability. For you, the subject is too tough.

In contrast, Japanese and certain other cultures cultivate an "effort" model of success and failure. Assiduous extended effort grabs you the gold ring of learning, and ability gaps are surmounted by increasing effort. Although "The Little Engine That Could" is an American institution among children's stories, it is as though Japanese children have read it more often and taken it to heart more deeply.

Naive theory #2, harbored by many parents, has just as much of a home in the minds of teachers and school administrators. Rexford Brown lists the idea that "most students do not have the intelligence required by a literacy of thoughtfulness" as one of the six most common reservations voiced by teachers and administrators asked about more thinking-centered approaches to teaching.

Of course, who says naive theory #2 is really naive? Maybe the parents and teachers and administrators are right. Maybe it's hard fact. Is it the case that effort is substitutable for ability to a considerable extent? Can students master ideas initially beyond them through protracted, motivated, and appropriately guided effort?

The news from research is good here. Although there are bound to be some limits in trading off ability against effort, many findings from laboratory and classroom research testify to the leverage of effort. In a way, the point is a simple one. Some people take longer to learn certain things. However, if we organize education so that those who need more time have the opportunity and motivation to put in more time, they achieve much more.

So naive theory #2 really is naive. But does it actually do any harm? Well, it seems to in some youngsters. Evidence on this point comes from research conducted by University of Illinois psychologist Carol Dweck and her colleagues. Probing students' tacit theories of learning, they have classified learners along a continuum ranging from "entity learners" to "incremental learners." The latter are more aggressive learners. They believe, akin to the Japanese model, that learning comes by increments; you have to hang in there and persist, winning your way to an understanding. In contrast, entity learners harbor the philosophy that learning something new is taking in an entire entity all at once. You either get it or you don't. Learning is a matter of "catching on" fairly quickly. If you don't catch on, the concept is beyond you for the time being, so why try? Interestingly, sometimes relatively bright learners, in an IQ sense, are also entity learners; they may lack stamina and strategies for dealing with situations when the learning gets tough.

If naive theory #2 does mischief in the minds of some youngsters, what about in the minds of teachers? A startling demonstration here is the classic "Rosenthal effect." In the mid-1960s, researcher Robert Rosenthal conducted a simple experiment in San Francisco. He informed some teachers that specific students showed higher IQ scores than others. In fact, the students identified as high-IQ were chosen at random by Rosenthal. At the end of the year, Rosenthal compared the performance of the students said to be gifted with those not. The supposedly gifted students actually had performed better—and not just by the measure of the teacher's subjective grades but on objective tests.

What had happened? Perhaps the teachers' manner toward the supposedly gifted students had built up their self-confidence. Perhaps they had helped these students in subtle ways. Whatever the case, the teachers' belief in ability translated into better learning for those students. But they were not more able. Rather, more was expected of them!

In summary, one might say that American schools are a virtual empire of ability. The teaching is there to feed those of greater ability all they can take and to herd along the rest. Ability, not effort, is seen as the primary determining factor in how much John or Jane can learn. Tracking sorts students into appropriate ability channels, moving each along at the pace dictated by intrinsic gifts and limitations. Students buy in or drop out at various stages in part according to their estimates of whether they have the ability for the learning to be done.

Of course, any teacher knows that motivation is important and that trying helps. It would be foolish to suggest that effort is not seen as a causal factor in learning. Nonetheless, the tacit American model is ability centered. Ability has priority as a causal influence. While effort helps, it cannot really overcome ability gaps.

In other cultures as well as in laboratory research, this premise has been challenged and has been proven false to a considerable degree. Effort can be the primary explanation for successes and shortfalls of learning, with ability playing second string to explain differences left over after effort has been taken into account. We need an effort-centered model.

A CONSEQUENCE: ECONOMIC EROSION

A chilling diagnosis of the ills of American education came my way recently via that very traditional conduit of information, the lecture. Marc Tucker is director of the National Center on Education and the Economy. At a recent conference, Tucker reported a systematic series of comparisons done between the educational practices of the United States and several other nations. He relayed a number of findings about the interlocked enterprises of education and economic productivity. The findings suggest why American schools are in trouble and where American society might end up unless something is done.

Economic prosperity and productivity are key elements in the picture. In the United States, the average standard of living has been declining slightly for a number of years. While the top 30 percent of wage earners have gained, the bottom 70 percent have lost even more. In other words, the culture is becoming economically polarized.

Several nations in the world have a higher standard of living than the United States, including Japan, Switzerland, Singapore, Denmark, and West Germany. They have high wages, very little unemployment, and high productivity. An especially interesting comparison looks at the relationship between "direct workers," those that actually assemble the products or provide the services, and "indirect workers," the administrators and support staff. In these countries, the ratio of indirect workers to direct workers is substantially lower. That is, there are fewer indirect workers per direct worker. Somehow, the direct workers are getting more of the work done by themselves!

A look at the organization of work in these countries reveals how this can happen. The direct workers typically do not operate in assembly line fashion. They function in teams and do varied tasks. They assemble. They troubleshoot. They refine. They test. In other words, within their own circle, they take care of many of the problems that otherwise would get spread out inefficiently through a complex hierarchy of administration and specialization. Their wages are higher than direct workers in the United States because they do more of the work, including the more thought-demanding sides of the work.

So how come direct workers are up to these challenges? Education! They are very well educated, both in the sense of basic schooling and the sense of technical preparation for their particular roles.

And how did they get so well educated? Marc Tucker's analysis identifies a number of characteristics of the educational process in these nations that ensure a generally and technically well-educated direct-labor force. Generalizing the pattern over nations, these are some key elements:

Examination Systems Independent of the Teacher. There are examination systems that gauge student achievement. Receiving educational credentialing requires passing these examinations. The teacher does not compose and administer the exams but rather is cast in the role of working with students to prepare them for the exams. The examinations are less fact-and-routine-procedure based, more open-ended and thought demanding. They may be unconventional in character; for example, involving project work or portfolios. There are general examinations and examinations related to particular professions.

Credentials Required for Employment. Employment is virtually unavailable without appropriate credentialing through the examination systems.

Safety Nets for Dropouts.   Inevitably, people vary in ability. Many do not pass on the first attempt at an examination. But the effort-centered model rules instead of the ability-centered model. You can try as often as you want. Since some people may not find conventional instruction suitable to their learning styles or other predilections, certain of these nations provide a myriad of alternative forms of education. Agencies provide intensive counseling and keep potential dropouts in the educational loop. The whole philosophy is effort based. "Keep in there. Keep trying in different ways. We'll counsel you and guide you. And you'll get your credentials."

A Labor Market.   One could imagine that well-credentialed individuals might have trouble actually locating a job. The system would break down at that point. However, these countries also have some form of labor market involving computer systems that keep track of job profiles and nationwide needs. This makes it much easier to match up a potential employee with a potential employer.

The circumstances in the United States contrast in virtually every respect with this picture. There is no nationwide, nor in most states even a statewide, achievement exam for those aiming to be direct workers. Exams are by and large composed and administered by teachers with pass/fail decisions made by the teachers, who are therefore placed in a conflict of interest. Typically, educational credentials are not required for direct workers. Contrary to popular belief, even a high school diploma, meaningless as it often is, has been shown not to be a determining feature in whether people get jobs. Despite our concern with at-risk students, there is no very effective safety net that rescues them and keeps them in the educational loop in some fashion. And there is no labor market.

The bottom line, according to Tucker, is that nations with a more effective system are steadily gaining in productivity and outperforming the U.S. labor force. American productivity is stagnant; it has not increased appreciably in many years. As poorer nations with a more effort-based philosophy catch on to the powerful configuration exhibited by these economic leaders, the United States is likely to find more and more nations above it on the productivity ladder. A trivial pursuit model of knowledge and an ability-centered rather than effort-centered concept of the causes of successful learning are more than mistakes: They exact a deadly cost in declining prosperity.

DEFINING THE PROBLEM

This entire chapter has been an exercise in one of the most fundamental steps of problem solving—defining the problem. So let's review. When we listen for shortfalls in educational outcomes, the alarm bells of American education sound the woes of fragile knowledge and poor thinking. Fragile knowledge goes far beyond the problem of missing knowledge—the dates-and-places ignorance which so troubles so many people. It includes not only missing knowledge but inert knowledge that does not function actively in thinking, naive knowledge representing entrenched misconceptions, and ritual knowledge reflecting superficial, schoolish performances without authentic understanding. As to thinking with the content that they learn, students generally perform rather poorly in solving word problems, making inferences, explaining concepts, constructing arguments, and writing essays.

When we listen to underlying philosophy and method, we find some broad contributing causes. The alarm bells sound out concerning two naive theories. Naive theory #1 is the tacit trivial pursuit theory of learning that drives the educational enterprise. Getting an education is by and large a matter of accumulating a large bank of fairly specific knowledge and routine skills from which you can make withdrawals to deal with particular situations. Naive theory #2 says that abilities count most in learning, much more than effort. You either get it or you don't.

As to consequences, these educational problems yield a pattern of economic stagnation and decline in the work force, as American industry proves unable to compete efficiently with other nations that have their acts together better.

With all this, it must be acknowledged that in many ways America in its vastness and eclecticism poses particular problems: racial and ethnic diversity, the malaise of the inner city, the (in many ways laudable) lack of the strong centralized education-

---

Key Ideas Toward 🏠 the Smart School

SHORTFALLS: THE ALARM BELLS

Shortfalls To Be Alarmed About

- **Fragile Knowledge.** Missing, inert, naive, and ritual knowledge. The fragile knowledge syndrome.

- **Poor Thinking.** Poor handling of story problems in mathematics. Poor inferences from reading. The knowledge-telling strategy when writing. Repetition rather than elaborative memory strategies.

Causes To Be Alarmed About

- **The Trivial Pursuit Model.** Overwhelming emphasis on factual questions. Little "language of thinking" in the classroom. Short-answer, right-or-wrong test questions. Emphasis on coverage.

- **Ability Centered Rather than Effort Centered.** Low achievement blamed on ability, not effort. "Entity learners" rather than "incremental learners."

A Consequence To Be Alarmed About

- **Economic Decline.** Need examination systems independent of the teacher, credentials required for employment, safety nets for dropouts, a labor market.

---

al policies characteristic of many nations. Many articles and books deal exclusively and pointedly with such particular problems.

But the agenda of this book is more general. The remaining chapters address fundamentals of teaching and learning, fundamentals for anyone and everyone. Yes, the United States and many other nations have special problems. But the reality of these special problems does not mean that we can ignore facts and fundamentals—the facts of inadequate achievement in knowledge, thinking, and prosperity and the fundamentally misguided naive theories that tacitly underlie much of current practice.

The straightforward, hard-to-argue-with goals mentioned earlier—retention, understanding, and the active use of knowledge—are being addressed by some nations in systematic and effective ways. They are demanding goals, and to achieve them we need informed, energetic, and thoughtful schools— smart schools. Which, by and large, we do not have. Not here. Not in results. Nor in method. In Poe's words, it's worth paying heed to the "moaning and the groaning of the bells."

CHAPTER 3

TEACHING AND LEARNING

Theory One and Beyond

We could call it the "savior syndrome." Like other folk in other circumstances, educators seem all the time to be looking for a savior. The savior *du jour* shifts around quite a bit. Once it was behaviorism, then discovery learning. More recently, "time on task" has been a popular idea: If only we could keep schoolchildren at it in a serious, engaged way for long enough, the kinds of learning that we want would surely occur. A current favorite is cooperative learning, where students work in small collaborative groups to master skills and ideas.

Yes, the "savior syndrome" label smacks of cynicism. It reveals a kind of impatience with the hunger for the quick fix, the *deus ex machina* that will put things right in the classroom. Education is a complex undertaking. The hope and eagerness with which the savior of the moment is greeted, assaulted, and all too often reduced to a trivialized version becomes tiresome.

But certainly no cynicism should apply to any of the candidate saviors, properly viewed. For example, the group-learning techniques that come with cooperative learning are marvelous things with immense promise for improving educational practice. Although not fashionable today, behaviorism has its place in giving us a clear way to think about motivation in the classroom in terms of how students get rewarded for various behaviors—some desirable and some not so desirable.

So the problem with the syndrome does not lie in the candidates. Rather, the savior syndrome is symptomatic of one of the most misleading premises of educational reform: What we need is a new and better method. If only we had improved ways of inculcating knowledge or inducing youngsters to learn, we would attain the precise arithmetic, the artful writing, the astute reading, and all the other outcomes that we cherish.

I don't think so. There are three reasons why a new and better method is a red herring. Here they are in brief (the rest of the chapter is devoted to elaborating them). 1. We have plenty of sophisticated instructional methods but do not use them, or not very well. 2. Most instruction does not even meet minimal criteria for sound methods, never mind sophisticated ones. Our first urgency is putting into practice reasonably sound methods. 3. Given reasonably sound methods, the most powerful choice we can make concerns not method but curriculum—not how we teach but what we choose to try to teach.

Therefore, educational reform toward smart schools should be driven not by method but by curriculum—not by more sophisticated visions of how to teach, valuable though they are, but by a broader, more ambitious vision of what we want to teach.

I'll build this argument by offering a conception of sound method, emphasizing how little we see of it, underscoring how much it can accomplish, and exploring briefly some more sophisticated methods. Then I'll return to the key point: Given reasonable method, our most powerful choice becomes what we try to teach.

INTRODUCING THEORY ONE

A rather good theory of teaching and learning can be stated in a single sentence. The theory is not terribly sophisticated. It does not require elaborate laboratory research to test and justify. But pursuing its implications can take us a long way toward a much improved vision of classroom practice. So simple is this theory, so much a rough-hewn, first-order approximation to the conditions that foster learning, that we will call it Theory One, saving higher numbers for fancier theories.

Theory One says this:

> *People learn much of what they have a reasonable opportunity and motivation to learn.*

How could so outrageously bland a statement about teaching possibly imply anything about better classroom practice? Admittedly, Theory One seems entirely too mousey for the job. But this is the Mouse That Roared. To see its power, we need to elaborate somewhat on the implications of the one-sentence version of Theory One. What is "reasonable opportunity and motivation to learn"? Without resorting to any technical knowledge about learning, one might commonsensically put down the following conditions:

- *Clear information.* Descriptions and examples of the goals, knowledge needed, and the performances expected.
- *Thoughtful practice.* Opportunity for learners to engage actively and reflectively whatever is to be learned—adding numbers, solving word problems, writing essays.
- *Informative feedback.* Clear, thorough counsel to learners about their performance, helping them to proceed more effectively.
- *Strong intrinsic or extrinsic motivation.* Activities that are amply rewarded, either because they are very interesting and engaging in themselves or because they feed into other achievements that concern the learner.

So there it is, Theory One, a commonsense conception of good teaching practice. Theory One aims simply to establish a baseline. For any performance we want to teach, if we supply clear information about the performance by way of examples and descriptions, offer learners time to practice the performance and think about how they are handling it, provide informative feedback, and work from a platform of strong intrinsic and extrinsic motivation, we are likely to have considerable success with the teaching.

THE DEVASTATING CRITIQUE LEVIED BY THEORY ONE

Theory One was a Mouse That Roared, I promised. Here's the roar. Simple though it is, Theory One yields a devastating critique of much educational practice. Consider, for example, explanation. If there is one thing that teachers need to do day in, day out, it is explain new ideas and reexplain old ones. In terms of Theory One, good explanation is first and foremost a matter of clear information. Then how well handled is the enterprise of explanation?

Some insight comes from research on "direct explanation" conducted by educational psychologists Laura Roehler, Gerald Duffy, and their colleagues. These investigators sought to characterize what good explanation demanded. Their analysis emphasized such features as the presentation of conceptually accurate, explicit, meaningful, and sequenced information. Good direct instruction includes information about not only the "what" but also the "how" and the "when" of the matter at hand; for example, not only what a particular technique is but how and when to use it. Good direct instruction involves monitoring students' evolving understandings and their points of confusion and uncertainty in order to clarify them. For example, in teaching the reading strategy of asking yourself questions to read for, a sample of direct explanation might sound something like this:

Okay, folks, we've talked about how to ask yourself questions. But when? When is it worthwhile? Certainly when you're studying for information and understanding. Because you'll remember and understand better. For instance, when you read a section in your science book, look at the title. Look ahead at the subheadings. Ask yourself, "What do I want to understand about this?" Make a short list of questions in your mind.

Now let's check if I've been clear enough. Roger, what's another time you think it would be worthwhile asking yourself questions before you read?

(Roger says: while reading a short story.)

Aha. I see some puzzled faces. Some disagreement maybe. Let's look at the pros and cons of that "when."

Explanation seems such a mainstay of teaching that one might think that good explanation would be routinely found in classroom practice. However, Roehler and Duffy found nothing of the sort. Their studies disclosed that teachers varied widely in the quality of the explanations offered. Some were very good, but some offered vague explanations. "Whats," "hows," and "whens" were sketchy, teachers did not probe their students to cross-check the students' evolving understandings, and so on.

While this and other research speaks to a less-than-Theory One level of practice in many classrooms, we need not rely on research to construct a critique. Common knowledge about typical practices will suffice. For example, history is usually taught by asking students to learn its "story" as it unfolds at particular times in particular places, for example, the French or the Industrial Revolution. Some typical aims of history instruction include: (1) cultivating students' understanding of important historical events, not just what happened but *why* it happened; (2) preparing students to understand current events in light of historical precedent and contrast; (3) providing students with an historical background so that they can understand allusions, the context of works of literature, and so on.

By the measure of Theory One—never mind loftier instructional theories—typical history instruction does an extraordinarily poor job of working toward these objectives. Take the first goal, cultivating understanding of why things happen as they do. A classic question students get asked here is "What were the causes of the U.S. Civil War?" And students can answer, at least when the text is fresh in their minds, because contemporary textbooks spell out the causes of the Civil War.

The catch? It's right there in Theory One: students need

thoughtful practice of their understanding, but asking students to recite causes from the textbook practices just their memory, not their understanding.

What could be done to engage learners in practicing their understandings instead? For a modest improvement, the teacher might ask, "The text has talked about three contributing causes. Which do you think is most important and why?" This demands that the students reason about what they have learned. For a bigger boost, the teacher might say, "A British textbook lists these three causes of the U.S. Civil War. They sound different from what we have been reading. What do you think are the strong points and weak points of this analysis from a British textbook?" For a more aggressive approach yet, the teacher might say, "Let's set up a debate for the entire class period tomorrow. One group will defend the British textbook's interpretation, another the U.S. textbook's interpretation."

These examples are not put forth as the ideal or only way to do a better job on understanding history. There are many innovative approaches to teaching history. But they do show some simple ways of getting Theory One's thoughtful practice into the picture.

Now let's look at the second goal, enabling students to see current events from an historical perspective. Again, the typical shortfall is lack of thoughtful practice. Normal history instruction does not engage students in making connections to contemporary events. History teachers do not often ask students to think about questions like these: "In the news over the last few days, we saw an attempted coup in Russia. How was this coup like and not like a civil war? Could a coup turn into a civil war? Were there any contributing causes anything like those of the U.S. Civil War?"

As to the third goal, the background function of historical knowledge in keeping with E. D. Hirsch's notion of cultural literacy, conventional history instruction provides information but again no practice in treating historical knowledge as a backdrop. Students do not usually read novels or poems in history class and are not primed to see such works of literature against their historic backdrops. History teachers do not usually model for students what it would mean to read a story or poem alert to this backdrop—what ideas would come to mind, how they would color the literary expression, what new meanings they would suggest. All this, indeed, is seen as the work of the English teacher, if anyone. The history teacher expects that such knowledge will "pop up" on appropriate occasions in English or other classes. But remember from chapter 2 the problem of inert knowledge: Knowledge does not pop up reliably.

To all this a skeptic might say, "Oh, you want to turn history into a current-events class or an English class." Not at all. The point is not that history classes should be dominated by discussions of today's newspapers and novels instead of history. The point is that typically there is no practice at all, not even a little, of performances that are often held to be goals of history instruction. We do not need a very sophisticated conception of teaching and learning to levy criticism on usual practice. It fares poorly by the most elementary measures of Theory One.

However, perhaps history, being one of the most reductively taught subject matters, has been unfairly used as the butt of this critique. What, then, about math? If we mean computation, the score is not so bad. Instruction does provide extensive information, elaborate practice with feedback, and so on. Practice could be more thoughtful, and motivation may be a weak link here. But computational achievements are reasonable if not stellar.

If we have in mind solving story problems, the "story" is different. Performance on story problems is chronically poor. Why? For one reason, schooling provides a good deal of practice —but not, typically, thoughtful practice. It's rare that students are encouraged to reflect on how they attack word problems. For instance, a teacher might build a discussion with students about how to tackle algebra problems around questions like these: "How do you begin? Do you read the problem more than once? Does that help? Does it help if you make a diagram? A table? A mental movie of what's happening in the 'story' of the problem? What helps for you?"

Another problem is clear information input. Here the process of problem solving is at stake. Yet, teachers do not normally model for students the mental processes involved in puzzling out a story problem. Yes, they work problems on the blackboard: "Step 1: You see that there are two key variables here—so let x stand for the distance to Plainsville and y the time of departure." But they do not usually dramatize the thinking process blow by blow. Yet they can, in this style for instance:

So we've looked over the problem. We have the car heading toward Plainsville. We need unknowns. What don't we know? Well, we don't know how far it is to Plainsville. That could be an unknown. Or when the car left. That could be another. The problem does say when the car arrived, so that's known. Now there's gas mileage—that's unknown. But do we need that information? Maybe not. Let's see now. What's our best choice of unknowns here?

As to the understanding of mathematics concepts, much the same argument can be made as for history. Understanding means more than repeating explanations found in the book, and youngsters typically do not see models of that kind of generative thinking, nor are they asked to engage in such thinking themselves. But they can be. For instance:

Now everyone pair up with someone near you. We've talked about common denominators and why they're needed. I'd like each pair to make up a way of explaining to someone two years younger what common denominators are and why they're important. You can use diagrams or anything you want. After you work in pairs for a while, I'll ask some of you to present your explanations.

Again, as in the case of history, repeating ideas from the text does not exercise understanding. To practice their understandings, learners must engage in activities that require reasoning and explanation.

In Appreciation of Teachers

Much of this critique seems to hit hard at teachers. While it's true that classroom practices commonly fall short of the desirable, teachers in general are not to blame, for two reasons.

First of all, many teachers inevitably share the trivial pursuit model endemic to the American culture. That this model is mistaken is not at all obvious. Although history gives us many champions of a more constructive approach to education—Socrates and John Dewey, for example—the weaknesses of a doggedly knowledge-oriented approach have become especially plain only in light of recent research in cognitive science.

Second, many teachers know Theory One intuitively and would like to follow through on it all the time. And some manage to do so part of the time. The trouble is that the realities of the school day make this difficult. Lee Shulman of Stanford University wryly puts the matter this way:

> Teaching is impossible. If we simply add together all that is expected of a typical teacher and take note of the circumstances under which those activities are to be carried out, the sum makes greater demands than any individual can possibly fulfill. Yet, teachers teach.

Theodore Sizer, in *Horace's Compromise*, writes eloquently of an English teacher, Horace Smith, who labors with great art and dedication in behalf of his students' learning. The catch is that Horace, like most teachers, has too much to manage. So he compromises. For instance, he assigns far less writing than he thinks ideal, although more than many teachers do, and offers far less feedback than he would like. Sizer puts Horace's plight this way:

> Most jobs in the real world have a gap between what would be nice and what is possible. One adjusts. The tragedy for many high school teachers is that the gap is a chasm, not crossed by reasonable and judicious adjustments. Even after adroit accommodations and devastating compromises—only *five minutes per week* of attention on the written work of each student and an average of ten minutes of planning for each fifty-odd-minute class—the task is already crushing, in reality a sixty-hour work week.

Many of the instructional ideas in this and later chapters will seem quite useless to teachers in their present settings. And they're right! Because most current educational settings neither labor very hard to build teachers' understandings of new instructional perspectives nor allow teachers the flexibility or freedom from the coverage fetish to pursue more enlightened instruction. This is why improvement in teaching practices has to go hand in hand with some restructuring of the way schools work as organizations (see chapters 7 and 9).

Theory One Revisited

To generalize, Theory One gives a poor grade to a good deal of educational practice. And now it's easier to see how. The first Theory One condition, clear information, should include clear explanations and monitoring of students' understanding of those explanations. But often this is not found. Theory One also says that students need clear information about process—about what the performances should look like blow by blow rather than just about the facts students are to use. However, typical instruction does not provide this process information; for instance, through teachers' modeling by thinking aloud while working problems.

Thoughtful practice should mean practicing the very performances one is seeking to develop. But surprisingly commonly, we do not actually engage students in the target performances but other, substitute performances. For instance, we do not actually ask youngsters to connect their historical knowledge to current events or to read literature with the historical backdrop in mind but rather simply test their knowledge base to check whether the historical data are there. When there is plenty of practice, as with story problems, it often is not very thoughtful—students simply do problem after problem without any encouragement to strategize reflectively on how they approach problems and what works for them.

As to informative feedback, apart from the general problem of being clear, the crowded curriculum and the number of students a teacher must deal with often simply do not allow for very much feedback. And as to motivation, it's plainly the case that many students find their school experiences quite disconnected from their out-of-school lives and professional aspirations.

Curing these problems will require helping teachers toward a richer and more discriminating conception of instructional method, the concern of this chapter. It will require building a new set of priorities in the educational milieu, priorities that give teachers the time and space to pursue a more ambitious agenda for students' learning. Chapter 7, concerning the "cognitive economy" of schooling, and Chapter 9, concerning the prospects of wide-scale educational change, speak to this challenge.

THREE WAYS TO PUT THEORY ONE TO WORK

Of course, Theory One is not a teaching method. Rather it is a set of principles that any good method should satisfy. That is, any good teaching method incarnates Theory One, fleshes out its principles in ways to suit the particular needs of the learner and the moment.

Good teaching demands different methods for different occasions. Theory One should underlie them all. Here's a case in point: In *The Paideia Proposal*, Mortimer Adler highlights three different ways of teaching. He calls them didactic instruction, coaching, and Socratic teaching. All three put Theory One to work in different ways. Let's take a look.

Didactic Instruction

By this, Adler means good, clear presentation of information by teachers and texts. The enterprise is most centrally one of explanation: laying out the whats, whys, and wherefores of a topic.

Recent research has clarified some of the components of good explanation. Earlier, I mentioned the work of Roehler, Duffy, and their colleagues on direct explanation. For another source, Gaea Leinhardt has outlined several characteristics of good explanation in instructional practice. By way of example, imagine a teacher teaching the concept of an "ecological niche." Leinhardt's principles and how they might translate into action follow:

• *Identification of goals for the students.* (Teacher: "We want to understand the meaning of an ecological niche, so we can use the concept to describe the plants and animals in ecologies and compare ecologies with one another.")

- *Monitoring and signaling progress toward the goals.* (Teacher: "Francis, when you said that sharks are predators in the sea, you made a smart connection: We hadn't talked about sea creatures at all. But sure, sharks are predators. What other sea predators can we identify?")
- *Giving abundant examples of the concepts treated.* (Teacher: "Let's compare the animals in our local forests with those in Australia, Alaska, and Madagascar.)
- *Demonstration, including offering complementary representations, highlighting links among them, and identifying conditions for use and nonuse of the concepts.* (Teacher: "As we watch this film about African animals, we'll stop it and talk about the niches we see. And we'll ask whether different animals are always in different niches or sometimes the same niche and why.")
- *Linkage of new concepts to old through identification of familiar, expanded, and new elements.* (Teacher: "Niche is an odd word. Who knows what a niche in the ordinary sense is?")
- *Legitimizing a new concept or procedure by means of principles the students already know, cross–checks among representations, and compelling logic.* (Teacher: "Is the niche concept really such a useful way of talking about ecologies? Well, let's explore that. Let's think about other situations where we talk about roles in a system; for instance, the roles of people in a business or a school.")

In intensive research on an adroit teacher's classroom practices, Leinhardt found all these elements at work.

How does Theory One match with Leinhardt's concept of good explanation? Plainly, the elements of didactic instruction spelled out by Leinhardt by and large concern clear information. They are elaborations of what it would take to be very clear with learners about what they are learning. Leinhardt also touches on informative feedback in her mention of monitoring and signaling progress toward the goals; and on motivation in the emphasis on clarifying the conditions for use and nonuse and on legitimizing.

Coaching

The second kind of teaching identified by Adler was coaching. Notice how neatly coaching and didactic teaching work together.

Without didactic teaching to present some kind of information base on a new topic, learners have nothing to practice. Given clear information, however, the question arises: How does the teacher's role shift? Coaching offers an answer.

The metaphor with sports is meant quite seriously. In football, gymnastics, hockey, or track, the coach stands back, observes the performances, and provides guidance. The coach applauds strengths, identifies weaknesses, points up principles, offers guiding and often inspiring imagery, and decides what kind of practice to emphasize. This role makes just as much sense in a writing teacher's or mathematics teacher's classroom as it does on the playing field.

Imagine, for example, a teacher coaching high school students writing short stories with good "narrative hooks," those opening sentences that draw a reader in, such as Charles Dickens's famous, "It was the best of times, it was the worst of times, it was the age of wisdom, it was the age of foolishness . . ." from *A Tale of Two Cities*. A teacher's comment to one student might sound something like this:

> Charles, I love your first line, "When I got to the cookie jar, there was only one thing left, and it wasn't a cookie." That's terrific. It really establishes a mystery. But then you give it away in the next paragraph. Maybe you should keep the mystery going for a while to keep the reader involved.

Again, how does Theory One fit in to the idea of coaching? Plainly, coaching highlights the two middle concerns of Theory One: thoughtful practice and informative feedback. Assigning practice, encouraging learners to be mindful of what they are doing, and offering feedback are the coach's principal activities. At the same time, the coach needs to strive for clarity, clear information again. Moreover, the coach's relationship with the learners commonly taps powerful mechanisms of motivation.

Socratic Teaching

Adler's third method of instruction was Socratic teaching. Both didactic teaching and coaching are relatively directive, working to inform and shape the performances of the learners. Where, it's fair to ask, are the students engaged in a more open-ended way, supported in their explorations of a topic but not told what to do all the time? Where is there occasion not just to learn answers but to learn the art of inquiry? Socratic teaching is a reply to that question.

In typical Socratic teaching, the teacher poses a conceptual conundrum or snags one from the ongoing conversation. The teacher urges exploration of the issue. What do you think? What positions could one take? What definitions do we need? Views are advanced, approaches proposed. The Socratic teacher acts as kindler and tender of the conversation, helping as the paradoxes vex too much, irritating with counterexamples and potential inconsistencies as premature satisfaction sets in.

Let's imagine a teacher talking with students about "zero."

TEACHER:	The "zero" is one of the great inventions of our number system. Let's have a little argument around zero to see if we can understand its importance better. Now pretend I'm a member of the Anti-Zero club. I say we don't need it. It just wastes space. Let me hear some arguments against that. Don't be shy!
STUDENT:	Yeah, well, but how do you write down nothing?
TEACHER:	Well, if there's nothing, you don't need to write down anything. You don't write down a 1 or 2 or anything.
STUDENT:	But see, suppose something comes out to nothing, like you have nothing in your bank account, what do you write down?
TEACHER:	You just leave a blank.
ANOTHER STUDENT:	Yeah, but how can you tell whether you know you have

	nothing or you just forget to write down what you have?
TEACHER:	That's a good point!
YET ANOTHER STUDENT:	Well, but wait a minute. Roman numerals don't have a zero, and they must have done something to show nothing. So it must be okay somehow.

Cognitive scientist Allan Collins has analyzed the key moves of Socratic teaching this way.

- Select both positive and negative examples to illustrate all qualities relevant to the issue under consideration.
- Vary cases systematically to help focus on specific facts.
- Employ counterexamples to question students' conclusions.
- Generate hypothetical cases to encourage reasoning about related situations that might not occur naturally.
- Use hypothesis identification strategies to force articulation of a particular working hypothesis.
- Use hypothesis evaluation strategies to encourage critical evaluation of predictions and hypotheses.
- Promote identification of other predictions that might explain the phenomenon in question.
- Employ entrapment strategies to lure students into making incorrect predictions and premature formulations.
- Foster tracing of consequences to a contradiction to encourage the careful formation of sound and consistent theories.
- Encourage the questioning of answers provided by authorities such as teacher and textbook to promote independent thought.

How does Theory One apply? As to clear information, the Socratic teacher normally does not supply piles of information. However, the teacher does police clarity of information supplied by the participants with probing questions and with the aim of encouraging all involved to examine the information critically. (Classically, Socratic interactions are undertaken concerning problems where people already have a fund of experience that they can draw on for information.) The Socratic teacher involves the learners in continuous thoughtful practice as they collaborate and contend to sort out the issue. The teacher provides immediate feedback by way of encouragement and critiques, encouraging others in the conversation to do the same. Finally, the teacher capitalizes on the intrinsic motivation of big, motivating questions that touch us all, such as Plato's "What is justice?" and on the engaging cooperative/competitive texture of lively conversations.

If Theory One is central to these three rather different ways of teaching, what accounts for the contrasts among them? In a word, agenda. Didactic teaching serves a need that arises in instructional contexts, that of expanding learners' repertoire of knowledge. Coaching serves another need: ensuring effective practice. Socratic teaching serves yet others: helping learners to work through concepts for themselves that they might not truly grasp in any other way, as well as giving them a chance to engage in and learn about inquiry. It is only a slight exaggeration to say that, if you combine the conditions laid down by Theory One with each of those agendas, you get the respective methods. In other words, Theory One has different incarnations depending on the instructional agenda of the moment. Three key incarnations of Theory One are didactic instruction, coaching, and Socratic teaching.

THE BOGEYMAN OF BEHAVIORISM

One of my favorite essays was authored by B. F. Skinner, founder of behavioristic learning theory and progenitor of a range of behavioristic classroom practices. The essay is called "On 'Having' a Poem." Behaviorism proposes that human behavior can be explained as a large set of inborn and learned reflexives— responses to stimuli. One doesn't even need to talk about thoughts or minds. Writing about creativity from a behaviorist's standpoint, Skinner proposed that we must eschew all talk about the poet's mind, a misleading concept lacking any real concrete meaning. Rather, a poet "has" a poem in much the same way that a hen lays an egg: a result of the physical constitution of the poet and the rewards in the environment that have "reinforced" over the years the poet's behavior of "having" other good poems.

Of course, I do not agree at all with Skinner's account of the matter. But I admire his style. The core metaphor—having a poem is like a hen laying an egg—is outrageous enough to press us to rethink our categories and premises.

So in return for such stimulation, it seems worth a brief detour to (a) moderate the barrage of criticism fired at behaviorism for the present ills of education and (b) spell out how behaviorism relates to Theory One.

Behaviorism is often blamed for the current problems of education. And not without some justification. In its heyday, behaviorism was the reigning theory of learning and teaching. It cultivated a kind of excess atomism in which performances were broken down into microperformances—the 30 key subskills of effective reading and such—that students never put back together again in meaningful, thoughtful performances, a behaviorist's Humpty Dumpty. Also, by ignoring human thinking as an invalid "folk theory," behaviorism discouraged some people from interacting with students in ways that made plain the workings of the mind.

However, with that acknowledged, the commonplace accusation that "this is an old-fashioned behaviorist classroom; we need to get beyond that" usually is simply false. Very few classrooms are run in an effective behaviorist manner. Well-crafted instruction in the style of behaviorism involves careful adjustments in the teacher's actions, how students work together, and other matters, so that what is most rewarding for students is pursuing the learning objectives, not side activities. The typical classroom, in contrast, allows students many other rewarding paths, some of them disruptive.

Indeed some of those unproductive paths are rewarding for students exactly because they are disruptive. I remember a high school English teacher of mine, let's call him Mr. Davis, who had the habit of saying "well" a lot. Some students cooked up the idea of forming a pool over how many "wells" Mr. Davis would say in a week. Almost everyone in the class invested. Several students became official talliers.

Mr. Davis found out about the pool quite soon and, to subvert students' efforts to guess the number, tried rather unsuccessfully to stop saying "well." The class that week enjoyed many a giggle at his efforts. The pool became the main interest of several days, although we went through the motions of normal English classes.

Of course, Mr. Davis made the wrong behaviorist move in trying to cut out his "wells." His behavior rewarded us, making the affair more rather than less interesting. He should simply have ignored the whole thing, minimizing the damage. To be sure, this example is mild compared with the harassment teachers sometimes face in inner city schools, which really can't be ignored.

The moral: Good control of the reward structure in teaching is a complex science and art. The typical classroom is as simplistic by the measure of behaviorism as it is by the measure of its successor, cognitive psychology. Moreover, behaviorism straightforwardly encompasses a number of important learning principles. In fact, Theory One is quite consistent with behaviorism. Providing information, arranging practice, offering informative feedback, and establishing motivation are all notions that a good behaviorist would subscribe to. This does not mean that Theory One is a behaviorist theory, because Theory One allows what behaviorism denies: talk about the mind and mental processes, including teacher modeling of mental processes. But it does mean that classroom practices that do not live up to Theory One do not live up to behaviorism.

If we want insight into the roots of educational malpractice, we can find some important hints in the influence of behaviorism on the classroom. But we need to look much further and in other directions—toward the Trivial Pursuit and Ability-Counts-Most theories discussed in the last chapter, for instance, both of which dominant the scene and work against the thoughtful process of teaching and learning demanded by Theory One.

BEYOND THEORY ONE

Theory One can be seen as a kind of a milepost, marking the first mile toward more sophisticated theories. Theory One is a pretty good theory of instruction. If we conducted education assiduously according to Theory One and its two easiest incarnations, didactic instruction and coaching, we would get considerably better results than we do.

But this is no reason for serene satisfaction. A variety of research on teaching and learning has refined our understanding beyond Theory One. A look at several approaches to teaching and learning illustrates the rich resources available to teachers.

A Constructivist Perspective

Many educators today take a constructivist view of educational practice. Such a view conceives the learner as an active agent, "constructing meanings" in response to the instructional situation. Constructivism, effort centered rather than ability centered, denies the notion that the learner passively absorbs information provided by the teacher or textbook. Rather, even when the task is sheer memorization, the learner plays a very active role, struggling to understand, formulating tentative conceptions, testing those conceptions out on further instances.

What does this mean in practice? Things like this:

- One might engage students in puzzling over and experimenting with what makes some things sink in water while others float. With artful coaching, they may recreate the principle of displacement.
- One might ask young students just learning arithmetic to invent their own ways of adding and subtracting, without teaching the standard algorithms. This actually works!
- One might ask students to build better more empowering conceptions of themselves as writers by keeping a writer's diary. What things work for them? What things don't? When their writing goes well or not, what seem to be the causes?

In other words, a constructivist approach puts students in the driver's seat to a surprising extent, asking them to find their way through large parts of the learning, but of course with teacher coaching.

How does this go beyond Theory One? Theory One is consistent with constructivism but does not lay specific emphasis on the importance of the learner's working through ideas with a good measure of autonomy to achieve understanding. (How much autonomy is controversial, even within a constructivist perspective.)

A Developmental Perspective

The challenges of learning can often be clarified through a developmental perspective that examines the age and sophistication of the learner, one that asks about developmentally appropriate attainments and means of instruction. Prior to the 1980s, a developmental perspective usually meant the theories of Jean Piaget, the famous Swiss developmental psychologist. Piaget held that youngsters pass through several developmental stages, culminating during adolescence in the stage of "formal operations," which enables thinking in a formal, logical way across diverse disciplines. Piaget argued that little could be done to accelerate development through these stages. Moreover, efforts to teach a topic would fail if they demanded patterns of reasoning beyond the learner's stage.

Not everyone was persuaded about the limits to learning suggested by Piaget. Jerome Bruner, writing in 1960, articulated one of the best-known statements about children's potential in education: "We begin with the hypothesis that any subject can be taught effectively in some intellectually honest form to any child at any state of development."

Research conducted in the 1960s, 1970s, and 1980s confirmed the ingenuity of many of Piaget's questions and methods of inquiry but undermined many of his principal tenets. Contrary to Piaget's belief that stage advance comes at its own pace, a number of teaching experiments have accomplished stage advance by using a variety of instructional methods. Contrary to Piaget's notion that stages have a universal cross-disciplinary character, it appears that the progressive mastery of more sophisticated patterns of reasoning is often discipline specific. And contrary to his precept that certain patterns of logical reasoning are simply not accessible to young children, investigators have found again and again that children can display such patterns of reasoning when the content is familiar, representations are concrete, and supports for short-term memory (for instance, paper and pencil) are available.

What are the implications for the practice of education? Here are some:

- "Advanced" ideas, like the control of variables, can figure in simple form in science experiments done in early elementary school. Formerly, such ideas were kept out of elementary science.
- Concrete or familiar materials can make very abstract ideas accessible; witness the classic experiments of Jerome Bruner with arrays of blocks representing the factoring of algebraic expressions.
- Familiarity counts for a lot and makes abstraction and complexity accessible. For example, one can encourage elementary school youngsters in reasoning about complex causal patterns, such as mutual escalation, with examples drawn from such familiar territory as family squabbles.

Moreover, in several specific areas there are stage-like or other models of children's developing understandings—for example, children's ways of approaching arithmetic problems, their understanding of narrative and metaphor, or their moral reasoning. These schemes, while not as sweeping as the original Piagetian conception, can provide discipline-specific and topic-specific guides to well-tuned instruction.

How does all this go beyond Theory One? By recognizing broad developmental trends and specific developmental patterns in subject matters simply not addressed by Theory One.

Cooperative and Collaborative Learning

There is considerable evidence that children can learn much better in well-configured cooperative groupings than solo. Most any cooperative grouping may help to achieve certain ends—for example, better socialization—but for gains in conventional educational objectives, careful design is needed. Investigators of cooperative learning David Johnson and Roger Johnson of the University of Minnesota at Minneapolis and Robert Slavin of Johns Hopkins University agree that effective cooperative learning calls for joint responsibility of all children for the group performance.

Here is a practical example, the well-known "jigsaw" method:

1. Students form groups of four and divide a given topic into subtopics, each student in a group taking responsibility for teaching the others one subtopic.
2. Say the subtopics are X, Y, Z, and W. The students responsible for X all leave their small groups and form a larger group that learns about X from the text, teacher, and other sources. Likewise for Y, Z, and W.
3. Then the students go back to their small groups and teach one another their subtopics.
4. After testing, each student receives as a grade the average performance of his or her group. Thus, each is motivated to see that all do well.

Researcher/educators William Damon and Erin Phelps draw a contrast between cooperative learning and peer collaboration. The jigsaw method typifies cooperative learning: Students work in groups on the same task and, within groups, often divide up the task into subtasks. In peer collaboration, pairs or small groups of students work on the same task simultaneously, thinking together as they puzzle over its demands and work through its complexities. The task may be specific to the group. Damon and Phelps argue that peer collaboration offers more "mutuality"—more extensive, intimate, and connected discourse. They suggest that peer collaboration serves better when youngsters face novel and complex concepts.

Cooperative learning and peer collaboration go beyond Theory One in using the dynamics of groups to promote thoughtful learning as youngsters talk and think together and in tapping the intrinsic motivation of social contact to keep students interested in their academic activities.

Intrinsic Motivation

Theory One avers the importance of extrinsic and intrinsic motivation but casts no vote between them. The tradeoffs of motivating students through either intrinsic or extrinsic means have been investigated in a number of studies. Briefly, performances motivated by such extrinsic rewards as grades, lollipops, or dollar bills tend not to persist once the reward structure is dropped. The activity is simply not seen as interesting in itself. In contrast, efforts to cultivate children's intrinsic interest in a rich activity, such as the reading of literature, are more likely to lead to sustained, self-motivated involvement.

This is obvious as far as it goes, but there is a more subtle finding: Strong extrinsic reward tends to undermine intrinsic interest. In other words, if an activity is both interesting in itself *and* rewarded in extrinsic ways, children's intrinsic interest tends to wane. In one classic experiment, children engaged in an art activity. Two groups received a reward in the form of a certificate while another group did not. Later, the children encountered another opportunity to work with the art materials or do other things. The children who had received the extrinsic reward of the certificate turned to the art materials much *less* than the unrewarded children. The extrinsic reward had undermined their intrinsic interest.

Moreover, intrinsic interest is related to creativity: People are more likely to perform creatively if driven by strong intrinsic motivation. In another provocative study, Teresa Amabile of Brandeis University asked college and graduate students serious about writing to rank order lists of reasons for their interest. Some writers rank ordered a list of intrinsic reasons ("You enjoy the opportunity for self-expression") while others rank ordered a list of extrinsic reasons ("You enjoy public recognition of your work").

Shortly before and after this activity, all the writers wrote haiku. A panel of judges carefully rated their output for creativity, with high reliability between judges. The poems written before rank ordering the lists showed about equal creativity, but the poems written afterward by the writers who rank ordered the list of extrinsic motivators showed markedly less creativity than the poems from the other writers. Amabile's interpretation: The poets who rank ordered a list of extrinsic motives experienced a temporary drop in intrinsic motivation. This in turn hurt the quality of their poems.

Here are some examples of educational practice that take these points seriously:

- A teacher coaches students in developing their own criteria of quality for stories and poems they write.
- A teacher involves students in writing story problems in mathematics for one another to heighten the intrinsic interest of the problems.
- On some quizzes, a teacher has students grade one another. But the teacher gives strong feedback about what kinds of answers make more and less sense and why.

This perspective on intrinsic motivation goes beyond Theory One in a very straightforward way: Theory One says nothing about interactions between intrinsic and extrinsic motivation, but there are important interactions to worry about when we want to build strong intrinsic motivation, as we often do.

Honoring Multiple Intelligences

Developmental psychologist Howard Gardner has articulated a Theory of Multiple Intelligences, arguing that conventional IQ conceptions of human intelligence are too monolithic. Gardner builds a case for seven different dimensions of human intelligence—seven intelligences—associated with distinctive symbol systems and modes of representation. For example, logical/mathematical intelligence involves ability with the formal notations of mathematics. Linguistic intelligence involves artistry with words on paper or in the air—the artistry of the poet, the novelist, the orator. Musical intelligence demands adroit handling of musical structures, instruments, and notation. Gardner's other four intelligences are spatial (architects, graphic artists), bodily/kinesthetic (sports, dance), interpersonal intelligence (politics, management), and intrapersonal intelligence (self-reflection).

Gardner makes the point that conventional educational practice focuses largely on linguistic and mathematical intelligence. Yet, he urges, the multiple character of human intelligence demands a wider horizon if we are to honor people's varied abilities. This would include finding ways to make music, the visual arts, dance and sports, interpersonal skills, and skills of self-reflection more substantive and salient presences in classrooms and curricula.

What might this mean in practice? Things like this:

- Involving students in projects that allow many alternative modes of symbolic expression—visual art, language, music.
- Creating group projects that invite students to work in media and symbol systems with which they feel most closely attuned.
- Bringing a greater diversity of symbol systems into subject matters; for instance, engaging students in writing essays in mathematics class, or essays about mathematics in English class, or doing cartoons with witty captions in English.

The idea of multiple intelligences goes beyond Theory One in highlighting the diversity of human ability and the consequent need to diversify instructional opportunities. Theory One says nothing directly about this.

Situated Learning

Recently, cognitive psychologists Allan Collins, John Seely Brown, James Greeno, Lauren Resnick, and others have underscored a troubling feature of typical classroom learning: its decontextualized character. What happens in school mathematics, writing, or the study of history, for example, bears little resemblance to what mathematicians, authors, or historians do. Nor does it resemble in-context uses of mathematics, writing, or history by nonprofessionals—in the supermarket, on the tax form, in formulating a personal statement for a job application, in understanding current events.

These scholars have also pointed out that, in authentic contexts, effective learning gets supported in a number of ways absent in the typical classroom. For example, apprentice-like relationships are common. Knowledge and skills figure conspicuously in making progress on tasks that need doing. A social network functions to support performance and sustain relevant learning.

They sum up the circumstances with a well-chosen term, "situated learning." Truly effective learning should be situated in a culture of needs and practices that gives the knowledge and skill being learned context, texture, and motivation. Much can be done to move classroom practices toward situated learning: for example:

- Students can learn writing skills by publishing a newsletter for fellow students.
- Students can learn principles of flight by experimenting with paper airplanes and other simple gizmos that fly.
- Students can learn about statistics by engaging in research relevant to their immediate surroundings; for instance, statistics for the school sports teams.

All this too goes beyond Theory One in that Theory One says nothing specific about the importance of situating learning in contexts with real audiences, needs worth pursuing, and so on.

Beyond, But . . .

Theory One is only Theory One. That has been the important message of the past few pages. There are many ideas in contemporary education—I've given only a sample—that add more sophistication to the basics of Theory One. But—and this is important—although these other perspectives add to Theory One, one should always keep Theory One in mind. Because in general these other perspectives do not automatically take care of the four core concerns of Theory One.

Take constructivism. Simply allowing youngsters to try to figure out something for themselves by experimentation does not ensure that they're getting informative feedback (because some experiments yield very obscure results) or that they're particularly motivated (because many things to investigate aren't automatically and instantly interesting to many children).

Or take cooperative learning. Simply putting students in small groups does not substitute for their having sources of clear information. The muddled accounts of important concepts in many science texts will still be just as muddled. And while students can give one another *informative feedback* up to a point, for subtleties the teacher's input may be crucial.

Or take situated learning. Learners will still need *clear informa-*

tion about how to tackle tasks. In many situations, they will not get good informative feedback automatically. For instance, the authors of a student newsletter might need to talk to fellow students to get reactions.

The moral should be clear. It's fine to go beyond Theory One, but many efforts to do so in the spirit of constructivism, cooperative learning, peer collaboration, situated learning, or any other approach tend to lose the basics of Theory One in the shuffle. Those basics do not typically take care of themselves. They need teachers' thoughtful attention, whatever the grander plan.

OUR MOST IMPORTANT CHOICE IS WHAT WE TRY TO TEACH

The challenge of educating youngsters presents innumerable choices. Two kinds of choices routinely faced are those about method—how to teach—and those about content—what to try to teach. Very often, method gets treated as the most critical choice. To be sure, there are concerns about excess content and reductive content, and there are important contemporary initiatives to reform content. However, most of the action rotates around methods—let's try cooperative learning, let's try discovery learning, let's try the Madeline Hunter method, and so on.

The implicit message is that we are fairly satisfied with what we are trying to teach . . . if only we taught it better, so that youngsters really understood it, thought critically about it, and used it. Hence the "savior syndrome," the continuing quest for the magic method that will finally inculcate in youngsters the knowledge and skill that we cherish.

I believe that this emphasis on the quest for new and better method is a mistake. Not how we teach but what we try to teach is our most important choice. Here's why.

Reason 1: *There is not that much choice to be exercised about basic method.* Any instructional method should incorporate the fundamentals of Theory One. Among basic incarnations of Theory One, such as didactic teaching, coaching, or Socratic teaching, choice is driven by need. What does the teacher or instructional designer need to do?

- Do you need to get across a complex bundle of ideas and information where the learners have little background? Then you had better employ didactic teaching to start with; there is nothing to coach yet, and a Socratic approach is ill suited to convey all that information.
- Do you need to ensure thoughtful practice and informative feedback? Then you had better coach. Students will need your help on what kinds of tasks to tackle, how to approach them, how to handle blocks, how to work with one another.
- Is there a puzzling concept that youngsters are not likely to grasp without working it through in their own minds in a very active way? Then you had better employ Socratic techniques, because Socratic techniques support students in open-ended inquiry.

But suppose the things to be learned have all these needs (as many things do)? Then weave together didactic, coaching, and Socratic approaches. Again, choice is driven by need.

Of course, there is much more choice to be exercised about fancier methods. Should we use cooperative learning here? What kind of cooperative learning? How can we build in more intrinsic motivation? Should we harness the seven intelligences? These are indeed worthwhile questions to ask and answer in context-appropriate ways. However, even if we never got to those questions and never used fancier methods, Theory One and its basic variations would take us a long way.

Reason 2: *The shortfalls we want to address by newer methods are often more a matter of what we try to teach.* For example, many educators would like students to develop better thinking and learning strategies. But they do nothing to teach such strategies. Many educators would like students to carry ideas from the classroom out into their lives away from school. But they do nothing to help youngsters make such connections. Virtually all educators want students to understand what they are learning, not just acquire rote knowledge and skills. But most educators do not get students to practice their understandings. Instead, students end up practicing remembering.

Notice the pattern: We want better thinking and learning strategies. We want connections to life outside of school. We want understanding. And we want other things. But by and large

KEY IDEAS TOWARD 🏠 THE SMART SCHOOL

TEACHING AND LEARNING: THEORY ONE AND BEYOND

Basic Sound Method

- **Theory One.** Clear information. Thoughtful practice. Informative feedback. Strong intrinsic or extrinsic motivation.

- **Three Incarnations of Theory One.** Didactic teaching, coaching, Socratic teaching.

Further Choices

- **Beyond Theory One.** A constructivist perspective. A developmental perspective. Collaborative learning. Care that extrinsic motivation does not undermine intrinsic motivation. Honoring multiple intelligences. Situated learning.

- **Our Most Important Choice Is What We Try to Teach.** Teach to the target performances actually desired. Use didactic, coaching, Socratic, or other methods as demanded by the target performances, meeting Theory One standards.

we do not actually teach those things—not in the sense of providing direct information about them, not in the sense of providing thoughtful practice or informative feedback, not in the sense of making plain those objectives and pursuing them directly with students to harness intrinsic motivation. This is the great paradox of education: To a startling extent, we do not really try to teach what we want students to learn.

In reconsidering what we try to teach, the single most helpful move may be to redescribe educational objectives in terms of performances rather than knowledge possessed. This idea smacks somewhat of the movement a few years back to frame educational goals as "behavioral objectives," long lists of overt, witnessable performances. Perhaps inevitably, such lists commonly trivialized the behaviors they aimed to cultivate. Nothing so destructively dissective is intended here. Rather, when I say "describe objectives in terms of performances," I mean describe in simple broad terms what we want learners to be able to *do*—explain a concept in one's own words, give fresh examples of it, and so on. The chapters to come offer many illustrations.

When we look at an educational setting and ask, "What performances are students actually asked to do?" the answer is always revealing. Often, it's plain that the students are only asked to display specific knowledge and routine skills. They are not asked to learn strategically, to make connections to life outside of school, to explain or inquire or practice understanding in other ways. Unsurprisingly, people learn to do much of what they actually practice doing and not a lot else.

So newer methods of teaching alone will not help. They are not even the heart of the problem, since we have plenty of solid and plenty of fancy ways to teach already. The heart of the problem is not teaching what we really want students to learn. If we face up to what we want students to learn, we then know a good deal about how to approach it: à la Theory One, provide information capturing the performance in question, provide needed background knowledge, offer thoughtful practice, generate informative feedback, and build motivation.

So let's make two slogans out of it all:

1. *Our most important choice is what we try to teach!*
2. *Our most important craft is solid Theory One teaching!*

What we try to teach will determine more than anything else what students learn, if we teach at least as well as Theory One asks. So the smart school needs to inform and energize. It must give teachers and administrators the time, encouragement, and knowledge resources (1) to think more deeply about what is worth teaching and learning and (2) to advance the craft of Theory One teaching. Both these are central to the smart school.

SCHOOLS

CHAPTER 4

CONTENT

Toward a Pedagogy of Understanding

Several years ago I made a presentation on youngsters' misconceptions about science and mathematics at a conference. I reviewed a few misconceptions and talked about their causes. Whatever the audience gained from the experience, I learned the most after the closing questions. I had packed up my transparencies and was on the way to another session, when two of the people who had heard the presentation drew me aside.

"We have a small question," one of them said. "Just a point of curiosity really."

"Okay, sure," I said.

"One of the misconceptions you talked about was kids' belief that you can take the square root of a sum. The square root of *a* square plus *b* square equals *a* plus *b*."

$$\sqrt{a^2 + b^2} = a + b$$

"Right, and that isn't so."

"Yes, we understand that. But our question is, *why* isn't it so? It looks as though it *ought* to be so."

The question took me aback. At first I had no idea how to respond. Had they asked me why some mathematical relationship *is* so, I would have tried to offer a proof or at least a qualitative explanation. But why does this relation *not* hold? Well, it just doesn't. You don't explain *that*.

Then I had an insight, which I gratefully explained to the two, about what made their question hard and what it said about our very different perspectives on the world of mathematics. Though an educator and cognitive psychologist now, I was trained as a mathematician. I knew from years of experience that every valid mathematical relationship is hard won. Relationships that "look nice," such as the one listed above, often do not hold up. The universe of nice-looking relationships is full of chaff, with the apparatus of mathematical proof winnowing out the grain.

However, my questioners' experience of mathematics would have been quite different. They had no exposure to building mathematical systems. They had learned mostly the received content of mathematics, the many beautiful relationships that *do* hold up. From this kind of experience, it is very natural to conclude that nice-looking relationships generally work out, to expect validity, and to react with surprise when a nice-looking relationship betrays that expectation.

In short, I learned that my questioners and I had very different understandings of not just the square root but something much broader—the whole enterprise of mathematics. They saw mathematics as a matter of formally validating relationships that looked promising and would probably hold up. I saw mathematics as a matter of drawing from a sea of possible relationships the few valid ones. It was those that needed explanation, not the many invalid ones.

The moral of the story is that understanding is a multilayered thing. It has to do not just with particulars but with our whole mindset about a discipline or subject matter. The story is testimony to the dangers of an overly atomistic take on teaching subject matters, one that does not pay heed to how individual facts and concepts form a larger mosaic that has its own spirit, style, and order. If a pedagogy of understanding means anything, it means understanding the piece in the context of the whole and the whole as the mosaic of its pieces.

Pedagogy is simply an erudite word for the art of teaching. A pedagogy of understanding would be an art of teaching for understanding. Yes, that surely is a large part of what education needs. Remember the "fragile knowledge syndrome" from chapter 2: An abundance of research shows that youngsters generally do not understand very well what they are learning. They suffer from deep-rooted misconceptions and stereotypes. And they are often just plain bewildered by difficult ideas: subjunctive tenses in English, Hamlet's indecision, Archimedes's principle of displacement, why it's hotter in the summer, how slavery could have taken such a strong hold in the South. We all want to teach for understanding, of course, and we often think that we are. But too often, quite apparently, we are not.

The last chapter drew a strong moral: Our most important choice is what we try to teach. This implies that teaching for better understanding is more than just a matter of superior method. It requires teaching something more or something else, choosing differently what we try to teach. To teach for better understanding, we should teach different stuff.

But what sort of stuff? What is understanding made of?

WHAT IS UNDERSTANDING?

The Role of "Understanding Performances"

Chapter 1 offered three hard-to-disagree-with goals for education: retention, understanding, and the active use of knowledge. Understanding plays a particularly pivotal role in this trio for two reasons. First of all, the kinds of things you might do to understand a concept better are some of the best things you can do to remember it well. Looking for patterns in ideas, finding personal examples, and relating new ideas to prior knowledge, for example, all serve understanding and also lock information into memory. Second, active use of knowledge comes hard without understanding. What can you do with knowledge that you don't understand?

But understanding is a somewhat puzzling objective for education. I have often been put off by goal statements in sample lesson plans or curriculum designs that take the form "Students will understand such-and-such." How, after all, can we tell whether a student has attained this precious state of understanding? It's not something that you can measure with a thermometer, nor very readily with a multiple-choice quiz.

A comparison between *knowing* and *understanding* underscores the mysterious character of understanding. Take Newton's laws. These are the cornerstones of classical physics. The first law of Newton says, more or less, that an object keeps going in the same direction at the same speed unless some force diverts it. This was not at all obvious before Newton's insight. After all, we do not very often see objects moving in the way Newton described. In our everyday world there are plenty of forces around to divert objects in motion. Friction slows them down to a stop. Gravity bends the paths of thrown objects into a curve that comes back to earth. So it's far from clear that, left alone, objects keep going at the same speed in the same direction.

If my goal as teacher is that a student *know* Newton's laws, I can check the student's achievement by asking for a recitation, or perhaps the writing of formulas. I can even insist that the student do some algebraic manipulations to show that the knowledge is not pure rote but at least somewhat operational.

However, suppose my goal is that the learner *understand* Newton's laws. Then if I have my students recite them, write them out algebraically, and even execute a few manipulations, I still can't tell whether my students understand. My students easily could be showing me "canned" performances with hardly any understanding of what the laws really imply or explain or why they are valid.

The mystery boils down to this: Knowing is a state of possession, and I can easily check whether learners possess the knowledge they are supposed to. But understanding somehow goes beyond possession. The person who understands is capable of "going beyond the information given," in Jerome Bruner's eloquent phrase. To understand understanding, we have to get clearer about that "beyond possession."

Understanding Performances

So let us view understanding not as a state of possession but one of enablement. When we understand something, we not only possess certain information about it but are enabled to do certain things with that knowledge. These things that we can do, that exercise and show understanding, are called "understanding performances."

For example, suppose that someone understands Newton's first law. What kinds of understanding performances might that someone be able to show? Here are several:

- *Explanation.* Explain in your own words what it means to go at a constant speed in the same direction and what sorts of forces might divert an object.
- *Exemplification.* Give fresh examples of the law at work. For instance, identify what forces divert the paths of objects in sports, in steering cars, in walking.
- *Application.* Use the law to explain a phenomenon not yet studied. For instance, what forces might make a curve ball curve?
- *Justification.* Offer evidence in defense of the law; formulate an experiment to test it. For instance, to see the law at work, how can you set up a situation as little influenced by friction and gravity as possible?
- *Comparison and Contrast.* Note the form of the law and relate it to other laws. What other laws can you think of that say that something stays constant unless such-and-such?
- *Contextualization.* Explore the relationship of this law to the larger tapestry of physics; how does it fit into the rest of Newton's laws, for example? Why is it important? What role does it play?
- *Generalization.* Does the form of this law disclose any more general principles about physical relationships, principles also manifested in other laws of physics? For instance, do all laws of physics say in one way or another that something stays constant unless such-and-such?

And so on in similar spirit.

Some of these understanding performances are quite modest

in their demands; for instance, making up a fresh example of Newton's first law at work. Perhaps a student knows examples about football, and so makes up one about baseball or soccer or playing frisbee. Others are quite challenging; for instance, the last one about generalization. The variety demonstrates some important points about understanding.

First of all, we identify understanding through generative performances, where learners "go beyond the information given." Understanding consists in a state of enablement to display such understanding performances.

Second, different understanding performances demand somewhat different kinds of thinking. To justify Newton's first law is not quite the same as to apply it, although there are parallels in the reasoning.

Third, understanding is not a matter of "either you get it or you don't." It is open ended and a matter of degree. You can understand a little about something (you can display a few understanding performances) or a lot more about something (you can display many varied understanding performances), but you cannot understand everything about something because there are always more extrapolations that you might not have explored and might not be able to make.

This performance perspective on understanding illuminates what a pedagogy of understanding should attempt: to enable students to display a variety of relevant understanding performances surrounding the content that they are learning. It also harks back to the basic principle emphasized in the introduction: Learning is a consequence of thinking. Notice how all these understanding performances demand thinking—to generate explanations, find new examples, generalize, and so on.

Finally, as mentioned earlier, this performance perspective on understanding connects to the previous chapter's moral that our most important choice is what we try to teach. If we want students to understand, we should make the choice of teaching them understanding performances about Newton's first law or anything we want them to understand. We should provide clear information, thoughtful practice, informative feedback, and good motivation, just as Theory One says. But we don't, by and large. We do not very often even engage students in understanding performances like generating explanations, fresh examples, and justifications. Then we wonder why they don't understand!

UNDERSTANDING AND MENTAL IMAGES

Suppose one day, sitting quietly on your living room sofa, you find yourself in an Eastern mood. Summoning your powers of concentration and contemplation, you levitate into the air. Rising up toward the ceiling, you pass through it.

The question is: Where would you find yourself? Perhaps in a bedroom or a bathroom. Perhaps in an attic. Perhaps in the apartment of the people who live above you. The curious thing about this exercise in imagination is that typically you can say where you would end up, even though the path through the ceiling is one you have never before traveled.

Notice that you've gone beyond the information given. Your trip through the ceiling is an understanding performance that reveals your understanding of the place you leave—an understanding more integrated than just a list of all the different routes you travel in your house.

This bit of mental gymnastics reveals at work one of the most important resources of mind we have—the mental image. Mental images help to explain how the trip through the ceiling works. Over the years, you have built up a mental image of your living space. It is like a map or a three-dimensional model. It shows how the various rooms relate to one another. Therefore, when asked what would happen should you float through the ceiling, you are in a position to answer. You look at the map in your mind—the mental image—chart your course, and read off your destination.

Mental images in the sense I use the phrase here are not limited just to environments or even to the strictly visual. People have mental images of what stories are supposed to be like.

What happens when you tell a child "Goldilocks and the Three Bears," but, seeing it's getting late, you stop at the point where Goldilocks is sleeping in the baby bear's bed, which is "just right." You say, "So that's all for tonight."

"But you didn't finish the story," your child says.

"Oh," you say. "Did I tell you the story before?"

"Nope," your child says. "But it doesn't sound done!"

Stories have a shape to them. They need mystery or challenge and resolution. Children develop a mental image of the shape of stories quite early in life—not a visual image, but a kind of general feel for how stories go. After the child has that image, you can't cop out with Goldilocks snoozing in bed.

Mental Images Enable Understanding Performances

There is an important connection between a pedagogy of understanding and this notion of mental images. Understanding performances might be called the overt side of understanding— what people do when they show understanding. But what about the internal side of understanding? What do people have in their heads when they understand something?

Contemporary cognitive science has a favorite answer: mental images (many psychologists would say "mental models" to mean the same thing). Roughly defined, a mental image is a holistic, highly integrated kind of knowledge. It is any unified, overarching mental representation that helps us work with a topic or subject. For example, our mental images of our homes and neighborhoods help us navigate them (as well as allowing journeys of the imagination through ceilings). Mental images of what stories are like help us understand and make up stories (as well as stop us from palming off nonstories on our children). Other mental images help us understand topics and themes in history, science, or any other subject matter.

How do mental images do this? They give us something to reason with when we attempt understanding performances. Because you have a mental image of your home, you can work with that mental image when I ask you to predict (an understanding performance) where you'd end up if you floated through the ceiling. Because you have a feel for the shape of a story, if I ask you to make one up, your general story image gives you something to work from. Whatever the understanding performance is—explaining, extrapolating, exemplifying—if you have the right mental images they will help you do it.

The mental images talked about so far concern very basic things such as the layout of your home or the shape of a story. But mental images can also concern very abstract and sophisticated matters. Consider, for example, the mental image of the organization of the chemical elements provided by the periodic table. The table itself is, of course, an overt image on paper. But in so far as people at least partially internalize what it says, it becomes a mental image too.

And notice how abstract it is, either on paper or in your head. The periodic table is a map of sorts, but not a map of a physical space. Rather, the spatial relationships on the periodic table denote cyclic patterns in the chemical behavior of the elements, with close neighbors on the chart sharing certain physical properties. The map thereby enables a variety of understanding performances, as people reason from the spatial relationships on the table to reach predictions about the chemical behavior of the elements.

For another kind of mental image, consider personalities. Ponder for a moment the mental images of characters you build up by reading *Othello*. To test their vividness, try this thought experiment. Suppose that Othello's neighbor stops by two-thirds of the way through the play and bears vehement witness to Desdemona's good conduct. Would Othello say, "Well, okay, I guess it was all in my head"? Certainly not! If you have a mental image of Othello (not in the literal sense of what he looks like but in the sense of a feel for his personality), you know immediately and intuitively that Othello would remain uneasy. He is compulsively suspicious of Desdemona's faithfulness. What about Iago? Hearing about the neighbor's testimony, would he leave town, fearful of disclosure? Certainly not! If you have a mental image of Iago's character, you know immediately this would be too meek for Iago. He would try some further treachery to discredit the neighbor and stoke Othello's fears all the more.

For an example even more abstract than the periodic table or a personality, consider my mental image of mathematics that figured in the introduction of this chapter, where a mathematical relationship that "looks nice" also looks suspect. Like any mental image, this one enables understanding performances. Because of it, I approach new mathematical propositions with appropriate expectations—skepticism and a demand for justification. Remember the people who approached me after the lecture on science and mathematics misconceptions, asking why one of the formulas I discussed wasn't true. They showed a more credulous mental image: mathematical relationships that "look nice" look true, too. And there would be consequences for their understanding performances. They would approach a new mathematical proposition with overconfidence in its likely validity and puzzlement if it fell through.

Understanding Performances Build Mental Images

So mental images equip people for understanding performances. And sometimes people get mental images through direct instruction—as when we teach the periodic table.

But the relationship between mental images and understanding performances is not a one-way street, from images to performances. It's a two-way street: Understanding performances build mental images.

For example, we do not normally learn our way about a new neighborhood by memorizing a map. We wander around. We cope with challenges, such as getting to the grocery store or the barber shop. We explain how to find X or Y to our spouse, who explains to us how to find Z or W. All these physical understanding performances of getting acquainted with a neighborhood build up a coherent mental image over time.

For another example, where do your children get their mental image of what a story is like? Certainly not from your giving them a formal definition of a story. Instead, from hearing lots of stories, asking questions about them, acting them out, and so on.

Or, for still another example, where did I get my "looks nice means suspect" mental image of mathematical relationships. No one ever told me point-blank as a mathematics student that neat-looking propositions should be viewed skeptically. I learned this by encountering many such propositions, by struggling with their proofs or disproofs, by calibrating my hopes and expectations to the real, albeit abstract, terrain of mathematics. By learning my way around the conceptual neighborhood of mathematics much as people learn their ways around real physical neighborhoods.

In summary, mental images and understanding performances occur in a kind of reciprocal relationship. Helping students acquire mental images by whatever means—including direct instruction—equips them for understanding performances. But also, involving students in understanding performances—efforts to predict, explain, resolve, exemplify, generalize, and so on— helps them build up mental images. So there is a kind of partnership between mental images and understanding performances. They feed one another. The two are, you could say, the yin and yang of understanding.

Understanding performances and mental images become the interlocking elements that yield a pedagogy of understanding. But how might one play out this conception? If our most important choice is what we try to teach, what kinds of understanding performances should we try to teach? And what kinds of mental images? The sections to come stake out further what to try to teach in a pedagogy of understanding.

LEVELS OF UNDERSTANDING

If you can't solve it in ten minutes, you can't solve it at all.

Many students of mathematics believe essentially this. It's their credo for mathematics problem solving. Mathematics educator Alan Schoenfeld at the University of California at Berkeley has written on students' mindsets about mathematics, one of them being this "ten-minute rule." Such an attitude undermines persistence, and although blind persistence is no virtue, intelligent persistence is one of the most powerful resources for learning and problem solving.

Notice an interesting feature of the ten-minute rule: It does not concern any particular piece of mathematical content, not square roots nor the Pythagorean theorem nor the quadratic formula. Instead, it's general. It's an overarching posture toward the mathematical enterprise. In fact, the ten-minute rule is a mental image about mathematics. Although expressed in verbal form, it's essentially a holistic attitude toward the character of mathematical problems. Either they yield quickly or they don't yield at all. Either you get it quickly or you don't. And, as images do, this image influences understanding performances.

Here is another example of a very general mental image about mathematics. Dan Chazen, an investigator of mathematics learning, has found that students of Euclidean geometry have some very odd ideas about the nature of proof. Catch students after successfully doing a proof, and ask them whether they might possibly find an exception. Often they will say, "Oh yeah, if you look hard enough. Maybe an unusual triangle or a quadrilateral where the theorem does not hold up."

This is an odd image of proof to have. A formal deductive proof establishes a theorem always and forever, with no exceptions. But somehow, many students miss this point and end up with a mental image of proofs as simply pretty good evidence that does not completely settle the question. Note again, as in the case of the ten-minute rule, how this attitude toward proof has no link to any specific theorem. It's general.

Why do I bring up these particular examples of mental images? To underscore two points: (1) mental images that students have are often pivotal to their understanding of a subject matter; (2) the mental images are often not part of what is ordinarily called content. They are more general and overarching. Typical content instruction rarely touches on them directly. But teachers, by listening to what students say, watching how they behave, asking general questions, and learning what research shows, can become more aware of these general mental images and can then include in their instruction direct attention to these overarching mental images that sometimes impair and sometimes empower students.

Is there any way of organizing the general images that students harbor? We might say that there are different levels of understanding involved in understanding a subject matter. Learners need to understand things not only about particular concepts but about the whole enterprise of a subject matter, the game of mathematics, of history, of literary criticism. The understanding of particulars sits within the context of these umbrella understandings.

Colleague Rebecca Simmons and I developed a four-tier analysis of levels of understanding. Our levels were:

Content.   Knowledge and know-how concerning the facts and routine procedures of a subject matter. The relevant performances are not by and large understanding performances but are reproductive: repeating, paraphrasing, executing routine procedures. The mental images are particular and, although important, somewhat parochial: the layout on paper of long division, a synoptic "mental movie" of the Civil War. Conventional education exposes students to a lot of knowledge at this level.

Problem Solving.   Knowledge and know-how concerning the solution of characteristic textbook problems in the subject matter. The relevant performances are one kind of understanding performance: problem solving in the textbook sense; for instance, solving word problems or diagraming sentences in English. The mental images involve problem-solving attitudes and strategies: The negative ten-minute rule fits here, along with its opposite, which says "you often *can* get a problem to yield by intelligent perseverance." Here too are familiar problem-solving strategies like dividing a problem into parts. Conventional education provides abundant practice in problem solving, but very little direct instruction in problem-solving-related knowledge!

Epistemic.   Knowledge and know-how concerning justification and explanation in the subject matter. The relevant understanding performances include generating justifications and explanations; for example, justifying a critical opinion in literature or explaining causes in history. The mental images express the forms of justification and explanation appropriate to the discipline. For instance, from the geometry example earlier, the "pretty good evidence" image of proof versus the "really reliable" image. Apart from Euclidean geometry, conventional education gives very little attention to justification and explanation. In contrast with problem solving, students are generally not even engaged in activities of justification and explanation.

Inquiry.   Knowledge and know-how concerning the way results are challenged and new knowledge constructed in the subject matter. The relevant performances include advancing new hypotheses (new to oneself at least), challenging assumptions, and so on. The mental images include the spirit of adventuring and a sense of what makes for a "good bet" hypothesis—potentially illuminating and valid. As with the epistemic level, conventional education gives very little attention to the inquiry level.

In summary, there is a great deal of important knowledge and know-how concerning a subject matter that simply does not sit at the content level. Conventional instruction gives the higher levels of understanding hardly any attention. Yet the very spirit and structure of subject matters, fields, and disciplines lie at these levels.

So do important contrasts among the subject matters. In mathematics, evidence consists in deductive proof. Examples will not do. In physics, just the reverse applies: Although you may deduce predictions from a given theory, the ultimate litmus consists in a check with empirical reality. Noting such contrasts and extrapolating their implications for activities within mathematics, physics, and other disciplines are parts of what it is to understand the subject matters individually and collectively.

A pedagogy of understanding therefore demands at least a Theory One treatment of subject matter knowledge at these levels. In particular, to run through Theory One again, students need clear information at all these levels: The instruction should present or otherwise cultivate the development of relevant mental images. Also, students need thoughtful practice with the understanding performances characteristic of the levels in order to sharpen the performances and strengthen the mental images. They need informative feedback to refine their performances. And they need intrinsic and extrinsic motivation, which should consist in good part in awakening learners to the power and perspective afforded by a more bird's-eye view of a subject matter.

The smart school gives teachers the opportunity to think, talk with one another, and learn some more about higher levels of understanding in their subject matters and the encouragement to pay serious attention to higher levels of understanding in their teaching. Such teaching is not terribly technical or demanding. It reaches only a little further than many proactive teachers already do. What might instruction in this spirit look like? Suppose

students are studying the well-known sonnet by William Wordsworth, "The world is too much with us."

- *Content level.* The teacher might go over the lines of the poem,
  clarifying terms and allusions, and would expect the students
  to "know" the poem and information about it on a quiz later.
- *Problem–solving level.* Interpretation is a typical problem in
  literature. The teacher might ask students to work up interpretations of key lines, such as "I'd rather be / A Pagan suckled in
  a creed outworn." What is Wordsworth saying there? What
  would it mean to be such a pagan, and why did Wordsworth
  think of that as a worthwhile contrast to people's usual
  "getting and spending" from line 2? Also, the teacher might
  suggest strategies that students could use to tackle such problems of interpretation and might coach them along.
- *Epistemic level.* The teacher might press for reasons for their
  interpretations: What's your evidence and argument that this
  line means what you say? Moreover, the teacher might engage
  the students in a discussion of what counts as evidence for a
  literary interpretation and what kinds of evidence one should
  look for.
- *Inquiry level.* So far, all has turned on teacher-generated
  questions, like the one about the "creed outworn" line. In
  addition, or instead, the teacher might encourage the students
  to find their own puzzles in the poem and might talk explicitly
  with them about what makes a literary puzzle worth pursuing.

Now some readers may be put off by this example, because it
does not truly involve students' immersing themselves in the
poem and finding their own personal reactions to it. That
approach is fine too!—full of understanding performances, in
fact. Both, in my view, are important parts of literary study.
However, I've chose this approach to show how readily straightforward literary criticism can reach beyond the content level to
encompass all the levels of understanding.

POWERFUL REPRESENTATIONS

How do we represent things to make them understandable?
Sometimes in stories. Here's an example:

A grammarian fell into a well one day and had difficulty climbing up the slippery sides. A little later a Sufi chanced by and heard the man's cries for succor. In the casual language of everyday life, the Sufi offered aid. The grammarian replied, "I would certainly appreciate your help. And by the way, you have committed an error in your speech," which the grammarian proceeded to specify. "A good point," acknowledged the Sufi. "I had best go off awhile and try to improve my skills." And so he did, leaving the grammarian at the bottom of the well.

This is a story from a literary and cultural tradition we do not so often encounter, the Islamic tradition of Sufi teaching tales, the same tradition that yielded the widely known parable of the three blind men and the elephant. It is a representation designed to cultivate understanding. Like many such, it has an analogical character. The tale does not so much concern Sufis or grammarians specifically as it concerns academicism, grace, and getting your priorities right. In fact, the story gives us a mental image about such things. If we take it to heart, we may understand some of our own foolishness better.

The Sufi tradition of teaching tales is just one example of the use of succinct stories in building mental images. And all such stories are but one kind of representation among many that can serve the pedagogy of understanding by helping people build mental images.

From Sufis to Physics

Take diagrams. Most diagrams used in science problem solving are specific to a quantitative problem: so much mass at such-and-such a height, or something of the sort. But qualitative diagrams can represent more general situations.

Imagine that you have been studying the mechanics of motion. This problem is posed: A rocket travels through space in free fall, unpowered. The captain, aiming to redirect the course of the rocket, turns it so that it points sideways to its direction of travel and fires the engines. Your task: Draw a diagram showing qualitatively the path the rocket will take.

Such a question can elicit a variety of responses. Some typical ones appear in the following diagram. You can probably find your response among them.

This is just the sort of question that commonly discloses students' misconceptions about the science they have been studying. Note how it involves no numbers and invites no routine calculations. In fact, responses *A* and *B* in the diagram are mistaken, whereas *C* is correct. The problem with responses *A* and *B* is that they treat the initial motion of the rocket as though it was somehow eliminated by the action of the newly fired engines. According to the laws of Newton, that initial momentum remains and continues to influence the trajectory of the object. So the right answer is version C, which shows a smooth turn as the momentum in the rightward direction builds up while the original motion remains.

A teacher might use a task like this and a diagram like the one below (perhaps having the students construct the diagram by generalizing from their own responses) to help students understand Newton's principles. The qualitative diagram highlights ideas that never tend to come up in normal quantitative diagrams.

Even better might be diagrams that actually move, to give students something closer to the experience of Newtonian motion. Happily, we have those. Educational psychologists Barbara

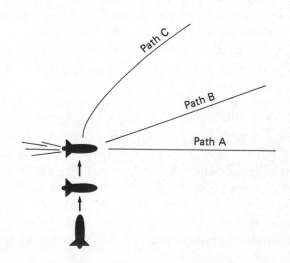

White and Paul Horwitz developed a computer environment called ThinkerTools that provides students with a Newtonian world to play with. In this environment, friction can be turned off or up. Gravity can be turned off and on and set to different strengths. Dots move about according to user-applied impulses, manifesting Newton's laws moment to moment. Moving objects can leave behind copies of themselves every second to show changes in their direction and velocity. In other ways, as well, the ThinkerTools environment demonstrates Newtonian motion clearly, allows learners to manipulate it, and makes key features of it salient by additional notational devices. In other words, ThinkerTools allows learners to build a better mental image of what Newtonian motion is like. Research done with the ThinkerTools environment has demonstrated that learners attain considerably more understanding of Newtonian motion than through more conventional instruction.

ThinkerTools is one case in point among many. A considerable body of evidence shows that carefully chosen representations can provide learners with mental images that enhance their understanding. Educational psychologist Richard Mayer recently reported an extensive series of experiments in which science concepts were taught both conventionally and accompanied by some sort of conceptual model, typically a visual representation that illustrated in some simple fashion what the concept meant and how it worked. For instance, a lesson on radar included a five-step diagram that showed a radar pulse moving outward from the source, striking an object, and bouncing back, with the total travel time measured to determine the distance. A lesson on the concept of density showed volume by the number of equal-sized boxes and density by the number of equal-mass particles in every box.

Mayer discovered that students' verbatim recall of the concepts taught did not differ much with or without the conceptual models. But when the conceptual models made up part of the lesson, recall of the gist of the message was superior. Moreover, the students showed much better performance on problems that asked them to extrapolate from what they had learned (understanding performances again). Such advantages appeared for weaker students but not for stronger ones, who, it seemed, constructed their own conceptual models. Interestingly, Mayer also discovered that conceptual models presented *after* a lesson yielded no positive effects. Mayer suggests that conceptual models presented after a lesson about a concept run up against students' already formed ideas and fail to penetrate.

Concrete, Stripped, Constructed Analogs

Colleague Christopher Unger and I generalized some key characteristics from many of the powerful representations that have proved effective in building students' understandings. Quite commonly, powerful representations are what might be called *concrete, stripped, constructed analogs.* There is a lesson to be learned about the use of representations by focusing on what each of these terms means.

- *Analogs.* Most such representations provide some kind of analogy with the real phenomenon of interest. For example, pictures of rockets and dots for their paths are not real rockets and trajectories. In the "ThinkerTools" Newtonian-motion computer simulation, dots on a screen are not real objects in motion, but behave like them.
- *Constructed.* Most commonly, the analogs are fabricated for the purpose at hand. Analogs based on common knowledge are often misleading. For example, one can characterize the atom as a small solar system, but in several ways the analogy is deceptive. By drawing the diagrams, programming the computer simulations, or telling the stories as we want them to be rather than relying on direct allusion to everyday experience, one can avoid this.
- *Stripped.* Most such representations eliminate extraneous clutter to highlight the critical features. For example, the diagram above lacks detail and the "ThinkerTools" environment does not show rockets or flying saucers in motion, but simply dots.
- *Concrete.* Most such representations make the phenomenon in question concrete, reducing it to examples, visual images, and so on.

Of course, not all representations that powerfully enhance understanding have to fit this profile. Representations of diverse sorts play important roles in learning and understanding. Still, it was with some amusement that I discovered, months after Unger and I had formulated the four criteria above, that the ancient tradition of Sufi tales fit them just as well as ThinkerTools!

The tale of the grammarian, for example, is an analog for a more general class of situations where fussy correctness threatens to override what's really important. The story makes the idea behind it concrete. The story is plainly constructed, not an actual experience. And finally, the story is stripped: nowhere near as elaborated in terms of character and setting as it would be were it presented primarily as a literary work. ThinkerTools may be a product of twentieth-century technology, but the human ingenuity to create powerful representations is ancient.

All this may sound rather technical, an unwelcome barrier for busy teachers. True! Although I've tried to cast some analytical light on what makes representations powerful, intuitions are worth trusting here. There is no need to worry about a checklist of key features of representations. Teachers—and students—can tap their intuitions. Does a representation look and feel as though it's making things clearer? If not, can you make up an image or analogy that works better? Can you trim down an image or analogy, getting rid of clutter to make the point clearer? What's really important is not technical criteria but the free and imaginative reach for diverse representations to build understandings.

GENERATIVE TOPICS

We've been discussing what to do with a topic to teach the topic for understanding: engage students in understanding performances, involve higher levels of understanding, use powerful representations.

But what about the choice of topics itself? Might some topics not lend themselves much more to a pedagogy of understanding than others do? To be sure, much can be made of any topic by sufficiently artful teaching. But this does not mean that all topics are created equal. One might speak of "generative topics," topics that particularly invite understanding performances of diverse kinds, topics that make teaching for understanding easy.

Again we are back to the theme of what we choose to try to teach. Many of the topics taught in the conventional treatment of the subject matters do not appear to be very generative. They are not chosen for their outreach, their import, their connectability. A pedagogy of understanding invites reorganizing the curriculum around generative topics that provoke and support a variety of understanding performances.

It is even possible to lay down some standards for a good generative topic. Here are three, stemming from collaborative work of colleagues Howard Gardner, Vito Perrone, and me:

- *Centrality*—the topic should be central to a subject matter or curriculum.
- *Accessibility*—the topic should allow and invite teachers' and students' understanding performances rather than seeming sparse or arcane.
- *Richness*—the topic should encourage a rich play of varied extrapolation and connection making.

But what are some good-bet generative topics? Here is a sample drawn from the collaboration mentioned above:

Natural Sciences.   Evolution, focusing on the mechanism of natural selection in biology and on its wide applicability to other settings, like pop music, fashion, the evolution of ideas. The origin and fate of the universe, focusing qualitatively on "cosmic" questions, as in Stephen Hawking's *A Brief History of Time*. The periodic table, focusing on the dismaying number of elements identified by early investigators and the challenge of making order out of the chaos. The question "What is real?" in science, pointing up how scientists are forever inventing entities (quarks, atoms, black holes) that we can never straightforwardly see but as evidence accumulates, come to think of as real.

Social Studies.   Nationalism and internationalism, focusing on the causal role of nationalistic sentiment (often cultivated by leaders for their own purposes), as in Hitler's Germany, in world history, and in the prevailing foreign policy attitudes in America today. Revolution and evolution, asking whether cataclysmic revolutions are necessary or evolutionary mechanisms will serve. Origins of government, asking where, when, and why different forms of government emerged. The question "What is real?" in history, pointing up how events can look very different to different participants and interpreters.

Mathematics.   Zero, focusing on the problems of practical arithmetic that this great invention resolved. Proof, focusing on the different ways of establishing something as "true" and their advantages and disadvantages. Probability and prediction, highlighting the ubiquitous need for simple probabilistic reasoning in everyday life. The question "What is real?" in mathematics, emphasizing that mathematics is an invention and that many mathematical things initially were not considered real (for instance, negative numbers, zero, and even the number one).

Literature.   Allegory and fable, juxtaposing classic and modern examples and asking whether the form has changed or remains essentially the same. Biography and autobiography, contrasting how these forms reveal and conceal "the true person." Form and the liberation from form, examining what authors have apparently gained from sometimes embracing and sometimes rejecting certain forms (the dramatic unities, the sonnet). The question "What is real?" in literature, exploring the many senses of realism and how we can learn about real life through fiction.

Many of these topics do not sound very much like those typically focused on in the subject matters. Compare them to "mixed numbers" or "factoring" from mathematics; "poetic feet" or "adverbs" from English; "Abraham Lincoln's early years" from history; and so on. To be sure, we have to remember what was acknowledged earlier: Much can be made of any topic. But truly generative topics reach for depth and breadth to a degree that more customary topics do not. They can provide the basis for foundational reorganizing of instruction, as indeed very similar topics and questions have in the Coalition of Essential Schools organized by Theodore Sizer and his colleagues.

This should not be taken as a blanket condemnation of the typical organization of subject matter instruction. Inevitably, there are a number of more specific and localized topics that invite weaving into the fabric of the subject matter. However, as underscored earlier, in general there is far too *much*. The trivial pursuit model has led to huge compilations of bits and pieces.

The smart school wants it just the other way. Working toward informed, energetic, and thoughtful learning, the smart school encourages teachers to think deeply about what they are teaching and why and gives them time and background information to help. In the smart school, there are fewer bits and pieces, and they cluster around more general and pregnant generative topics.

AN EXAMPLE OF TEACHING FOR UNDERSTANDING

Concretely, what does all this mean for classroom practice? What happens in the truly thoughtful school? Suppose, for example, that youngsters in a class have just read one of the tales from the Sufi tradition alluded to earlier.

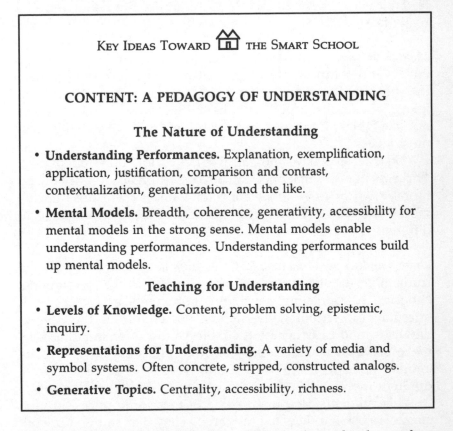

KEY IDEAS TOWARD 🏠 THE SMART SCHOOL

CONTENT: A PEDAGOGY OF UNDERSTANDING

The Nature of Understanding

- **Understanding Performances.** Explanation, exemplification, application, justification, comparison and contrast, contextualization, generalization, and the like.

- **Mental Models.** Breadth, coherence, generativity, accessibility for mental models in the strong sense. Mental models enable understanding performances. Understanding performances build up mental models.

Teaching for Understanding

- **Levels of Knowledge.** Content, problem solving, epistemic, inquiry.

- **Representations for Understanding.** A variety of media and symbol systems. Often concrete, stripped, constructed analogs.

- **Generative Topics.** Centrality, accessibility, richness.

The Conventional Classroom.   The teacher asks the student for a definition of fable. The teacher then asks the students to recount what happened in the story. And why do we call it a fable? Does it fit the definition? Then the students discuss the point or moral of the story. And that's that.

The Thoughtful Classroom.   The fable is a locus for a much richer and more complex array of activities:

Generative topics.   The fable is one example within an ongoing topic concerned with allegory and fable. "Why do we have fables?" the teacher asks. "Do all cultures have fables?" "Where do you think fables come from?" As the youngsters get the spirit of connection making, the teacher encourages them to ask their own questions: "Why do fables stick around for so long?" "Why do fables sort of sound alike?" "Are any of the fables we read really helpful?"

Mental images.   The teacher uses many classic exemplars of fables, and contrasting examples of nonfables are used to help the students develop a feel for what fables are like. "What about jokes?" the teacher asks. "Are jokes fables? How are they like and not like fables? Can you find a joke that's more like a fable than most jokes?"

"Do jokes ever have 'morals,' like fables do?" one student asks. The class ponders that one. Can anyone think of a joke that has a moral? Two or three jokes are told. One of them does have a moral. The class discusses how jokes and fables are the same and different.

Understanding performances.   Questions like those above ask the students to engage in understanding performances, explaining, choosing, extrapolating, developing arguments, and so on. Such questions can encourage learners to relate fables to their everyday lives, find cases where the fable would offer sound advice, make up cases where the fable would offer poor advice, create another fable with the same moral, revise the fable to offer a different moral.

While students can pursue some of these enterprises through class discussion, others are too large. They demand group work or work at home to afford time to think things through and craft a product.

Levels of understanding.   The teacher involves students in exploring how you know what a fable really means. "How do you test your interpretation against the story?" the teacher asks. "Is this different from other ways that we test ideas in literature or in other fields?" "Let's work through an example. We'll all write what we think the moral of this fable is. Then we'll see if we agree. If not, we'll look for evidence. And we'll pay attention to what kinds of evidence we need."

The students give it a try. Of course, they all don't draw the same moral. Thinking on the Sufi story about the grammarian, maybe one child says, "It means that you shouldn't say bad things to people who might help you."

"Okay, can you find some evidence for that in the story?" the teacher asks.

"Well, the grammarian, he says what's wrong with the way the Sufi talked. And then the Sufi walked away."

"Good. How about another moral?"

Another student answers. "It's about what's important. Getting out of the well is more important than grammar. It's life or death."

"And what's your evidence?"

"Well, it's sort of the same. The grammarian tells the Sufi his mistakes. But the grammarian isn't thinking about his own situation. He's not thinking about what's important."

After a little more of this, the teacher shifts focus. "Okay, we'll see what other morals there might be in a moment. But lets stand back and look at what we're doing. We're looking for evidence in the story. How do we do that? What do we look for? What's evidence?"

After a pause and a little puzzlement, the students begin to respond. "Well, you sort of read it over and look for things the story says that fit." "You think about what happens in the story." "You can't just make it up. You have to find some words that say the evidence." "Sometimes you can use the same evidence in more than one way." In this sort of exchange, teacher and students begin to deal directly and explicitly with the epistemic level of understanding.

Powerful representations.   The teacher asks the students to make up unifying metaphors that express the students' mental images of fables. One child suggests, "A fable is like a peach, with a tasty outside but a tough center. That's the moral."

Another says "A fable is like a joke, only not always funny. It's like a joke 'cause it tells the story but you have to get the point yourself."

Of course, all this is simply by way of example. Many different and rich lessons cultivating students' understanding could be built around the same fable. To offer a formula for a pedagogy of understanding would defeat the enterprise at the outset, working against the extrapolative character of understanding performances.

But to disdain formulas is not to eschew guidelines. The notions of understanding performances, mental images, higher levels of understanding, powerful representations, and generative topics offer a broad framework for changes in what we try to teach in the smart school.

CHAPTER 5

CURRICULUM

Creating the Metacurriculum

What do you do when you don't understand something if you want to understand it better? For example, what would you do if you wanted to understand something like Abraham Lincoln's Gettysburg Address, long division, or a suit of armor, just by thinking about it? What questions would you ask yourself about it?

This was the question my colleagues Heidi Goodrich, Jill Mirman, Shari Tishman and I concocted for youngsters to probe their ideas about how to approach a problem of understanding. We wondered what their ideas were about the challenge of understanding and what strategies they knew. One thing we quickly discovered was that even fourth and fifth graders had some pretty sophisticated notions. One fourth grader wrote:

First I would ask myself: What is it? Then, why we need it? How does it work or how it happens? If for example I can't

understand a word, I read the title and think about what the
title means. Then I would read the sentence before it and
after it twice. Next I would read that sentence and replace
the word with a word that might fit in its place.

Some chose to generate specific questions rather than mention
their general strategies.

1. How do you make a Lego? 2. How do we think? 3. How
do we move? 4. How did we get the alphabet? 5. How do
taste buds taste? 6. How do we hear? 7. How do we read? 8.
How do I do this test? 9. What is this test about? 10. How
hard is this test?

Apparently, not very hard for this curious youngster. Of
course, whereas these are two particularly rich responses in their
distinctive ways, there were also sparse responses.

First when my teacher asks me if I understand I would not
answer yes. I would only answer *that* if I knew the answer
and if I didn't know the answer I would ask her to explain it
more clearly.

And, even more baldly:

I have no idea what goes on in my head when I don't
understand something.

However sparsely or richly, all these youngsters, cued by a
simple question, proved able to reflect upon their own thinking
and learning. Moreover, many of the children revealed quite
specific and sophisticated ideas about the thinking and learning process. Their responses illustrate "metacognition"—
thinking about thinking (including learning). The liveliness of
their answers and the practical utility of many of their strategies speak to the importance of what we could call the metacurriculum.

THE IDEA OF THE METACURRICULUM

The basic idea of the metacurriculum is a simple one. It says that our usual notions of subject-matter content leave out higher-order knowledge.

But what does higher-order knowledge mean? For a start, let's proceed by way of example:

- From the previous section, fourth and fifth graders' ideas about questions to ask themselves to understand something are higher-order knowledge—knowledge about how to get knowledge and understanding.
- General problem-solving strategies like "divide a problem into subproblems" are higher-order knowledge—knowledge about how to think well.
- Familiarity with ideas like hypothesis and evidence—and with what you do with such ideas, such as make hypotheses and test them by seeking evidence—is higher-order knowledge about thinking.
- Knowledge about what evidence is like in different subject matters—formal proof in mathematics, experiment in science, argument from the text and from historical context in literature —is higher-order knowledge about the way the subject matter works.

As these examples suggest, what makes higher-order knowledge higher order is its aboutness. Higher-order knowledge is about how ordinary subject-matter knowledge is organized and about how we think and learn.

People sometimes worry that higher-order knowledge consists only of generalities disconnected from the subject matters. But on the contrary, much of it specifically concerns particular subject matters and is arguably an essential part of understanding a subject matter. Look again at the last bulleted item above. Certainly, understanding how mathematics or science or literature works requires understanding what evidence is like in those disciplines.

Of course, not all higher-order knowledge is knowledge about particular disciplines. Much of it concerns people's knowledge of how they think and learn. This is often called "metacognitive" knowledge, because it is knowledge about how cognition works. The fourth grader with all the questions like "What is it?" and "Why do we need it?" showed considerable metacognitive knowledge about how to build an understanding. My colleague Robert Swartz and I have defined four levels of metacognition: tacit, aware, strategic, and reflective. Tacit learners are unaware of their metacognitive knowledge. Aware learners know about some of the kinds of thinking they do—generating ideas, finding evidence—but are not strategic in their thinking. Strategic learners organize their thinking by using problem solving, decision making, evidence seeking, and other kinds of strategies. Finally, reflective learners not only are strategic about their thinking but reflect on their thinking-in-progress, ponder their strategies, and revise them.

Whether about the subject matter or one's own thinking, all these kinds of higher-order knowledge are parts of the metacurriculum. The idea of the metacurriculum puts more flesh on the basic notion expressed two chapters ago that *our most important choice is what we try to teach.* The normal curriculum deals with conventional content and rarely touches the metacurriculum, another kind of content that addresses the learner and the subject matters from a higher-order perspective.

Motivating the Metacurriculum

Nice, this higher-order perspective. But is it necessary? Do we really need it for the smart school?

We do if we want to accomplish the hard-to-argue-with goals advanced in chapter 1. It was already argued there that conventional educational practice does not achieve what we want for any of these objectives. We do not see the retention, or the understanding, or the active use of knowledge that we would like to see.

But how does the metacurriculum speak to these shortfalls? By dealing directly with all three. In particular, the metacurriculum includes skills of memorization, thus dealing directly with retention. It treats the conceptual organization of the subject matters and thinking, thus dealing directly with understanding. And it includes attention to transfer of learning, thus dealing directly with the active use of knowledge.

Besides this general argument, there is the testimony of various individuals and organizations who have thought hard about the dilemmas of education in recent times. For example, in the widely read report *High School: A Report on Secondary Education in America,* Ernest L. Boyer, president of the Carnegie Foundation for the Advancement of Teaching, speaks to the need for enhanced literacy in a broad sense. He includes not just better mechanics of reading and writing, but higher-order skills of dealing thoughtfully with texts.

In like spirit, the report of Project 2061, an effort to reconceive the content of science and mathematics instruction, urges attention not just to selected conventional content (Newton's laws, atomic theory) but to several "meta-aspects" of science and mathematics (the nature of scientific inquiry, the evolution of scientific thought, the practice of scientific thinking). Recent recommendations of the National Council of Teachers of Mathematics emphasize the centrality of flexible problem solving to the learning of mathematics.

Building the Metacurriculum

If the metacurriculum is so important, what does it look like? First of all, the metacurriculum is not a separate curriculum, with its own class periods. The metacurriculum should be blended in rather than added on. The metacurriculum is infused into the usual teaching of the subject matters, enriching and amplifying them. Without pretending to exhaustiveness, we can certainly list some key components of this metacurriculum. Here they are in preview, with upcoming sections saying more about each of them:

- *Levels of understanding.* As in the previous chapter, kinds of knowledge "above" the level of content knowledge in their abstraction, generality, and leverage (e.g., problem-solving strategies).
- *Languages of thinking.* Verbal, written, and graphic languages that assist thinking in and across subject matters.

- *Intellectual passions.* Feelings and motives that mobilize the mind toward good thinking and learning.
- *Integrative mental images.* Mental images that tie a subject matter or large parts of it together into a more coherent and meaningful whole.
- *Learning to learn.* Building students' ideas about how to conduct themselves most effectively as learners.
- *Teaching for transfer.* How to teach so that students use in other subject matters and outside of school what they learn in a particular subject matter.

If the metacurriculum reminds us of anything prominent these days on the educational scene, it is thinking skills. For more than a decade, many educators have worked hard to understand the nature of complex cognition and sought ways to teach students how to think better. Indeed, this has been one of my own major areas of research and materials development.

However, the metacurriculum is much more than thinking skills. It is a larger concept in several ways. Whereas thinking skills generally do not focus on the subject matters, the metacurriculum concerns their conceptual organization as well. Whereas thinking skills usually are seen as cross-disciplinary, the metacurriculum emphatically includes discipline-specific skills. Whereas thinking skills by name and nature center on thinking, the metacurriculum includes integrative mental images and teaching for transfer.

Certainly, the inspiration for the metacurriculum comes from contemporary efforts to teach thinking skills. But ambitious as they are, those efforts may not be ambitious enough to mesh well with the larger enterprise of education. By going further, the notion of the metacurriculum may help to make plain how essential to youngsters' learning a higher-order perspective is.

Let us look at some pieces of the metacurriculum in more detail.

LEVELS OF UNDERSTANDING

The notion of levels of understanding is already familiar from the previous chapter. It means here what it did there: Attention should be paid not just to facts and routines but to the problem-solving, epistemic, and inquiry levels of understanding. Recall that the problem-solving level concerned how to solve typical problems in a discipline. The epistemic level had to do with the nature of evidence and explanation in a discipline. The inquiry level addressed the kinds of questions and explorations characteristic of the discipline.

This is a good place to underscore how very useful such higher-order knowledge can be. Investigations of mathematical problem solving conducted by Alan Schoenfeld have shown substantial gains from instruction in good problem management and the use of problem-solving strategies. For instance, students who learn to monitor their progress on problems, asking themselves "Am I making progress with this approach?" "If not, can I find another approach?" "How can I check my answer?" and so on, make better use of their knowledge of mathematics in the solving of problems.

How about the epistemic and inquiry levels? Researchers Posner, Strike, Hewson, and Gertzog argue that the acquisition of science concepts with genuine understanding depends in part on the "conceptual ecology" within which the particular concept sits, including matters of standards of inquiry, how things are supposed to fit together, what's a puzzle and what isn't, and so on. A number of interesting interventions in science and mathematics learning operate at the epistemic and inquiry levels emphasized by Posner and his colleagues.

For example, educator-software designers Judah Schwartz and Michal Yerushalmy developed a software environment called The Geometric Supposer. The Supposer makes it very easy for students to do geometric constructions on computer. Students can bisect a line segment, drop an altitude, or try out other constructions freely and flexibly. This allows them to poke around with geometry, looking for interesting relationships and formulating conjectures that could become theorems. Of course, a conjecture that passes the test of "coming out right" when worked out several times on the Supposer still needs a proper proof.

Students using the "Supposer" commonly rediscover important classic theorems rather than learning them by rote from the textbook. The moral: The Supposer works at the inquiry level, making Euclidean geometry an inquiry-oriented subject, which it usually is not. Moreover, the Supposer has payoffs at the epistemic level (evidence and explanation), because it emphasizes the confusing distinction between particular constructions where a conjecture holds up and an actual logical proof.

For another example, experiments by John Clement and colleagues on youngsters' understanding of Newton's laws encourage students to use analogy to detect logical incoherences in their own conceptualizations of physics phenomena. For instance, some of their experiments concern force and bending: If you place a book on a table, does the table bend slightly and push back on the book? The answer is crucial to learners' understanding of Newtonian mechanics. Many students say no at first. They agree, however, that if you place a book on a spring, or a very thin board, those certainly bend and push back. So where to draw the line? By imagining thicker and thicker boards, many students realize that a logically simpler picture comes from saying that even thick tables push back and finally, that any push has an opposing push—there is always a reaction force in Newtonian terminology. The moral: Clement's technique works at both inquiry and epistemic levels. As to inquiry, it involves students in reasoning out something for themselves, albeit with the teacher's support. As to the epistemic level, it highlights argument by analogy and the importance of simplicity in explanation.

For a third example, specialists in the teaching of thinking Robert Swartz and Sandra Parks have developed a number of lessons to demonstrate the infusion of thinking strategies into subject matter instruction. One illustrative lesson focuses on decision making in history. The lesson looks closely at Harry Truman's decision to use the atomic bomb to end World War II. Students read a testimonial from Truman about the care with which he took the decision and how troubling he thought it to be. Then the students brainstorm alternative plans, putting themselves in Truman's shoes: What else could have been done? They analyze the consequences of other possible plans, including a land invasion. Along the way, they read original source documents that inform their reasoning. Representatives of the American military comment on likely losses from a land invasion. Japanese generals articulate their steadfast determination to carry the war to the limit.

At the beginning of the exercise, many students view Truman's decision as appalling. By the end, many are less sure. They have learned something about the historical circumstances and the importance of examining options and consequences. The moral: The Truman lesson operates at the inquiry level by projecting students into an active historical role. The lesson also carries an epistemic message about history: the evidential weight of original source materials.

With such examples in mind, problem-solving, epistemic, and inquiry knowledge become obvious essentials for the content of the metacurriculum.

LANGUAGES OF THINKING

As mentioned earlier, one natural part of the metacurriculum is the teaching of thinking skills, an enterprise that has generated considerable activity and controversy in education over the past two decades. Some thinking skills fall naturally within the levels of understanding just discussed. Others, though, seem less related to the disciplines: skills of decision making, everyday practical problem solving, or communication. Since levels of understanding by no means soaks them all up, they deserve separate discussion.

One problem with the thinking skills movement has been the narrow sound of the term "skills." Indeed, hardly anyone associated with efforts to teach thinking is happy with it. A much broader and more flexible way to understand the enterprise is as cultivating languages of thinking.

The Resources of English

One language of thinking is part of ordinary English. Chapter 2 mentioned a clear example: the investigations at the Ontario Institute for Studies in Education of David Olson, Janet Astington, and Richard Wolfe. They looked at the extent to which certain school textbooks included the ordinary everyday vocabulary of thinking that English provides—terms such as "hypothesize," "believe," "predict," and so on. Disturbingly, their studies revealed that such words rarely appeared in textbooks at all. Authors apparently avoided them on the grounds that students wouldn't understand.

The consequence of this dumbing down of textbooks is dismaying. Students rarely encounter, and so lack familiarity with, a very fundamental vocabulary concerned with the critical and creative exploration of ideas. Therefore, one important part of the metacurriculum has nothing to do with thinking skills in any special sense. It simply says, "Let's get back into place in the schools an important part of our common linguistic heritage."

Arthur Costa, a former president of the Association for Supervision and Curriculum Development and a vigorous campaigner and consultant toward the smart school, directly addresses teachers' use of language in a well-known article called "Do You Speak Cogitare?" By "Cogitare," Costa means ways of using the English language that exercise the vocabulary of thinking and foster thoughtfulness. Costa emphasizes by contrast how teachers can frame their utterances differently to promote thoughtfulness. For example:

- Teachers can use the vocabulary of thinking. Instead of saying, "Let's look at these two pictures," a teacher might say, "Let's *compare* these two pictures." Or instead of "What do you think will happen when . . . ?" "What do you *predict* will happen when . . . ?"
- Teachers can handle discipline in ways that encourage thoughtfulness. Instead of saying, "Be quiet!" a teacher might say, "The noise you're making is disturbing us. Is there a way you can work so that we don't hear you?" Instead of "Sara, get away from Shawn!" a teacher might say, "Sara, can you find another place to do your best work?"
- Teachers can provide questions rather than solutions. Instead of saying, "For our field trip, remember to bring spending money, comfortable shoes, and a warm jacket," a teacher might say, "What must we remember to bring with us on our field trip?"
- Teachers can press for specificity. When a student says, "Everybody has one," the teacher might say, "Everybody? Who

exactly?" Or when a student says, "This cereal is more nutritious," the teacher might say, "More nutritious than what?"

By shifts of locution such as these, Costa shows how teachers can use language artfully to make the classroom a more thoughtful place. Ultimately, as children do in any language environment, they will begin to pick up and internalize the idiom.

The Language of Strategies

Besides the everyday language of thinking ("believe," "predict," and so on), there is the language of thinking strategies. There are numerous efforts to improve particular kinds of thinking—problem solving, decision making, causal reasoning. Usually in such efforts, students are introduced to concepts and strategies for handling better the kind of thinking in question.

Good causal reasoning involves a set of significant terms and concepts—cause, effect, sufficient vs. contributing cause, multiple causes, and so on. There are standards to abide by and cautions about what to avoid: For instance, correlation is not sufficient evidence for causation. An increase in crime rates with the advent of television (correlation between the two events) does not prove that television causes crime. Maybe both were caused by some other event. Maybe it's coincidence. This is an important pitfall to know about: Many students (and not only students!) take correlation as strong evidence of causation; it is not.

Causal reasoning is a good "language" to cultivate in students because there are numerous applications in the curriculum: exploring causes of war, drugs, crime, or on the not-so-grim side, what makes a rocket work, an air conditioner cool, or even a poem speak to its audience with power and eloquence. The concepts, words, and strategies of the language of causation include some everyday ideas—like cause and effect—but also more technical ideas—like contributing cause and correlation. These are not so much a part of our commonplace linguistic heritage, but they are ideas to keep in mind in order to reason well about causes and effects.

There is considerable evidence that some thinking concepts

and strategies can be taught to students in a fairly direct way with worthwhile results. For example, several years ago a team of researchers, including myself, wrote and tested a course called Project Intelligence (now distributed in the United States under the name Odyssey). The course was developed at Harvard University and the Cambridge consulting firm of Bolt, Beranek, and Newman under contract with the government of Venezuela.

The course taught a number of concepts and strategies in the areas of classification, decision making, inventive thinking, problem solving, and more. The lessons on decision making introduced a simple but powerful tool for organizing the exploration of a decision. You make a table with brainstormed options down the side and brainstormed criteria across the top. The boxes of the table give you a place to evaluate each option by each criterion. The lessons on inventive thinking highlighted the concept of design. The lessons introduced powerful questions that you can ask about any design—"What are its different purposes?" "How do its features serve those purposes?"—to develop students' appreciation for the ingenuity of ordinary objects like pencils and doorknobs. Then the students learned design strategies to help them invent simple gadgets and tackle other creative problems.

Project Intelligence was tested with a particularly elaborate set of measures. The course showed a major impact on seventh-grade students' cognition, including measures of the particular thinking concepts and strategies taught *and* measures of general scholastic ability and intelligence. One unfortunate feature of the study was that we did not have a chance to do follow-up work, to see how the students performed six months or a year later. However, the initial results were very encouraging.

A number of positive findings for this and other programs are discussed in *The Teaching of Thinking* by Raymond Nickerson, David Perkins, and Edward Smith. Accordingly, the teaching of concepts and strategies for reasoning about cause and effect, the soundness of beliefs, decision situations, and the like becomes an important part of the metacurriculum.

Thinking on Paper

"Languages of thinking" inevitably suggests verbal languages. But this is somewhat misleading because some interesting programs and experiments have actually involved visual symbols. Joseph Novak and his colleagues at Cornell University have conducted a number of studies of students' use of "concept mapping," a way of diagramming complex conceptual relationships. Similar techniques are called "webbing" and "mind mapping." The general idea is to create a network of lines connecting words and brief phrases. For example, to diagram the ecology of a pond, you might connect "tadpoles" to "frogs" with a line labeled "grow into." You might connect "frogs" to "flies" with a line that says "eat."

In some cases at least, students find that concept mapping represents an effective means of reviewing and consolidating their understanding of subject matter content. In the same spirit, Beau Jones, Jay McTighe, Sandra Parks, and John H. Clarke are among the investigators and developers who, concerned with effective reading and related performances, have explored pictorial formats for helping students generate and organize ideas. For instance, a neat graphic technique for comparing and contrasting uses two intersecting circles to compare, say, a sonnet by Shakespeare with one by Wordsworth. In the intersection of the two circles, students list features common to both. In the circle for each sonnet but outside of the intersection, the students list features distinctive to one or the other.

Pictorial languages of thinking have an advantage. They "download" onto paper complex patterns of thinking—the whole ecology of a pond or a dozen or more contrasts between sonnets by Shakespeare and Wordsworth. The downloading is important. One problem with pushing students' thinking beyond typical classroom levels is that it introduces an additional cognitive load for students. Another problem is that sessions largely conducted orally afford limited opportunity to look back and reexamine a line of thought. Thinking on paper helps solve these problems. Students do not have to hold so much information in mind at once, and they can look back at what they have written to rethink and revise it.

In this process the powerful resources of two traditional text forms, the essay and the story, should not be overlooked. Both can be potent means of laying out ideas. They do not take the place of resources like concept mapping, which are less formal and more flexible, but they do offer formats for the shaping and refined expression of ideas. Nor should we neglect other forms of writing that afford more flexibility than essays or stories—thought diaries, brainstormed lists and notes, and the like.

The Culture Connection

The notion of languages of thinking has another advantage over talk of skills: its cultural spin. It suggests that education is as much a process of acculturation as of learning particular pieces of knowledge. To achieve thoughtful learning, we need to create a culture of thoughtful learning in the classroom. This is a matter of how teachers talk to students, students to teachers, and students to one another. And talk here is of course a matter not just of the words used but of manner and style and goals.

For example, the "whole language" movement has over the past several years inspired and enabled many teachers to draw their students into classroom cultures of thinking and writing that draw on a number of different text forms. A theory-based perspective on teaching and learning rather than a method or package, whole-language teaching emphasizes how skill in reading and writing develops through authentic involvement in reading and writing activities. In this approach, students do not write mock pieces as exercises for the teacher; they write diaries, stories, advertisements, and arguments that have genuine contemplative and communicative functions—a reflective diary, a contribution to a school newspaper, stories for other students to read and enjoy.

All this reflects a developmental understanding of how language facility evolves. The whole-language perspective emphasizes how instrumental natural language learning is. Toddlers learn their mother tongues because each bit of skill and understanding can help them do something that makes sense and looks worthwhile in context. The same mechanisms can be harnessed in the classroom, where learning activities should not be exercise-like rituals directed toward some vaguely promised goal of mastery but rather should make sense and look worthwhile in a context of communication.

Whether classrooms attain a culture of thoughtfulness has been a direct object of research. Fred Newmann of the Wisconsin

Center for Education Research at the University of Wisconsin-Madison has investigated what might be termed "the thoughtful classroom," examining a number of variables concerning how much a teacher models, expects, and makes time for thoughtfulness in learning. Many of these variables have to do with patterns of language use.

Newmann and his colleagues gauged the extent to which teachers explored explanations and conclusions and encouraged students to offer reasons for claims and to reach for imaginative ideas. They looked for students actively sustaining attention to a topic, engaging in discussion with one another, and raising questions. Newmann discovered that in classrooms with these and similar characteristics, students picked up a thoughtful mindset. They tended to write more elaborated and probing statements on a given topic.

Teachers face challenges when they seek to draw students into a culture of thoughtful learning. For example, working-class students who achieve their way into more difficult studies emphasizing reasoning and imagination may find the problems recognized by Harvard educator Sara Lawrence Lightfoot in *The Good High School:*

> To the working-class student who has strived mightily to gain a loftier place, the intellectual play may seem threatening and absurd. With such high stakes, how can he dare to test out alternative propositions? He must search out the right answer. How can he spin out fantasies of adventurous projects? He must take the sure and straight path.

Lightfoot goes on to note how artful teaching can draw in students through staging debates, maintaining a lively pace, and other means. The "play" of which she speaks is, of course, the serious but engaging enterprise of thoughtful learning.

In summary, then, the general area of languages of thinking offers a major body of content for the metacurriculum, including (1) restoration to the classroom of such familiar English thinking terms as belief, hypothesis, evidence; (2) cultivation of concepts and strategies for decision making, problem solving, and related kinds of thinking; (3) introduction of ways of thinking on paper, such as concept mapping and use of traditional text forms, to help manage the problem of cognitive load and afford more opportunities for capturing thoughts and reflecting on them; (4) generally fostering the culture of a thoughtful classroom.

Complicated for teachers? Difficult for at-risk students and slow learners? Yes, if you had to do it all in a semester. But not everything has to be achieved or even attempted at once. Imagine instruction over the years keeping the language of thinking in active use, occasionally introducing a deeper perspective on key kinds of thinking such as causal reasoning or decision making, occasionally acquainting students with concept mapping and other tools for thinking on paper, and always working to keep prior ideas alive and carry them a little further. Time is one of the great resources of public education. Despite the crowded curriculum, and especially since some of the stuff crowded into it is not worth doing, there is ample time to build a smooth ramp up to the truly thoughtful classroom.

INTELLECTUAL PASSIONS

Culture was mentioned earlier as a matter of language and communication. But culture is also a matter of passions—what is felt about what—about thinking and learning, for instance. We need to make room for the role of affect in schooling, generally, and in thoughtful teaching and learning, specifically. In a short essay on the role of aesthetics in education, Arthur Costa puts it this way:

> The addition of aesthetics implies that learners become not only cognitively involved, but also enraptured with the phenomena, principles, and discrepancies they encounter in their environment. In order for the brain to comprehend, the heart must first listen.

However, schools generally give little reason for the heart to listen. In his recent examination of school reform, *In the Name of Excellence,* Robert Toch writes with concern of the general neglect of the human side of schools. He uses the voices of children to indict a system that leaves them disaffected from education:

"School? It's just a getting out of the house thing. Kids don't come to learn, they just come," said a high school junior from California. A senior from Virginia put it this way: "I'm just doing my time." About efforts to reform schools, Toch warns:

> . . . to date, the widespread disinterestedness among students and the schools' contribution to the problem has received scant attention within the excellence movement. In its eagerness to strengthen the quality of academics, the movement has neglected this crucial *human* element of the crisis in public education.

Of course, thinking, good thinking, *is* spirited. Philosophers more than psychologists have underscored this point. John Dewey, who shaped educational theory throughout the first half of this century and helped to found the progressive movement in education, emphasized the importance of cultivating both habits and attitudes of reflective thought. He urged the importance of three attitudes particularly: open-mindedness, wholeheartedness, and responsibility.

Israel Scheffler, noted philosopher of education at Harvard University, writes of the "cognitive emotions," a calculated oxymoron. While emotions are sometimes considered the enemy of good thinking, Scheffler urges that certain emotions—love of truth, commitment to fairness, zest for exploration—serve the agenda of thinking. Indeed, those very phrases demonstrate passionate language about thinking. Teachers who couch what they say in a passionate language of thinking and honor commitment to thinking in their other behavior telegraph to their students a committed culture of thinking.

In the same vein, Richard Paul, a west-coast philosopher and prominent member of the thinking skills movement, speaks of "strong sense" versus "weak sense" critical thinking. Roughly, weak sense critical thinking is the craft of reasoning— formulating sound reasons, combining them into a well-structured arguments, rebutting counterarguments, and so on. Paul emphasizes that one can become adroit in this craft without an authentic commitment to fairness, without openness to genuinely divergent points of view. Such a commitment involves the will and the passion to maintain open-mindedness about very different perspectives from one's own—not in the empty sense of "anything goes" amiable tolerance but with thoughtful reflection. It is critical thinking in this strong sense, Paul urges, that teachers need to model and encourage in the classroom if students are to divest themselves of prejudice and other forms of narrow thinking.

Also concerned with commitment in thinking, philosopher Robert Ennis urges the importance of "thinking dispositions." The idea of a disposition contrasts with the idea of ability: Whereas the ability to swim refers to know-how, the disposition refers to inclination. You can have the know-how without the inclination or the inclination without the know-how; both are important. Ennis emphasizes that building up thinking abilities counts for little unless teachers also cultivate thinking dispositions. Teachers can emphasize and model appropriate thinking dispositions during lectures and discussions, they can strive to bring in alternative points of view, they can honor divergent perspectives within the classroom. Without such attention, dispositions toward good thinking are not likely to take, whatever technical skills youngsters learn.

Recently, colleagues Eileen Jay, Shari Tishman, and I developed a model of good thinking that makes dispositions its central theme. We propose that seven dispositions make up the essence of what it is to be a good thinker:

1. The disposition to be broad and adventurous.
2. The disposition toward sustained intellectual curiosity.
3. The disposition to clarify and seek understanding.
4. The disposition to be planful and strategic.
5. The disposition to be intellectually careful.
6. The disposition to seek and evaluate reasons.
7. The disposition to be metacognitive.

Our concept of dispositions, a little different from that of Ennis, actually includes abilities within dispositions, so that dispositions become the most central thing, the heart of good thinking.

Classrooms offer ample occasions to cultivate all these dispositions. For instance, in discussions about an essay or a concept in mathematics or science, students have an opportunity to clarify and concretize what was said. In planning a paper or an experiment, students have an opportunity to be planful and strategic. In taking a test or organizing homework time, students have an opportunity to be metacognitive. And these are only a few of many, many occasions. But they are opportunities likely not to be taken unless the teacher encourages such dispositions by naming them, modeling them, creating time for them, helping students see how to pursue them, and rewarding them.

Teachers I know already have an intuitive feel for thinking dispositions. But the low-energy culture of conventional schools and the initial attitudes of many students work against them. In contrast, the high-energy culture of the smart school (see chapter 7) gives teachers the time and encouragement to celebrate and cultivate thinking dispositions.

INTEGRATIVE MENTAL IMAGES

Central to a pedagogy of understanding, and no less to the metacurriculum, is the idea that the teaching of the subject matters involves much more than teaching bits and pieces of content. Learners need an integrative sense of the subject matter: "How does it all hang together?" They need overarching mental images of its structure, so that they see how its strands interweave to make a whole fabric.

The last chapter emphasized how powerful representations could clarify particular, hard concepts by providing learners with mental images. Here it's worth adding that carefully constructed, powerful representations also can integrate a subject matter.

Steven Schwartz, other colleagues, and I developed supplementary materials and a teachers' guide to provide a higher order approach for students learning computer programming. We called the package a "metacourse." One important feature of these materials was an overall organizing image of the computer as a data factory, with a laborer in the factory that moved around following the commands in the program. The data factory image gave students a general tool for imagining just what the computer did with a program—what a program "meant" to the computer. The intervention proved quite successful in boosting students' programming achievement in comparison with that of control groups.

We have been developing a similar intervention for elementary algebra. For that, we adopted a different overarching metaphor: the "algebra workplace." In the imagery of the algebra workplace, algebra parts hang on the wall above a work table and toward the left—letters, numbers, equal signs, plus, minus, and so on. Hanging above the work table on the right are algebra tools such as commutativity and adding the same thing to both sides of an equation. Doing algebra is treated as a matter of working at the table to build and modify algebra objects, using the parts and the tools.

Of course, powerful as analogical imagery is, it is not the only kind of mental image for integrating a field. Sometimes, well-chosen categories can provide a mental image to do the job.

University of Massachusetts scholar Edwina Rissland, investigating instruction in mathematics, developed a triad of organizing concepts: concepts, examples, and results. The three work together as a team. Take, for instance, a concept like right triangle. This concept has typical examples: standard diagrams of a right triangle. It also has special-case examples: an isosceles right triangle or the well-known 3-4-5 right triangle, which is 3 units long on one side, 4 units on the other, and 5 units on the hypotenuse. Then there are associated results, most obviously the famous Pythagorean theorem, which says that the sums of the squares of the two sides equal the square of the hypotenuse. Indeed, the 3-4-5 right triangle illustrates this relationship: 9 (3 squared) plus 16 (4 squared) equals 25 (5 squared). Rissland reports that the framework of concepts, examples, and results, used persistently as an organizing scheme for instruction, seems to help learners considerably toward mastery of mathematics.

The previous section mentioned concept maps, a technique developed by Novak and others. These network-like diagrams allow constructing integrative representations of complex disciplines and subject matters. They give teachers and students another resource to use in representing whole subject matters or large parts of them.

In summary, integrative mental images of varied kinds can help students toward a cohesive understanding of particular subject matters and, more broadly, of the interrelations among the subject matters.

LEARNING TO LEARN

One of the most basic results in the psychology of learning is that humans—and even some animals—do not just learn: They learn to learn. They develop behaviors and concepts serving the endeavor of learning itself. This process begins very early. Youngsters who are just beginning to talk fairly well already have and express ideas about the way memory works. As the quotes at the beginning of this chapter illustrate, fourth graders can have quite sophisticated notions about how to learn.

Unfortunately, the conceptions of learning that students arrive at are not always the best ones. Just as many students have misconceptions about key ideas in physics or mathematics, many students have misconceptions about learning. As mentioned in chapter 2, University of Illinois researcher Carol Dweck and her colleagues have investigated youngsters' theories about the nature of learning and their own learning processes. They distinguish between what they term "entity learners" and "incremental learners." An extreme entity learner believes that "you either get it or you don't." Learning something is a matter of "catching on," and if you don't catch on in a few minutes, you probably will not catch on at all. In contrast, "incremental learners" see learning as more a piecemeal process requiring persistence. Students with an entity attitude toward learning have a theory about the nature of learning that is fundamentally mistaken and counterproductive. The more productive incremental attitude is worth cultivating.

Investigators also have examined students' monitoring of attention—a matter of staying on the task at hand versus drifting off it. Very often, poor learners are poor attention monitors: They have not learned to track their own cognitions very well and do not notice when they drift off task. In contrast, youngsters good at attention monitoring can not only stay on task but track "in the background" what else is going on.

In general, research has shown that in the course of the years, and starting relatively early in life, people develop a number of conceptions about good learning—what strategies are good for reading, understanding, and memorizing, for example. With age, the strategies gradually get more sophisticated, in some learners reaching a high degree of refinement.

For instance, Michelene Chi of the Learning Research and Development Center at the University of Pittsburgh investigated how different students used examples in studying physics. She found that some students had developed the craft of learning well from textbook examples. These students paid careful heed to the logic of examples, working through them step by step and trying to explain to themselves how each step functioned. Other students looked at examples more casually and tried to solve new problems by loose analogy with textbook examples. Chi's research showed that the students who looked at examples carefully also understood and solved new physics problems better.

Other investigations at the Learning Research and Development Center involved students working with microcomputer environments designed to support discovery learning of electrical and economic principles. Important differences among students were found. Some students paid systematic attention to control of variables when they did experiments in the computer environments; others did not. Some kept careful records of their steps, made systematic plans, and tested hypotheses. Understandably, the students who approached the task in a more sophisticated way learned considerably more from the environments.

All this concerns the learning strategies that students spontaneously develop. What happens when learning strategies are taught to students? At least sometimes, substantial advantages can result. In an integrative study of attempts to teach metacognitive reading strategies, the researchers Haller, Child, and Walberg synthesized 20 studies to find an average "effect size" of .71. This means that on the average, these treatments improved students' reading on the measures in question by 70 percent of a standard deviation. An effect size this large is considered very good in instructional interventions. Among the most potent strategies were backward and forward searching in the text to clarify obscure points and self-questioning strategies to monitor progress and regulate one's reading.

Others have taken a more broad-band approach to elevating

students' learning abilities. A number of years ago, Benjamin Bloom and Lois Broder conducted an investigation of more and less effective college students and created a pilot program to boost the academic performance of the lower achievers. They painstakingly analyzed differences between better and worse students, finding a number of counterproductive behaviors in the weaker students: impulsive responses to problems on the basis of superficial cues, little effort to understand a problem thoroughly, indifference to gaps in their knowledge, and a general "either you get it or you don't" attitude. They worked with students both individually and in groups and had them think aloud and compare their approach on sample problems to that of model problem solvers who were careful and systematic. The students treated individually, and those in groups that met for at least seven sessions, showed markedly better performance and grades.

Another approach to developing students' academic abilities was developed by Charles Wales and Robert Stager at West Virginia University around 1970. Called "guided design," the approach engages groups of students in working step by step through open-ended problems that use subject matter knowledge. The guidance in guided design comes partly from an organized pattern of problem solving that highlights such steps as identifying the problem, gathering information, and generating and evaluating candidate solutions. The guidance also comes by way of sample resolutions of these steps, given to students after they have made some progress on their own. The sample resolutions are not to be taken as "right answers" but as further fuel for thinking about the problem. In 1970, the approach became the core of a required freshman course for engineering students at West Virginia University. An examination of student performance over the next several years suggests that, because of the guided design component, the students performed better academically and a greater percentage graduated from the program.

None of this means that efforts to get students to learn to learn always works. Indeed, the general consensus in the educational community seems to be that many study skills programs are remarkably ineffective for a variety of reasons. For instance, they often stand separate from the academic mainstream, carry no credit, and are seen as embarrassingly "remedial" by students.

Nonetheless, there are enough success stories to make the case that learning to learn can happen in useful ways in educational settings when we make it central and important enough for students to pay serious attention.

TEACHING FOR TRANSFER

It's a basic premise of education: We don't learn fractions arithmetic to pass the fractions arithmetic quiz. We don't diagram sentences for the sake of diagraming sentences. Ideally at least, the subject matters speak to one another and to life outside the walls of the classroom.

This point engages what has become one of the most important and contentious themes in the psychology of learning—transfer of learning. "Transfer" means learning something in one situation and then applying it in another, significantly different one—for instance, putting the math you learn in school to work in physics class or the supermarket. The dilemma for educators is that often, transfer does not occur. For example science instructors commonly complain of having to reteach mathematics to their students, even though the students seem to be doing well enough in their math classes. Why has their mathematical knowledge not traversed the corridor between the math room and the physics room?

A graphic way to tell the story of transfer as it has played out over the years involves three theories: the Bo Peep theory, the Lost Sheep theory, and the Good Shepherd theory.

The Bo Peep Theory

The Bo Peep theory of transfer is the tacit theory that operates in typical classroom settings. This theory says that useful transfer happens automatically. It takes care of itself. Like Bo Peep's sheep, appropriate knowledge gets drawn to its points of utility: "Leave them alone and they'll come home/wagging their tails behind them."

The trouble with the Bo Peep theory is that an overwhelming body of evidence shows it to be false. All too often, desirable transfer does not occur spontaneously. Youngsters do not think to use their mathematics skills in the supermarket, their social studies knowledge in the workplace, their reading skills acquired in English class in history, and so on.

The classic findings on the question of transfer were established not long after the turn of the century by the notable educational research pioneer E. L. Thorndike. Among his various studies, he investigated whether Latin "trained the mind," as it had been said to do. Comparing matched groups of students who had and hadn't studied Latin, Thorndike found not one whit of difference. In other, more straightforward experiments, Thorndike also found little transfer.

The Lost Sheep Theory

A continuing history of negative findings concerning transfer has fostered what we can call the Lost Sheep theory. The Lost Sheep theory simply says that transfer is a lost cause. People do not on the whole carry knowledge and skills from one context to another. Indeed, some psychologists argue, knowledge and skill may be too context bound by nature to allow much useful transfer. Moreover, when knowledge in context A genuinely and usefully does apply to context B, people commonly fail to see the connection.

Although this claim has been vigorously defended by some, in my view it is simply mistaken. It results from an oversimple conception that does not specify when transfer should be expected and when it should not. Indeed, one reason against general pessimism about transfer is that despite the spate of negative findings, some experiments seeking transfer show positive findings.

Researchers Clements and Gullo investigated transfer of cognitive skills from learning a computer language. They taught the language in an especially mindful way, the teacher working closely with the students to prompt them to ask themselves thoughtful questions about what they were doing and try to answer them. While most investigations of transfer from learning computer programming have been negative, these investigators found enhanced performance on certain tests of flexible thinking.

For another example, consider the Philosophy for Children program developed by philosopher Matthew Lipman and his colleagues. This program involves separate courses for several grades, beginning in middle elementary school. The courses involve the students in reading short novels, especially written for Philosophy for Children, that bring up in a fairly natural way philosophical issues concerning the sureness of our conclusions, what the right thing to do is, and the like. Teachers engage the students in probing discussions of these issues as the students go through the novels. The program in no way directly teaches reading skills, much less mathematics skills. Nonetheless, research seeking spinoff effects found that students who had participated in Philosophy for Children showed better performance in reading and mathematics, as well as in more general tests of reasoning.

For yet a third example, University of Arizona investigator Gavriel Salomon and colleagues engaged students in using a computer-aided reading tool called the Reading Partner. The tool prompted students with questions to ask themselves while reading, such as "What image can I make of what I read?" "What can I predict from the story's title?" "What's a summary of the preceding paragraphs?" and "What are the key sentences here?" The students were strongly encouraged to respond to these cues. Their reading improved substantially. More to the point, a month later the investigators administered a writing task to the students. Those who had worked with the Reading Partner showed better writing performance; they had made fertile generalizations from reading to writing.

So transfer does sometimes happen. But why sometimes yet so often not? More refined models have begun to clarify when to expect transfer. Gavriel Salomon and I presented a theory that distinguishes between two fundamentally different mechanisms of transfer—"low road" and "high road." Low road transfer depends on the reflexive activation of well-practiced patterns. It is automatic and mindless. In contrast, high road transfer depends on effortful, mindful abstraction of principles from one context to apply them in another.

Salomon and I argue that the studies that have failed to find transfer generally did not establish the conditions for either low road or high road transfer. Students had not thoroughly practiced the knowledge and skills in question in diverse contexts to set them up for low road transfer. Nor had they been encouraged in mindful abstraction that would have led to high road transfer. But contrast the studies that did find transfer: Clements and colleagues teaching a computer language emphasized thoughtful self-questioning; the Philosophy for Children program stressed thoughtful analysis of issues; the Reading Partner highlighted questioning oneself about the text read. In other words, all promoted mindful high-order reflection. They established the conditions for high road transfer.

The Good Shepherd Theory

All this amounts to the third, and preferred, theory of transfer—the Good Shepherd theory. The Good Shepherd theory acknowledges that the Bo Peep theory will not do: Transfer does not occur spontaneously nearly as often as we would like. At the same time, the Good Shepherd theory denies the Lost Sheep theory: Contrary to its pessimistic claim, strong transfer is quite possible. The thing is, one cannot expect transfer without "shepherding" it, by setting up the learning conditions that foster transfer.

In an ingenious series of experiments, Ann Brown, of the University of California at Berkeley, investigated whether children would transfer abstract concepts from one context of application to another. In one study, she and colleagues showed that children as young as three could catch on to the parallels between similar problems and solve one problem by analogy with another, provided the children were asked ("shepherded," one might say) to look for similarities. For instance, the children saw the connection between someone helping a boy out of a hole by reaching down with a hoe and someone helping a girl adrift in a boat by reaching out with a fishing pole. In another study, she and colleagues demonstrated that youngsters just as young could learn to look for such connections over a series of problems so that they did not have to be prompted every time.

From these and other studies, Brown concluded that transfer is more likely when (1) the knowledge to be transfered figures in cause/effect relationships; (2) there is emphasis during learning on flexibility and the possibility of multiple application; (3) there is some effort to disembed the principle from the initial learning context. The latter two conditions correspond to Salomon and Perkins's conditions for high road transfer.

Shepherding Transfer

In summary, it seems that students can transfer knowledge and skills from subject matter to subject matter and to a variety of out-of-school contexts, provided that the instruction sets up the conditions for transfer. Regrettably, most instruction proceeds in ways that do not favor transfer. But a number of instructional practices can help.

They fall into two broad categories called bridging and hugging. Bridging means that the teacher helps the students to make connections between what they are studying and other areas— something from another subject matter or their out-of-school lives.

Bridging is not hard to do. It simply means taking time to get students to make outreaching connections. A teacher might ask students studying the U.S. Civil War to explore analogies with topical events in Northern Ireland or the secessionist movement in Canada. When students are studying oscillators in physics class, the teacher might provoke them to find oscillating systems in their everyday lives (dripping faucets, swaying tree branches, backyard swings) and try to identify the energy sources that keep the oscillators going.

Hugging, in contrast, means keeping the instruction close to (hugging) the very target performances one wants to cultivate, so that transfer is less of a problem. This is commonplace in music and drama instruction: One practices the very thing one is to perform. But the principle often gets bypassed in more academic instruction. For example, students may put in practice time on topic sentences largely by selecting topic sentences among multiple choices or identifying topic sentences in paragraphs. Neither one gives intensive practice in actually writing paragraphs with topic sentences.

Once teachers are alert to the routine lack of hugging, it's easy to build well-hugged instruction into the school day. Rather than choosing topic sentences from lists, students might better spend most of their practice time composing paragraphs with an emphasis on good topic sentences. For feedback, they can exchange papers, each trying to identify his or her neighbor's topic sentences. The teacher can adjudicate problems and confusions. This gets kids writing paragraphs, but one can easily go further. More holistic approaches to developing writing skills would recommend full-fledged writing activities with a communicative emphasis, good topic sentences being one among several agendas.

One special kind of hugging is called problem-based learning. In this technique, students learn a body of knowledge by working at problems that require the knowledge, which is not presented in advance but looked up as needed. Research conducted by John Bransford and his colleagues shows that problem-based learning leads to more flexible and generative application of the knowledge later. It's a matter of hugging: Because students learned the knowledge in the context of problem-solving tasks, the knowledge is better organized in their minds for later problem solving.

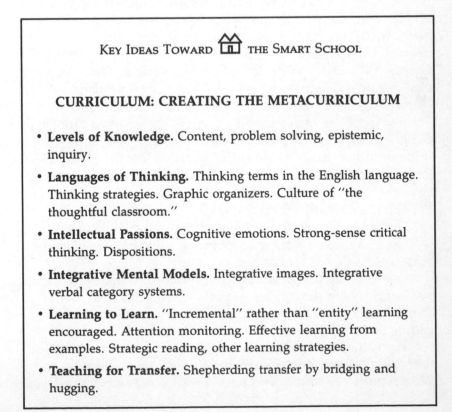

KEY IDEAS TOWARD THE SMART SCHOOL

CURRICULUM: CREATING THE METACURRICULUM

- **Levels of Knowledge.** Content, problem solving, epistemic, inquiry.
- **Languages of Thinking.** Thinking terms in the English language. Thinking strategies. Graphic organizers. Culture of "the thoughtful classroom."
- **Intellectual Passions.** Cognitive emotions. Strong-sense critical thinking. Dispositions.
- **Integrative Mental Models.** Integrative images. Integrative verbal category systems.
- **Learning to Learn.** "Incremental" rather than "entity" learning encouraged. Attention monitoring. Effective learning from examples. Strategic reading, other learning strategies.
- **Teaching for Transfer.** Shepherding transfer by bridging and hugging.

AN EXAMPLE OF TEACHING THE
METACURRICULUM

I hope that the foregoing pages have made something of a case
for the metacurriculum. But making a case is not quite the same
as painting a picture of what it would really be like. Just as at the
end of the last chapter—for a pedagogy of understanding—we
can imagine. Indeed, we do not have to imagine very hard,
because in many places many teachers are teaching parts of the
metacurriculum—teaching languages of thinking, teaching for
transfer, employing overarching mental images, cultivating the
critical spirit.

Suppose our class is studying the U.S. Constitution, certainly a
hallowed topic in the content curriculum. In the conventional
course of events, students would probably find themselves
reading parts of the Constitution, learning something about the
function and importance of particular components, such as the
Bill of Rights, and answering fact-oriented questions that dis-
played their knowledge of what the Constitution said. The
metacurriculum would call for something more, something
deeper. For example, the class might start by exploring the
Constitution using some language of thinking. One language
from my own research and materials development work is called
"knowledge as design."

Knowledge as design asks learners to analyze things as
designs that serve a purpose. Familiar with the approach, a
student might ask, "What's the purpose of the preamble?"
Puzzling among themselves, the students begin to come up with
answers:

"The preamble is a kind of preview, just like it says."

"The preamble says what the purpose of the Constitution is."

"The preamble is kind of inspiring; it says that we all commit
ourselves to these ideas as one people."

Knowledge as design has been introduced to the students not
just as a thinking strategy but as part of learning to learn. They've
come to recognize its set of key questions as a good tool for
getting inside a topic.

Okay so far, the teacher thinks. But the teacher wants to push
the conversation deeper, urging the students beyond these
surface purposes to hidden ones. "Fine," the teacher says. "But

you know, I'm really curious about this. It's so well expressed and it says so much." The teacher quite honestly but quite deliberately is displaying an intellectual passion, curiosity. The teacher wants students to see this and value it. "What else is going on here? Can you find any more subtle purposes, ones hard to see at first?"

"Well," one student might answer, warming up to the hunt for something mysterious, "it's a little deceptive, this 'We the People,' because there was a lot of disagreement. And the people really weren't everyone. Like only males could vote, for instance. So it pretends there's a unity that isn't really there."

"Do you think the authors of the Constitution meant to gloss things over there," the teacher says. "Or did they think there was more unity?"

The students disagree, giving the teacher a chance to bring in a higher level of understanding. "Well, let's see now," the teacher says, deliberately sounding skeptical—more intellectual passions. "Can we really tell at all how people might have been thinking 200 years ago? What kind of evidence could we possibly have?" This question provokes a commonsense exploration of how historical interpretations get justified—the epistemic level of understanding.

Concerned with transfer, the teacher wants to connect the discussion with other situations. During the next period, the teacher broadens the compass of the discussion, bringing in other documents that have set nations upon a path—the Declaration of Independence, the Magna Carta. "You know, documents like these really do change the world. How are these the same? How are they different?" the teacher asks. Probes like this are bridging questions. They foster transfer from other topics the students already have studied in the history course.

The teacher wants to bring matters closer to home, for more transfer. "Do we in the class or school or town have any documents like this?" Perhaps a student recalls that the school has a constitution, as some schools do. Perhaps the students have never read it. What are their rights and responsibilities? Maybe they had better find out.

Or perhaps, if there is no constitution, one ought to be drafted. The students might undertake this. What would they like their rights and responsibilities to be? And who else would have to agree? And would they? And why or why not? Such a project would prove an arena for problem solving, decision making, understanding, and a dozen other kinds of thinking.

Suppose students pursued some such project. Reflecting back and going for the big picture, the teacher might ask, "What generalizations can you make about your document, and the U.S. Constitution, and the Magna Carta? What's important that they all have in common? Make a chart, make a diagram." This is an invitation to construct some kind of integrative mental image that captures key features of documents that declare rights and responsibilities. Instead of offering such an image on a platter (which is fine sometimes), the teacher nudges the youngsters to construct their own images.

Of course, as with the example at the end of the last chapter, this is just one cut through the apple of opportunity. If probing the purposes of the preamble sounds too analytical for the students in question, the teacher might ask them to act out different people—housewives, small farmers, slave owners, businessmen—reacting to the preamble. From that, the purposes might be drawn. If finishing a constitution for the school, or even starting one, makes too big a deal of what was supposed to be a short unit, the teacher might stop with a period's worth of discussion and save major projects for another occasion.

Whatever the style, there are ample opportunities to orient instruction toward higher levels of understanding, introduce and exercise languages of thinking, cultivate intellectual passions, seek out integrative mental images, foster learning to learn, and teach for transfer. The smart school makes the most of these opportunities. It informs and energizes teaching by giving teachers time and support to learn about the opportunities and by arranging curriculum, assessment, and scheduling to encourage tapping them.

Opportunities, yes, and necessities as well. Because those three seemingly innocuous goals of education—retention, understanding, and the active use of knowledge—not only invite but demand much more attention to the metacurriculum. We are simply not likely to see much of the three without contributing directly to students' overarching conceptions of the subject matters and to their artful orchestration of their own mental resources.

SMART

SCHOOLS

CHAPTER 6

CLASSROOMS

The Role of Distributed Intelligence

Here is a tale of three notebooks. Alfredo begins the first as a lad fifteen years of age, in his history class, where he and the other students are studying the League of Nations and the United Nations. In this notebook, he enters a variety of information about the two organizations. The history teacher encourages thoughtfulness, and Alfredo, reflectively inclined himself, adds to his notebook a number of ideas about what happened and why and what it meant.

But there is something odd about Alfredo's notebook: What is written there does not count as part of what he has learned. With the final exam coming up in two weeks, Alfredo makes sure that most of what appears in the notebook is also in his head, because the final exam will be closed book, including the essay questions. What is written in the notebook does not count, even though it reflects effortful organization and added reflection. To be sure, side effects of the cognitive effort Alfredo has invested will help

131

him to remember the content, but the notebook itself earns no credit.

Alfredo keeps his second notebook around the epic series of Dungeons and Dragons games that he and several friends maintain. The status of this notebook is quite different. There is no question that the diagrams of dungeons, the notes about crucial hazards, and so on comprise part of what Alfredo has learned. When he doesn't happen to remember, he looks it up. Not only is Alfredo's notebook a resource for him, but the kids are resources for one another. In contrast with the classroom setting, in Dungeons and Dragons the youngsters cooperate as well as compete. They rely upon each other's knowledge and thinking.

Alfredo's third notebook gets started fifteen years later, when Alfredo is a young engineer, part of a technical team designing a new bridge over the Hudson River. Not only is a team of people involved but also a team of physical supports for cognition. Alfredo's notebook, full of ideas and specifications, joins with a computer-aided design system, books full of specifications and regulations, journals with engineering advances, memos from various team members to each other, a physical mock-up of the proposed bridge design, hand calculators, and much more.

Compared with the Dungeons and Dragons game or the engineering profession, the typical classroom begins to look like an odd place. Emphatically and in manifold ways, schools address what might be called the "person-solo." It is the person-solo who should acquire knowledge and skills. It is the person-solo who should work out math problems and write essays. It is the person-solo who should have all knowledge and skill in his or her head rather than tucked away in easily accessible sources.

At least, someone might say, youngsters are encouraged to work out their ideas with pencil and paper; so schools do not ignore the role of physical supports in cognition. Well, sometimes. Thought about more carefully, the pencil and paper tolerated in exams seem to have another purpose: Students are not so much encouraged to think on paper as to use the paper and pencil to display their thinking. The paper and pencil are there not as powerful vehicles for supporting cognition but as a conduit of communication for showing the teacher in-the-head cognitions.

At least, someone else might say, there are open-book exams. Yes, open-book exams are in the right spirit, recognizing that in out-of-school contexts people routinely draw fluently on all sorts of information sources. But they are only a token reflection of this overwhelming trend.

To attach a metaphor to this contrast, we could compare the person-solo with the "person-plus." The solo mode of operation —noncollaborative and without extensive physical and information resources—is an oddity. People normally function in their homes, workplaces, and playplaces in person-plus kinds of ways, with intensive use of physical and information resources, interaction, and interdependency. Plainly, this is no accident. People operate as persons-plus because it is empowering and engaging.

THE IDEA OF DISTRIBUTED INTELLIGENCE

Lest we take schools too much to task for a unique shortfall, there is at least one other bastion of the person-solo perspective. It is, regrettably, psychological theory and experimentation. The classic question of psychology is "What goes on in the mind," or, from the standpoint of B. F. Skinner's behaviorist psychology (which does not believe in minds), "How does the individual organism react to stimuli?" Just as in the classroom, psychological experiments typically proceed with a minimum of physical and social support for the subject. Psychologists wonder what the subject can and will do without much equipment, and certainly without another person, to help. There are exceptions, but they hardly impugn the reality of the trend.

However, in several quarters a new assessment has been made of this entrenched "personcentric" view of the human organism. Roy Pea of Northwestern University has written recently about what he calls "distributed intelligence." Others, including myself, have picked up this theme. We argue that human cognition at its richest almost always occurs in ways that are physically, socially, and symbolically distributed. People think and remember with the help of all sorts of physical aids, and we commonly construct new physical aids to help ourselves yet more. People think and remember socially, through interaction with other people, sharing information and perspectives and developing ideas. The work of the world gets done in groups! Finally, people sustain thinking through socially shared symbol systems— speech, writing, the technical argot of specialties, diagrams, scientific notations, and so on.

A more modest term than distributed intelligence for this dispersal of intellectual functioning across physical, social, and symbolic supports is "distributed cognition." But there is a point to Pea's more provocative use of the term intelligence. Taken broadly, intelligence refers simply to effective cognitive functioning. And intelligence is at stake here. People can function more intelligently in person-plus than in person-solo kinds of ways.

Defenders of classic notions of intelligence would complain, "But this isn't real intelligence. Real intelligence is in people's heads. Part of what you're talking about lies in the hand calculator or the notebook, not in the person." The rebuttal would be, "But the person-with-calculator-and-notebook is the actual functioning system. The person-plus system is what gets things done in the world. Its intelligence is more to the point than that of the person-solo."

Another contribution to the notion of distributed intelligence or distributed cognition comes from University of Arizona researcher Gavriel Salomon, long-time observer and investigator of the role of technologies in learning, writing with Tamar Globerson and myself. The authors draw a distinction between the effects *with* and *of* technology, including computers and television but also such ordinary technologies as paper and pencil. Effects *of* are the residues left when we are away from the technology. Perhaps, for example, we speak more articulately because we have written so many paragraphs. Effects *with* a technology are the empowerment that results when we have the technology at hand, actually thinking on paper, writing with word processors, communicating with telecommunications systems, and so on. Both effects *with* and effects *of* are part of the person-plus phenomenon, to be sought and cherished.

One might sum up the person-plus perspective in two principles:

1. The surround—the immediate physical, social, and symbolic resources outside of the person—participates in cognition, not just as a source of input and receiver of output but as a vehicle of thought. The surround in a real sense does part of the thinking.
2. The residue left by thinking—what is learned—lingers not just in the mind of the learner but in the arrangement of the surround as well; yet it is just as genuinely learning for all that. The surround in a real sense holds part of the learning.

These precepts imply a very different posture toward Alfredo's school notebook than most classrooms tolerate. The notebook is both an arena of thinking and a container of learning. Alfredo does not just think and put his thoughts down in the notebook. Alfredo thinks with and through the notebook. Alfredo has not just learned what he remembers from his writings in the notebook. Alfredo, the person-plus, functions with his notebook available as a resource. What is in the notebook, whether the person-solo remembers it or not, is part of what the person-plus has learned.

Of course, this does not mean that knowledge in notebooks is always just as good as knowledge in your head. Which is the best place to store up knowledge depends on matters like how often the knowledge is used, how quickly you can get to it when you need it, and so on. But the best place is often not in your head. Often, you can maintain far larger and more accessible and accurate knowledge structures in a notebook or a computer database. What really counts is not where the knowledge is— inside or outside the skull—but what might be called the "access characteristics" of relevant knowledge—what kind of knowledge is represented, how it is represented, how readily it is retrieved, and related matters. Whatever place—in the surround or in the head—gives the person-plus the best access characteristics is the place to use.

DISTRIBUTING COGNITION IN THE CLASSROOM

Outside of schools and psychological laboratories, person-plus is more the rule than the exception. We operate in close alliance with our physical, social, and symbolic surrounds. What would it mean to nudge classroom practice in that direction? Without trying to be comprehensive, here are some ideas drawn from a variety of innovative practices in education.

Distributing Cognition Physically

The traditional means of distributing cognition in the classroom almost all have to do with input—texts, lectures, posters, films, and so on. Output—what students say and write—is much less varied in format, a matter of problem sets and fill-in-the-blank and essay questions. And this output is usually not seen as a process of thinking something through on paper. Rather, it's a way of exercising and testing students' person-solo, in-the-head thinking.

But rich opportunities exist for changing that. One of the most familiar is the keeping of journals where students write about themes from their subject matters and their own evolving understanding of those themes. Such journals look to be good both for the students' understanding of the subject matter and their own metacognitive development.

John Barell, a figure in current efforts to cultivate thinking in the classroom, has discussed some singularly impressive examples of youngsters' journal reflections on what they are learning in school and what they are not learning. One journal format that Barell developed helps students to articulate and assess both their problem-solving and problem-finding skills. Here, a high school student thinks through a troubling problem she is trying to solve, a problem not unlike the one we struggle with in this book.

> I guess I could call myself smart. I mean I can usually get good grades. Sometimes I worry, though, that I'm not equipped to achieve what I want, that I'm just a tape recorder repeating back what I've heard. It scares me . . . I do my work, but I don't have the motivation. I've done well on Iowa and PSAT tests but they are always multiple choice. I worry that once I'm out of school and people don't keep handing me information with questions and Scantron sheets I'll be lost.

School is kind of unrealistic that way. Kids who do well often just repeat what the teacher has said . . .

Other modes of journal keeping enable students to track their thinking about a particular assignment as they work through it.

Yet another innovation that has received considerable attention concerns student portfolios. Not just in writing but in science, mathematics, and other subjects, students build portfolios of key products—essays, notes, diagrams, and so on. A portfolio is a selective enterprise: Not everything goes into it, just those items that students think most powerfully reflect their understandings and their expressions of those understandings. The portfolio functions as an object of review and assessment for the teacher, but also as a gauge of progress and occasion of reflection for the learner.

An extension of the idea of portfolios is the "process-folio," developed by the Arts PROPEL project under the direction of Harvard University educators Howard Gardner and Dennis Wolf. In contrast to a portfolio, which presents the best end-products of a student's work, a process-folio is a record of learning that focuses on the student's process of working through a creative activity. Arts PROPEL process-folios are used both for in-class and across-district comparison of student work in the arts. They provide an excellent way to document project work over time and to aid reflection alone or with other individuals.

It's easy to hear teachers saying at this point, "I don't have time to read dozens of journals. I don't have time to review dozens of portfolios." True, if we think of journals and portfolios as traditional student products—yesterday's math assignment— that get handed in for the teacher to go over—each one, every time—in detail. However, in the smart school, we can think in different ways. Although this is not the place for a disquisition on journal or portfolio technique, there are all sorts of tricks to their efficient use. One is that the teacher keep in touch with students' work, but not look at everything from each student all the time. Another is that, part of the time, students function as respondents for one another.

Computer technology has provided a range of new physical vehicles for supporting students' cognitions. The hand calculator is a notable and notorious example. Some years ago, youngsters' use of hand calculators generated considerable furor. This has settled down somewhat. The perspective in many quarters that both person-solo arithmetic and person-with-calculator arithmetic have roles to play: It is simply not an either/or proposition. Nor need the use of hand calculators undermine hand arithmetic proficiency. Moreover, hand calculators afford person-plus learning opportunities that should not be missed. By empowering students to handle large numbers easily, hand calculators allow them to focus on other facets of mathematical understanding.

Heavy-duty computer resources are also making themselves felt. These include word processors, computer programming environments such as Logo, spreadsheets, computer-aided drawing systems, databases—and, of course, special-purpose tutorial environments for cultivating particular skills: sometimes routine, such as arithmetic operations, and sometimes not so routine, such as aspects of higher-order thinking.

For example, working out of the Media Laboratory at the Massachusetts Institute of Technology, Idit Harel involved fourth graders at an inner-city public elementary school in Boston, Massachusetts, in a software-design project concerning fractions arithmetic, one of the all-time killer topics in the elementary curriculum. The students' challenge: to write tutorial programs in the computer language Logo to help third graders understand fractions basics better.

Of course, the real point was for them to understand fractions and programming better. The students designed their programs over a number of weeks, writing before and after each computer session in their Designer's Notebooks. The notebooks served as vehicles for planning and reflection, cultivating metacognition. Harel gathered data to show that this design experience gave the students a much better understanding of fractions and a much better understanding of the Logo computer language than the usual instruction in either. Harel also points up changes in their attitude toward mathematics and in their general reflectiveness.

For another example, desktop publishing can be a vehicle for lively learning activities with multiple payoffs. In Scottsdale, Arizona, at the Kiva Elementary School, students studying ancient Egypt synthesized their knowledge into a *National*

Enquirer–style, four-page newspaper called *King Tut's Chronicle.*
Headlines blared "Cleo in Trouble Once Again?" Readers could
check out their horoscopes and the latest price of mummified
cloth and pyramid blocks on the stock market. A "Dear Cleopatra" column offered advice, while news on Nile boat races
satisfied sports fans. An unusual lesson in history, yes—but also
lessons in contemporary media, writing, and cooperation, all
rolled into one.

Distributing Cognition Socially

Any educator conscious of the contemporary scene will know
what this most often means: cooperative learning. As mentioned
in chapter 3, considerable research has shown that techniques of
cooperative learning can boost student achievement. Educational
psychologists Ann Brown and Annemarie Palincsar, reviewing
the research on cooperative learning, emphasize that what
beneficial effects occur are not to be attributed merely to the
formation of groups. All turns on what happens in the groups—
how materials are used, what kinds of interactions are encouraged, and so on.

Socially distributed intelligence inevitably depends on the
physical distribution of intelligence. For example, it is often
advised that cooperative groups share a common workspace and
resources, with one set of source materials for all the group
members and one scribe to catch and organize the ideas of the
group. If the group develops a chart, there is one draft in front of
all, a common focus around which the members interact.

Another interesting facet of cooperative learning concerns
specialization. In the simplest of cooperative learning arrangements, everybody tries to get better at the same thing—say,
doing algebra manipulation problems. The structure of assessment in the classroom encourages the group members to help
one another out. For example, each group member may receive
for a grade the average of the test scores of all members tested
individually. Thus, it is worth each learner's while to improve the
skills of all.

But more elaborate cooperative learning techniques introduce
specialization of function. Remember the well-known "jigsaw"
method outlined in chapter 3: The materials to be learned are

divided into about four parts. Students are organized into home groups of four. Each student leaves his or her home group to join a learning group that studies one part of the material. Then the students return to their home groups; they must teach one another what they learned in the learning groups.

Of course, everyone need not end up knowing the same thing and having the same skills. Although we would like students to master a common core, there is ample room for specialization. Note that in the world of persons-plus outside the walls of schools, specialization is normal: We rely on one another. This immensely practical arrangement has the additional benefit of honoring individual worth.

A broad view of the potentials of working together comes from William Damon of Brown University and Erin Phelps of Radcliffe College. They write of "peer education" as an encompassing category that includes peer tutoring, cooperative learning, and peer collaboration. In peer tutoring, same-age or slightly older students tutor others in their areas of strength. In cooperative learning, students in a class get grouped into learning teams with the same learning goal; often, they divide the work within groups so that each student plays a distinct role, as in the jigsaw method just mentioned. In peer collaboration, pairs or small groups of students work together simultaneously on the same task, which may be individual to the group.

Damon and Phelps highlight two dimensions of importance in understanding the tradeoffs of these different forms of peer learning: equality and mutuality. Equality refers to the equal status of the participants. For instance, peer tutoring offers more equality of status than typical teacher/student relationships, but still maintains some hierarchy: The tutor has a dominant position. Cooperative learning and peer collaboration alike score high on equality.

Mutuality asks to what extent the discourse among learners is extensive, intimate, and connected. Peer collaboration ranks high in mutuality. Peer tutoring varies in mutuality according to the tutor's interactive skills and the learner's openness to the learning experience. Cooperative learning varies in mutuality depending on the extent to which tasks are divided among different students and on competitiveness, a motivator often used in cooperative learning.

The bottom line: Damon and Phelps argue on principle and research evidence that equality and mutuality contribute to good learning in peer learning situations. Therefore, peer collaboration serves well. Since peer tutoring and cooperative learning do not necessarily rate high on equality and mutuality, Damon and Phelps urge making the most use of versions of the two that do.

What do different sorts of peer learning look like? The jigsaw method, just sketched above, is a cooperative learning technique. For a different sort of example, consider "pair problem solving," a peer collaboration method good for developing metacognition and problem-solving abilities.

Pair problem solving was devised by mathematics/science educators Arthur Whimbey and Jack Lochhead and employed and investigated extensively by them. This tactic focuses on problem solving and organizes students into pairs. One student tackles the problem, reporting his or her thoughts. The other has two responsibilities: (1) to understand the first student's thinking, right or wrong (for instance, by asking questions to clarify when the first student has not said enough); (2) not to intervene, even if the first student makes mistakes. (However, if a student is especially prone to minor errors, Whimbey and Lochhead recommend that the listener draw seeming errors to the attention of the problem solver to support getting through the problem.) After the problem solving itself, the students discuss the problem and switch roles for the next problem.

What does this actually sound like? Suppose we have a familiar type of story problem: *If Aaron can rake the lawn in three hours and Boris in four, how long will it take them to do the job together.*

PROBLEM SOLVER:	Well, let's see. Certainly they'll do it faster together, 'cause Aaron will do one part and Boris another part.
LISTENER:	Okay.
PROBLEM SOLVER:	The trick is to figure out how much time they save. Or how much time they take. Let's see . . . I suppose it would kind of average out.
LISTENER:	What do you mean by "average out?"
PROBLEM SOLVER:	Well, if Aaron takes three hours and Boris four hours, the two of them to-

	gether might take three and a half hours, sort of splitting the difference. But I'm not sure.
LISTENER:	So let me see if I understand. Aaron is better off working without Boris. Boris actually makes things take longer.
PROBLEM SOLVER:	Yeah, I guess so. Wait a minute, that doesn't make sense. 'Cause Boris does part of the lawn so Aaron doesn't have to do it all. So it's not the average. Well let me start over.

Lochhead explains the logic of pair problem solving this way. Metacognitive awareness and reflection are important aspects of effective problem solving. But this is a difficult skill for students to sustain when they are worrying about the problem at the same time. Pair problem solving splits metacognitive awareness into two roles. The problem solver gets practice articulating ongoing thoughts, and the listener gets practice making sense of them and probing for clarity. The need for the two to communicate captures thoughts that otherwise would stream by in the rapids of moment-to-moment cognition. Eventually, students are pressed to combine the two roles, reporter and interpreter, in themselves, internalizing the initially social process of reflection.

Of course, peer learning techniques should not be seen as the only approach to distributing cognition socially. Socratic teaching, discussed in chapter 3, is another pattern of cooperative cognition in groups of medium size. Joint class projects can involve two dozen students, each in a somewhat specialized role. Drama activities distribute roles. And so on, through an abundance of opportunities.

Distributing Cognition Symbolically

In a way, to speak of physical and social distribution of cognition is already to include symbolic distribution, because symbol systems of various kinds—words, diagrams, equations—are the medium of exchange among people. But some direct attention to symbol systems is worthwhile.

One of the prejudices to be broken down in efforts to distribute cognition symbolically concerns the entanglements of particular symbol systems with particular subject matters. Mathematics, for example, is usually seen as the stamping grounds of formal notations. Yet in recent years many mathematics educators have advocated essayistic writing in mathematics: Youngsters discuss their approaches to particular problems, their understandings of key mathematics concepts, how mathematics connects to some slice of life outside of school, such as household budgets or government tactics to stabilize the economy.

Likewise, there is no particular reason why stories in literature always have to be talked and written about. Stories can be diagramed, taxonomized, mimed, turned into plays. Imagine students reading Dickens's *A Christmas Carol* and then improvising before/after vignettes around the characters. (Bob Cratchit asks for a raise before Scrooge's experience with the ghosts and after.) Three or four pairs of children take a crack at the improvisation. That provides a basis for discussing "character," what it means and why it's important.

The symbolic distribution of intelligence also recalls the emphasis in the last chapter on languages of thinking. One barrier to distributing cognition symbolically in the classroom is the impoverishment of classroom language, the failure to cultivate a common vocabulary about inquiry, explanation, argument, and problem solving. Distributing cognition symbolically calls for a concerted effort to bring languages of thinking into play in the classroom and reawaken them frequently, week by week, hour by hour.

Another important direction for the symbolic distribution of cognition concerns text forms. By and large, schooling relies on the essay, the story, and whatever forms of note taking students fall into spontaneously. But the fact is that neither essay nor story forms are very good for exploring alternatives and organizing patterns, although both can express what one has thought about. More telegraphic and flexible kinds of thinking on paper serve thinking better than these more extended and constrained forms. Remember again from the last chapter the importance of graphic organizers, ways of thinking on paper. Brainstormed lists, concept maps, charts, and two-dimensional tables are among the simple layouts that can be useful as students work to build a conception of something.

In analyzing a short story, for example, students may be better advised to begin with a concept map of it than just to think about it in their heads or start immediately to write about it. In planning an experiment in science, some students may prefer to lay out the steps in a diagram, with branches for contingencies, rather than in a written list. Sometimes key points about a period of historical development might be better captured on sortable three-by-five cards than laid down linearly in a notebook in the order served up by the text. As these points make plain, part of the agenda in distributing cognition symbolically is to foster a wide range of flexible symbolic resources, a kind of broad-band literacy.

Physical, social, and symbolic distribution of intelligence in the classroom—a whole brew of innovations toward the smart school. But where do teachers and administrators gain the know-how to put such ideas into practice? There is no one answer, but also no lack of answers. First of all, it's important to recognize that a good start can be made without any special help. In a school setting that encourages experimentation, any teacher can try some of these ideas. It is not difficult, for example, to ask students to keep a personal journal on something for a few weeks or to call for an essay in math class or a diagram of a short story. As to cooperative and collaborative learning, most teachers have had some introduction to these techniques already.

To be sure, many practices benefit from much more information and advice. Refined use of cooperative learning methods requires techniques for setting up joint responsibility of every student in each group for the other students' learning. Innovations involving computers call for some minimal technical tutorial. But a veritable industry of consultants and published materials stands waiting to supply such needs. And in the smart school, with its commitment to informing and energizing instruction, teachers and administrators have time to experiment and learn.

THE FINGERTIP EFFECT

Many of the foregoing examples are familiar. If anything is new, it is not the individual ideas but the way of seeing them. They all are part of the mission to redistribute cognition more broadly in the classroom, a person-plus approach to instruction that suggests many ways of reorganizing the learning process.

However, lest all this seem too utopian, there is a fundamental factor that threatens the whole enterprise. I like to call it "the fingertip effect."

The fingertip effect is a belief that many innovators have had in the impact of a new technology or other innovation, such as cooperative learning or peer tutoring. The essence of this belief can be stated in a sentence: *When we put opportunities at learners' fingertips, they take the opportunities.*

For example, the fingertip effect forecasts that when we make word processors available to young writers, they will take the opportunity of making structural revisions of their stories and essays, something very inconvenient with paper and pencil. When we make programming languages available and familiar to learners, they will discern powerful analogies between programming and other areas, carrying over skills from one to another. When we make cooperative groupings part of the classroom, students will seize the opportunity to adopt mutually supportive patterns of thinking and learning. And so on.

In short, belief in the fingertip effect is belief in the immediate opportunism of the human organism. The forecast that follows boils down to this: All we have to do to mediate change is to set up physical or social structures (word processors, cooperative groups) that afford opportunities. Change will then follow naturally, as learners seize those opportunities.

The trouble with the fingertip effect is that it doesn't happen. Not with any reliability. Not in the short term. The impact of word processors on students' writing is a classic case. It is simply not true that students gravitate toward fundamental structural revisions of their texts when given the conveniences of word processors. Rather, they tend to use the word processors for minor, local revisions such as correcting spelling.

Likewise, it is simply not true that organizing youngsters into cooperative groups immediately yields great benefits. Initially, the participants do not know how to work well in groups. Also, certain group structures turn out to foster achievement more effectively than others. While the opportunities to collaborate are created simply by grouping students, *follow-through* depends on much more than the existence of opportunity.

Once it's recognized that the hoped-for fingertip effect does not routinely occur, reasons why are easy to find. Here are some of them.

Opportunities Not Recognized.   Students who have had little chance to engage in structural revisions in text do not even recognize its importance. There is nothing in their experience to spur them to seize the opportunity. In contrast, people with ample experience in writing "the hard way," who have coped with the vexations of structural revision by paper and pencil or typewriter, will immediately begin to exploit such resources. In general, the new opportunities afforded by an innovation commonly cannot be recognized by novices.

Cognitive Burden.   It's also important to realize that the opportunities afforded by innovations often bring with them a bewildering array of new things. A word processor, for example, does not await attentively for you to tell it what to write. There is a lot to learn about what it will do and what keys make it do those things. Cooperative groups bring with them puzzles of decision making, communication, task tracking, and responsibility that youngsters are not used to dealing with. "Here we are in a group. Okay. Who's boss? Is there a boss? How do we decide what to do first?" and so on. Quite apart from whether they are in a position to discern opportunities in principle, students commonly run headlong into considerable confusion and disorientation.

Motivational Structure.   Just because an opportunity appears does not mean that learners feel motivated to take it. A common problem in cooperative groups is that the ablest member ends up doing the task. The others copy, getting an almost free ride. To be sure, the opportunity for more evenhanded collaboration is there . . . but why bother? The ablest member will do a better job solo. And the ablest member often likes it that way—it's more quickly done and better done, he or she thinks. Accordingly, advocates of cooperative learning have had to discover how to configure groups and group responsibilities carefully to ensure full participation.

None of this should be surprising. There is no reason why

simply providing a resource should yield immediate and pro-
found transformations. But belief in the fingertip effect needs
explicit identification because, not uncommonly, innovators have
argued for the immediate transformative power of simply putting
something into place—computers, television, typewriters, cooperative groups, or whatever. When such initiatives fail, as they
commonly do, blame falls on the medium. "Computers can't
help, after all."

This is too hasty. The problem is not the new medium but the
lack of mediation. The lesson of the fingertip effect is that the
discovery of opportunities needs to be guided. Teachers can help
students to unearth the opportunities of technical resources, such
as computers and calculators. Teachers can arrange fruitful
interaction patterns in cooperative groups.

Some innovative software environments provide cuing systems to remind students of opportunities. For example, writing
environments developed by Gavriel Salomon, mentioned earlier,
and by Collette Daiute of the Harvard Graduate School of
Education, prompt students occasionally with reminders about
good things to ask themselves. Salomon's Writing Partner from
time to time poses questions like this:

- Do you want your composition to persuade or to describe?
- What kind of an audience are you addressing?
- What are some of your main points?
- Does this lead me to the conclusion I want to reach?

As these examples make plain, the questions put forward by
the Writing Partner are not meant to raise subtle points about
composition but quite basic ones—which, however, the learner
can easily neglect. Such writing environments go beyond the
conventional word processor, which offers opportunity aplenty
but little guidance, by stimulating opportunity finding and
opportunity taking.

Part of the lure of the fingertip effect seems to lie in the
cherished belief that educational transformations should be
natural, not forced. The image of simply putting something into
place—say, a word processor—and seeing wonderful learning
experiences unfold organically is seductive. But innumerable lost
hopes argue for a more hard-headed posture toward the fingertip

effect. We must not expect new technologies, the grouping of students, and like innovations to do the job by themselves. We must accept the responsibility of mediating students' good use of these person-plus resources.

WHO'S BOSS WHEN?

If intelligence can be distributed in various ways, a provocative question arises: "Who's boss when?" Put more formally, people, societies, and even some machine systems have what might be called an "executive function." There are mechanisms that guide the overall activity, confronting decision points and deciding when different tasks should be undertaken. So we can ask: When cognition is distributed, how, specifically, is the executive function distributed?

It is not hard to recognize a number of scenarios. Most often, we think of people as deciding for themselves. Decision making is a person-solo undertaking, whatever other cognitive functions might be distributed. But this is only one possibility. For example, during conventional instruction, the teacher decides what is best to do next. The students carry out the teacher's agenda, their own executive function limited to minor decision points within that agenda. A text or workbook includes a tacit and sometimes explicit set of executive guides: Read the chapter from the beginning; answer the questions at the end of the chapter; fill in the blanks.

In summary, in all sorts of ways, learners (and others) commonly cede executive control to some part of the surround—the text, the worksheet, the teacher. Now all this may seem to be a setup for a revolutionary statement I'm about to make, something along the lines that learners need to be liberated from the autocracy of the surround. But nothing of the sort is intended.

On the contrary, ceding executive function to the surround is one of the most effective cognitive strategies we have. In everyday life, we do it all the time. When you follow a map or a set of directions for assembling a bicycle, you are ceding executive function, and soundly so. The map "knows" more about the landscape than you do. The manufacturer knows more about how to put the bicycle together than you do. To be sure, you retain the right (and the risks) of override. But unless there are reasons to exercise that right, you do well to take advantage of the prefabricated executive.

Further, we as a whole society cede executive function to certain political units—mayors, presidents, governors, and so on. We cede legal judgment to written law, precedent, and a judicial system. In cases of civil conflict, we may cede judgment to a mediator. In cases of management, the wise manager commonly cedes large classes of judgments to subordinates to avoid the overwhelming task of keeping track of everything himself or herself.

With all this in mind, two questions about the executive function seem particularly important:

1. Is there an appropriate executive function anywhere in the person-plus system in question?
2. When learners cede executive function, do they ever get it back?

The first question is important exactly because the answer is commonly no. Indeed, this connects to the problem of the fingertip effect. Why is it that students do not seize the opportunities that various technologies afford? Because, all too often, the technologies are presented as a kind of cognitive sandbox. The invitation is to build what you can in the sandbox. But neither in the student nor in the technology is there any executive function guiding the student to recognize and exercise the opportunities.

And why is it that at first students often have trouble working fruitfully in cooperative groups? Consider their previous experience. Earlier, they did what they or the teacher wanted. But cooperative learning brings new questions of distribution of executive function within the group. Learners need, with appropriate guidance, to feel their way into consensus patterns, tie-breaking tricks, and the like to function well.

The second question—do learners get the executive function back—is important because a good deal of educational practice vests executive function in teacher or materials "temporarily." But the students never recover it.

A prime example is problem selection. Textbooks and teachers do virtually all the problem choosing for students, deciding which problems are worth attention and usually in what order.

After a period of practice, the assignments stop. Then we are puzzled when students fail to see the opportunities to apply what they have learned on a final exam with mixed problem types. Here's John or Jane looking at the math final, for example. Now problem number seven . . . is that a related-rates problem? Do I need to use simultaneous equations? Wasn't there a formula? Poor John and Jane. Before, they always knew what approach to use because the exercises at the end of the chapter always went with the method in the chapter. Now, they don't have that crutch.

Likewise, learners commonly fail to see applications of what they have learned in another subject matter or in everyday life—the problem of transfer of learning. No wonder! They've had no experience identifying problems and thinking how what they already know might connect to those problems. They have never exercised the executive function of deciding what problems to tackle and how.

This is no reason to conclude the opposite: that teachers, texts, and computer tutoring systems should turn over the task of navigating through learning opportunities to the students from the first. Some people do argue for something like this, but I see no evidence that it is particularly effective. If anything, students have no idea what to do with initial near-total freedom, not only because they are not used to the elbow room but because they lack the knowledge base about the topic that would inform wise decisions.

Rather, the main implication is that sooner or later the executive function should return to individual students or groups of students so that they learn how to guide their own thinking and learning. But when exactly?

Suppose that some students are just learning a cooperative learning technique. They most likely will need step-by-step direction. Suppose that they already have employed this technique two or three times with considerable direction. Then the teacher can say, "Remember how we did that? Who can tell me?" A few questions and answers in that spirit will get students off on the right track. Or suppose that the students have grown familiar with the technique. The teacher need only say, "Okay, it's our usual group thing. Let's go!"

In other words, when to pass the executive function to learners has a fairly straightforward answer: Pass along as much as you can as soon as you can. Teachers who know their students can best judge this. It's a matter of the nature of the task and the sophistication of the students and, often, a matter for teachers to experiment with as they learn what their students can handle. But youngsters are really shortchanged when they rarely exercise the executive function at all. This is one of the most significant gaps in conventional education.

AN EXAMPLE OF PERSON-PLUS TEACHING

We have made our way from Alfredo's three notebooks to an enlarged view of educational practice. Most classroom conduct, like most psychological research, leans toward an emphatically person-solo perspective on cognition, neglecting the many ways in which people tap the resources of the surround (including other people) to support, share, and conduct cognitive processing.

A smart school should be different. Let's take a person-plus approach to thinking and learning. Let's treat the person-plus-surround as one system, scoring as thinking what gets done partly in the surround and treating as learning traces left in certain parts of the surround (such as a notebook). Let's challenge the hegemony of the person-solo posture.

Mounting such a challenge means paying attention to several things. First of all, opportunities must be sought (and in many current innovations *are* sought) to distribute cognitive functioning more widely, with the help of physical artifacts such as computers, of social configurations such as cooperative groups, and of shared symbol systems such as various languages of thinking. Second, we must be wary of the misleading belief in the fingertip effect—the idea that simply introducing ways of distributing cognition will make things happen. Rather, the taking of opportunities needs to be mediated. Third, the distribution of the executive function—who decides what to do—needs particular attention to ensure that somewhere in a system there is always a good executive function and that it eventually ends up with the learners.

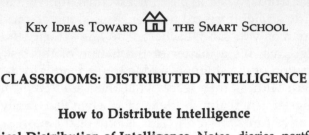

KEY IDEAS TOWARD THE SMART SCHOOL

CLASSROOMS: DISTRIBUTED INTELLIGENCE

How to Distribute Intelligence

- **Physical Distribution of Intelligence.** Notes, diaries, portfolios, calculators, computers, and the like.

- **Social Distribution of Intelligence.** Learning in groups with common group test. Pair problem solving. Socratic teaching, drama activities.

- **Symbolic Distribution of Intelligence.** Essays in mathematics and the sciences. Diagrams, taxonomies in literature. Varied text forms—stories, essays, lists, concept maps, charts, two-dimensional tables.

What to Watch Out For

- **The (Unreliable) Fingertip Effect.** Benefits of new physical, social, and symbolic configurations not automatic. Needed: help in recognizing opportunities, managing the cognitive burden. Careful design for motivation.

- **Executive Function in Managing Tasks.** Good executive somewhere in the system, not necessarily the student. The student eventually gets the executive function.

So what would this actually look like? Imagine a class facing a puzzle: How would you arrange a fair race between a dog and an ant? Of course, this puzzle is not all there is to the project these youngsters are undertaking. It is simply a motivating device. The students are investigating the general theme of animal locomotion. Within this theme can be found a number of questions relating to biology, mathematics, and physics. For example:

What different strategies for locomotion do animals display (for instance, two-leg walking, or four-leg, or six- or eight-, or as many as in millipedes, along with flying insect-style, flying bird-style, and so on)?

In what ways are these modes of locomotion adaptive for the life-style of the organism involved? What are their trade-offs (for example, flying has high energy demands but affords speed, escape from ground creatures, and a bird's-eye view)?

At what speeds do animals travel, and how are they measured—in absolute terms, relative to the size of the creature, relative to predators' speeds (plenty of mathematics enters here)?

Of course, merely posing such questions does not demand a person-plus perspective. Person-plus enters during the students' pursuit of the project. They work in small groups—socially distributed cognition. They brainstorm questions to pursue regarding animal locomotion and capture them on paper— physically distributed cognition. They employ symbol-handling techniques introduced by the teacher for supporting exploratory thinking, such as listing, concept mapping, and flowcharts— symbolically distributed cognition.

Skeptical of the fingertip effect, the teacher does not expect that these social, physical, and symbolic resources will automatically help the youngsters progress in their inquiries. The teacher coaches the students to ensure that distributed cognition works well. The teacher helps the groups to divide their work into roles—Alan will handle the stopwatch, Beatrice will handle the frogs, Carlos will handle the ruler. The teacher helps students think about what kinds of graphic organizers would serve them well. Comparing animals' speeds? What about a table of numbers or a bar graph? Classifying different ways that different animals move? How about a concept map? And so on.

As the different groups choose their particular topics of inquiry within the general theme of animal locomotion, distributed cognition broadens and deepens. One group employs field notes and sketches to investigate how ants crawl. Another uses videotape to examine with stop-action the gaits of humans and dogs. The groups employ the language of mathematics—numbers, formulas, and tabular arrangements—to calculate and compare rates of motion.

Toward the end, the groups collaborate on a large concept map, covering much of the wall of the classroom, that assembles and organizes what they have discovered about animal locomotion. And they may even stage a race between a dog and an ant, with different finish lines chosen to represent each creature's functional context.

Inquiry projects such as this, because of their richness and length, inherently call for a person-plus approach. Otherwise, how is one to divide the work and manage the flood of ideas and information? Moreover, outside of school settings, the activities of life tend to be project-like: many-sided, complex, ongoing, as in pursuing a hobby, advancing a profession, or even simply planning a picnic. Accordingly, this animal locomotion example is something of a pitch for project-based learning as well as for a person-plus perspective. In addition, recalling the last two chapters, it plainly involves understanding performances and the metacurriculum in several ways.

However, if project-based learning seems too complicated an enterprise to mount in a particular classroom, there is ample room for the benefits of a person-plus perspective anyway. Students can work in groups to address the exercises at the end of the chapter. Students can deploy concept mapping and other symbolic devices to synthesize what they have learned from textbook readings. They can maintain portfolios of their best essays or proofs of theorems. They can cooperate on papers. The serious use of distributed intelligence in the classroom comes in many sizes and shapes, some larger and more complex, others that can be started today on a whim, something for virtually everyone.

A person-plus agenda for education acknowledges the broad trajectory of the development of civilization, from one-pebble-per-sheep accounting systems to hieroglyphics to the alphabet and beyond. It's remarkable how vigorously people have recruited into the cognitive enterprise not only other people but the quiescent physical things around us, arranging and transforming them so that they become—to use a lovely phrase coined by Gavriel Salomon—"partners in cognition."

smArt

SCHOOLS

CHAPTER 7

MOTIVATION

The Cognitive Economy
of Schooling

"Why are we studying this?"

No teacher likes to hear this question! Such words of skepticism about the educational enterprise are among the least welcome utterances that students voice. When someone asks, "Why are we studying this?" any teacher hears the message all too well. To one student at least, it's not obvious at all. There's no point to the enterprise. So why expect me to buy in?

So what do we do? We bemoan students' blindness. We wonder why they don't recognize the importance of knowledge and skill for their futures. We wonder why they don't tune in to the rich rewards of Shakespeare or algebra. But sometimes students who offer such misgivings may be seeing all too clearly. Here, for example, is a bundle of questions one fourth grader wrote down about fractions:

155

1. How much is one half of a fraction? 2. Why do we use fractions? 3. Why [sic] do fractions have to do with math? 4. Do they have to do with anything else?

Dumb questions? Not at all! Such questions as these do not sound like the obtuse recalcitrance of a student without vision. On the contrary, they are all too pointed. "Why do fractions have to do with math?" suggests that the math curriculum has not made plain how different sides of mathematics relate to one another. "Do they have to do with anything else?" suggests that links have not been made between the mathematics class and the rest of life. With such a persistent lack of connectivity, why indeed are these students studying fractions?

Certainly, we need to work to connect things up more. This is one of the agendas of a pedagogy of understanding, as discussed in chapter 4, and of teaching for transfer, as discussed in chapter 5. But the "Why are we studying this?" question and its kin point up an even larger concern about educational practice: What is it that could and should keep students learning at their best? And let's not forget teachers: What is it that could and should keep them teaching at their best? How, indeed, should we talk about the complex networks of motives that all too often produce low energy and negativity? And how can we see ways toward more vigorous and thriving smart schools with their high positive energy?

Here is a way of talking about all that. We can call it "the cognitive economy."

THE IDEA OF A COGNITIVE ECONOMY

Consider the economy of a classroom. Not the money economy —how much teachers get paid and textbooks cost. Rather, the metaphorical economy of gains and costs that students encounter.

As in any economy, there are a myriad of gains and costs. The central gain for students is the knowledge and skills that they acquire. But besides this there are a number of other gains as well: intrinsic interest in some of what is taught, a sense of mastery, good grades, credentialing, teacher approval, peer status, and social interaction (not just in the halls, but in cooperative learning and peer collaboration). As in a real economy, many of these gains have value because of their later consequences: credentialing and skills for the sake of a better fate in the job market, for example.

As in a real economy, there are also a number of costs. Time and cognitive effort are the most obvious. But there are others as well: boredom, fear of failure, actual experiences of failure, feelings of isolation, and uncomfortable competition.

Teachers are also players in the economy of gains and costs in the classroom. One central gain for teachers is their students' academic achievement. On the whole, teachers feel very committed to student learning. Another gain is pleasure in the artful exercise of the craft of teaching. Another includes the respect of students, principal, other teachers, parents, and the community. And of course there are salary and professional advancement. But there are costs aplenty. They include time, effort, boredom, lack of appreciation, lack of control, and feeling beleaguered by dozens of agendas.

What kind of an economy is all this? Not a money economy, because money, although part of the picture, does not seem so central as other gains and costs. Let's call it a cognitive economy. After all, schools and classrooms deal with the cognitive achievement of their students more than anything else. Of course, many other noncognitive factors play important roles in schooling. But that's okay. We speak of Iowa as having a corn economy and the Arab countries an oil economy, even though Iowans and Arabs deal with many other things. We do so because those economies rotate around corn and oil, respectively. In just this sense, classrooms and schools have a cognitive economy—matters rotate around the cognitive achievement of students, whatever else goes on.

To clarify the idea of a cognitive economy a little further, it must be acknowledged that the economic metaphor is a loose one. For instance, there is no equivalent of money in the cognitive economy of the classroom; certainly not grades, because they are only one of several kinds of gain, and they do not function as a medium of exchange.

But there is a liberating advantage to the loose fit. In particular, lacking an equivalent of money, the cognitive economy of schools and classrooms does not press us to reduce all costs and benefits to some standard cognitive currency. While the common yardstick of the dollar in Keynesian economics yields mathematical rigor, it also generates unsettling equivalences: How many dollars is health worth? How many dollars is a life worth? In the cognitive economy of schools and classrooms, we can frame costs and benefits more loosely but flexibly in terms of the diverse qualities that count—effort invested, confusions encountered, experiences cherished, understandings gained, skills attained. Most of all, rewards in a cognitive economy need not be selfish in character. Altruism counts as well.

How the Idea of the Cognitive Economy Gives Reason

We usually discuss why students and teachers behave the way they do in terms of motives. And talk of motives is okay as far as it goes. But it fails to capture something crucial and widely neglected about the educational scene: Students and teachers are rational agents.

Talk simply of motivation suggests a picture of students and teachers responding blindly to the pushes and pulls in the school setting, even, in behaviorist terms, the "contingencies of reinforcement." But the economic metaphor pictures all as rational agents, players in the economic game, considering the costs and gains and generally responding rather reasonably. When a student says, "Why are we studying this?" the student has good reason for the question in the context of school as it is. Because the gains the student wants to see coming his or her way are often either not obvious or not there at all.

In *The New Meaning of Educational Change*, Michael Fullan has recently commented wryly on teachers' rationality and innovation: "Teachers' reasons for rejecting many innovations are every bit as rational as those of the advocates promoting them." Fullan highlights some of the criteria teachers spontaneously use in sizing up an innovation: Does the change address a real need? Will students show an interest? How do I know the change will have the desired impact? Is it clear what I, the teacher, need to do? What about the time, energy, skills I need? What about conflict with other agendas? Often, proposed innovations make little sense from this very rational teacher perspective.

Of course, the reasonableness of people in the cognitive

economy should not be overdrawn: People in real economies only behave with limited rationality, as stressed in the classic work of cognitive scientist and economist Herbert Simon of Carnegie Mellon University. Nonetheless, it is terribly important to recognize that students are not generally acting foolishly or blindly when they ask questions like "Why are we studying this?" Teachers are not acting irresponsibly when they hang back from an innovation, saying, "I really don't have the time."

Eleanor Duckworth, an academic colleague at the Harvard Graduate School of Education, writes eloquently of "giving reason to people"—probing to understand their logic when they seem to be struggling obtusely. They almost always have an intelligent cut, albeit sometimes a mistaken one. Giving reason is part of a pedagogy of understanding. And it applies just as much to motives as to concepts. We should also give reason to students who seem to be questioning or even disdaining the educational enterprise and to teachers who respond coolly to yet one more agenda. They are generally behaving quite sensibly.

THE COOL COGNITIVE ECONOMY
OF THE TYPICAL CLASSROOM

Let us give reason to the cognitive economy of the ordinary classroom. We don't have to be happy with it, but at least we can understand how it works.

Remember how smart schools need high positive energy. Basically, this is a matter of the cognitive economy. One might call the cognitive economy of the typical classroom a "cool" rather than a "hot" cognitive economy—one that does not motivate the energy needed for complex cognition of students but runs at an altogether lower level of cognitive demand. Let us probe why it functions in the way it does.

The Costs of Complex Cognition

One reason for the cool, low-energy, cognitive economy is the cost of complex cognition. Of course, reformers usually focus on the gains and feel them to be high. Complex cognition has more intrinsic interest and promises more payoff outside of school and later in life. But consider the cost to learners: Complex cognition demands much more effort. It creates greater risk of failure. It introduces the discomforts of disorientation, as learners struggle to get their heads around difficult ideas. Peer status for complex cognition is certainly mixed; who wants to be known as a "brain"? And very commonly, so far as grades and teacher approval go, complex cognition buys students no more than the simpler path of getting the facts straight and the algorithms right. No wonder, then, that students perfectly reasonably do not automatically gravitate toward complex cognition.

The Lack of Connectivity and Consequences

For complex cognition, or equally, for basic knowledge and skills, one can ask, "What does it connect with? Where are the gains?" As intimated by the fourth grader's questions about fractions, often the curriculum does not make plain the intellectual or practical significance of even the basics, never mind complex cognition. To be sure, there are consequences of lackluster performance for grades and teacher approval (but see below). However, at least some of the consequences for everyday life are doubtful. How does school knowledge prepare the ghetto dweller to cope? In terms of the labor market, as mentioned in chapter 2, research shows that possession of a high school diploma makes virtually no difference in access to jobs for students who are not college bound.

A Sole-Source and Single-Choice Economy

Teachers-*cum*-texts constitute almost the sole source of information in the typical classroom. And the fare offered by the teacher-*cum*-text usually is not a menu, but take it or leave it. Plainly, real economies gain much of their vigor from multiple sources for goods and from the flexibility that members of the economy have to seek after their own individual interests. Analogously, students might learn from one another much more than they typically do and might have more choices about what they learn within a subject matter than they typically do. None of this is to deny the importance of a core of knowledge and skills that all students should acquire to some reasonable degree of mastery. Nor is it to argue for a wide range of electives at the expense of a solid core. But the sole-source, single-choice, cognitive economy of the typical classroom seems far more extreme than needed to provide for the common core.

The often abysmal quality of textbooks makes the typical sole source an unfortunate one, with plenty of cognitive cost in boredom and little cognitive gain in insight. Textbook publishers have responded to market pressures and economies of scale by producing textbooks that try to meet a myriad of requirements in different states and the pressures of a hundred special-interest groups. One common tactic is called "mentioning." Publishers say something somewhere in their texts about as many nations, ethnic groups, ideas, issues, and people as they can. Inevitably, it's an exercise in overweening superficiality. Textbooks also use readability formulas to control the difficulty level, formulas that have nothing to do with clarity of exposition and less with engaging style. The result: bad writing in "readable" textbooks.

Teachers' and Schools' Conflict-of-Interest Position

Of course, the students are not the only players in this cognitive economy. As a key source of information and guidance, the teacher also holds a unique position as the administrator of grades and advancement. Indeed, the gains and costs from the standpoint of the teacher put teachers in a bit of a bind. On the one hand, research shows that teachers have very high intrinsic motivation. They value youngsters' learning and will work hard to foster it. The gain of seeing youngsters learn spurs them onward in their efforts to teach their best.

However, there are costs of setting high standards, costs associated with the culture of the school and the society outside the school. Teachers get paid not only for teaching but for moving students along through the grades. It is embarrassing for a teacher to hold back many students. Students are discouraged, and parents can be furious. Complaints come to the principal. In many contexts, complaints may also come to the principal if teachers attempt something "highfalutin," peer collaboration or the teaching of thinking or writing without due attention to spelling, for instance.

So teachers feel pressed not to demand too much. Demanding

a lot creates a lot of trouble and a lot of cost. So teachers behave entirely reasonably: They do the best they can to encourage good learning but without demanding it. Inevitably, there sets in grade inflation, and more generally, "standards inflation," not a bad analogy to the phenomenon of inflation in real economies.

The same logic applies to whole state educational systems. Over the past few years, efforts to legislate tougher graduation requirements in many settings have generally backfired. Schools have responded not by finding better ways to teach challenging subjects but by padding the menu with watered-down subjects. A few years ago, Florida legislated stiffer high school graduation requirements—three years of science and mathematics, for instance. With what result? Weaker students enrolled on a massive scale in a new, academically negligible "Fundamentals of Biology" course and other "Fundamentals of . . ." courses acknowledged to require little intellectually of students. "Informal Geometry" calls for no formal proofs, while "Fundamentals of Math II" essentially repeats "Fundamentals of Math I," which is itself a low-demand remedial course. Such courses attract not only the weakest students but a fair number of moderately able students looking for the easy way out.

The Token Investment Strategy

Teachers are beleaguered with agendas. Responsible for teaching the traditional subject matters, they are also asked to impart basic knowledge about health, sex, and the risk of AIDS, imbue youngsters with citizenship values, detect students with special needs or talents and respond appropriately, build students' writing skills whatever the subject matter, foster good thinking, ensure "fun" participation, meet with parents, and so on and so on.

How to manage it all? Very commonly, teachers adopt an adroit strategy: "token investment." They invest a little bit of their resources in everything. In the cognitive economy of typical classrooms and schools, this strategy makes very good sense. 1. It does something for the students about each agenda, even if not as much as one would like. 2. It protects the teacher against the accusation from principals, parents, or students of doing nothing about an agenda, a high-cost accusation.

The token investment strategy should not be seen as selfish and uncommitted. On the contrary, it often constitutes an heroic effort to accomplish as much as possible. The Horace Smith that Theodore Sizer writes about in *Horace's Compromise* is a case in point. As mentioned in chapter 3, Horace is a conspicuously committed teacher, who asks students to write often, responds to their work, and so on. But to serve all his students and all the agendas, he spreads himself thin. He ends up spending only about five minutes a week on each student's written work and ten minutes planning each class, considerably less effort on any one thing than he thinks appropriate. This is the compromise.

Students, too, are not strangers to the token investment strategy. Student lives are full of demands and desires—some of them academic, many of them not. How to manage the many agendas? Often, token investment. Students quickly learn that it is much better to do a little something on an assignment than nothing, which would trigger a harsh response from the teacher.

Effective though the token investment strategy is in the cool cognitive economy of the ordinary classroom, it of course has at least two flaws from a larger perspective. First of all, students would arguably gain more in the long run by in-depth attention to certain priorities. Second, for many of the agendas, token treatment of many of the agendas arguably benefits students not at all. While the token investment strategy presumes that the small investment in X will achieve a modicum of learning about X, often, without more ample and recurrent treatment, X never takes hold in students' minds at all. In a day or a week, it is gone.

Coverage

While innovators criticize the overemphasis on coverage and teachers generally acknowledge its ills, the impulse to coverage persists. Beyond condemning coverage, we need to recognize the cognitive-economic forces that sustain it.

Coverage can be seen as a special case of the token investment strategy. Students receive a token exposure to a large number of topics in, let us say, science. As in general with the token investment strategy, this puts teachers, texts, and curricula in a highly defensible position. "Students had an opportunity to learn this" can be the response to a parent who complains about a question missed on the final exam or the SAT, to a congressperson who complains that youngsters do not know basic facts about government, to a scientist who complains that students do not know how many planets circle the solar system.

To be sure, there is more to the dominance of coverage than the defense-oriented, token investment strategy. As discussed in chapter 2, a trivial pursuit conception of knowledge and understanding pervades much of education. However, the cognitive economy has a role in sustaining this conception. As happens throughout human affairs, pragmatics reinforce ideologies. Just as in the days of the Crusades, the lure of booty from the East encouraged ideological commitments to a Christian world, so the defensibleness of coverage subtly encourages commitment to a conception of learning as the accumulation of information and skills.

CREATING A HOT COGNITIVE ECONOMY

We have to do better. Certainly, if we want to attain those three crucial achievements of retention, understanding, and the active use of knowledge, a different cognitive economy is in order—a hot rather than a cool one, a cognitive economy that sustains high-energy, complex cognition in the classroom rather than the low-energy, simplistic cognition of facts and routines.

But how to build a hot cognitive economy? The basic rule is this: An innovation has to make sense in economic terms— cognitive economic terms. An innovation that demands complex cognition of students has to bring with it (a) conspicuous gains and (b) minimally increased costs. After all, the greater cognitive demand is itself a cost that must be offset for the innovation to make sense.

So what might work? What will not work is simply upping cognitive demand—more Shakespeare, calculus sooner, history based on original source materials, no wimpy courses. All that may or may not be a good idea, but by itself it simply increases cognitive complexity, which is a cost, while doing nothing to minimize cost or ensure real and visible gains persuasive to the students.

What can work are the strategies suggested in earlier chapters.

They have not been casually chosen, but selected with an eye toward their viability in the cognitive economy of a classroom. A list for review may help bring the prospects into focus:

- *Theory One*, the basic theory of teaching and learning that asks for clear information, thoughtful practice, informative feedback, and strong intrinsic or extrinsic motivation, can reduce the cost of complex cognition by making it more accessible and by reducing students' risk of failure and can increase the gain by helping students to learn more.
- *Intrinsic motivation* in particular can be boosted by giving students more choice about exactly what they work on and more information sources than teacher and text, instead of the sole-source, single-choice economy typical of classrooms (this does not mean an "anything goes" setting).
- *Coaching and Socratic teaching* can reduce the cost of complex cognition in risk and fear by supporting students in the learning process in ways that didactic instruction cannot and can increase the gain by helping students to learn more and by providing a more interesting, interactive style.
- *A pedagogy of understanding, with its focus on understanding performances, mental images, and powerful representations,* can reduce the cost of complex cognition by making difficult ideas more accessible and can increase the gain through greater learning and through the increases in intrinsic motivation that come with understanding what one is learning.
- *Higher levels of understanding,* patterns of problem solving, explanation and justification, and inquiry appropriate to the subject matters can increase the gain by helping students feel more oriented to a subject matter and more empowered to do things with it.
- *Generative topics,* when they become the bread and butter of the curriculum, can increase the gain by making the subject matters more intrinsically interesting and more connected to applications beyond the classroom. Good choice of a limited set of generative topics can help teachers evade the token investment strategy, where they spread themselves thin.
- *From the metacurriculum, languages of thinking, integrative mental images, and learning to learn* can reduce the cost of complex

cognition by making difficult topics more accessible and can increase the gain by empowering students as thinkers and learners.

- *The intellectual passions*, modeled and encouraged by teachers, can increase the gain by developing proactive, thoughtful mindsets in students.
- *Teaching for transfer*, with ample attention day by day, can increase the gain by making the payoffs of more demanding studies clearer and preparing learners to transfer school learning to other classes and to applications beyond the classroom.
- *The physical distribution of intelligence*, via writing and other media, can reduce the cost of complex cognition by reducing cognitive load.
- *The social distribution of intelligence*, via peer tutoring, cooperative learning, and peer collaboration, can reduce the cost of complex cognition through group support and the comfort of groups when tasks are hard and can increase the gain through the enjoyments of working with others and the payoffs of learning how to do that well.
- *The symbolic distribution of intelligence*, through drawing a number of different symbolic forms into instruction in the different subject matters (stories, concept maps, diaries, improvisatory drama, picturing) can reduce the cost of complex cognition by making ideas accessible in symbol systems better suited to the topic and/or different individual learners and can increase the gain by equipping all students to work with a diversity of symbol systems.

So what's the catch? If all this worked that well, we would see it in every school district. And there is a catch; in fact, two of them.

Catch #1.   These strategies for the hot cognitive economy all require up-front investment. Although they can pay for themselves once in place and part of the system, there is a high initial-effort cost, and some dollar cost, in expanded programs of teacher development, rearranging old patterns of administration, getting students used to the new pattern, assembling appropriate materials, and so on.

Often, we do not see a hot cognitive economy because the

transition to it is hard. But the smart school has a commitment to making the up-front investments needed for a hot cognitive economy. Moreover, for a somewhat reduced cost, sources such as Michael Fullan's *The New Meaning of Educational Change* tell us much about how to manage such change processes less painfully, as the next chapter explores.

Catch #2. Besides needing to pay the initial cost of change, schools need visions of what to change to. Otherwise, it's easy to get lost. In a way, there is too much to try out. Education abounds with new ways to teach fractions or Dickens, scientific thinking or good citizenship, a vast and confusing menagerie of options. What's required—but found much more rarely than individual, promising innovations—are holistic visions of schooling that provide an overall direction. Many current efforts to restructure schools come with visions that lean in the direction of the smart school. I hope that the idea of the smart school as outlined in this book will bring into clearer focus what such schools could be like.

SCHOOL RESTRUCTURING: A COGNITIVE ECONOMIC REVOLUTION

A conspicuous feature of the United States educational landscape over the past few years has been efforts to "restructure" schools. As mentioned in chapter 1, behind this initiative lies the recognition that many organizational features of schools—short class periods, too many subject matters, overauthoritative leadership —make more enlightened instructional practices tough to launch and tougher to sustain. School restructuring strives to take down these barriers, liberating teachers, administrators, and students to pursue a brighter path.

One of the best known examples of restructuring high schools is the Coalition of Essential Schools, founded by Theodore Sizer of Brown University. Sizer and his colleagues do not offer a detailed model for what such a school should be like. Rather, Sizer articulates a set of principles, his well-known "nine points." Through these nine points, Sizer urges a focus on only a few academic subjects, with emphasis on adolescents' using their minds well. He calls for simple and universal goals, a limited number of important skills suitable for all students. But students of different abilities and interests may pursue them in different ways. Education must be personalized rather than impersonal, emphasizing individual needs and supportive individual relationships among teachers and students.

Sizer envisions the student-as-worker in contrast with the teacher-as-deliverer-of-instructional-services. Teachers coach students, who engage in meaningful extended inquiry. Graduation requires an "exhibition" by a student, demonstrating his or her grasp of the school's expectations. Through such exhibitions, students must show that they can accomplish worthwhile inquiry or other projects. In the long term, Sizer urges that such a program need only cost 10 percent per student more than a traditional high school.

Notice how Sizer's vision remakes the cognitive economy of the conventional school. With more time for fewer subjects and skills, the cost in frustration of students and teachers reaching for depth becomes much lower. With student-as-worker, both students and teachers get rewarded for nontraditional roles—the student a serious inquirer and the teacher a coach rather than lecturer. The emphasis on exhibitions from students wires student-as-worker to graduation requirements. Sizer's budget estimate calls for more dollar investment, but not that much more, keeping the dollar cost of a hot cognitive economy reasonable.

The Coalition of Essential Schools does not expect each participating school to cast itself in the same mold. The faculty and students at a Coalition school need to find their own way, albeit with input about what others have done. One well-known incarnation of Sizer's principles is the Central Park East secondary school in New York City. Most of the instruction gets organized into two broad subject areas, humanities and mathematics/science, to help knit together particular subjects. Teachers generally manage more than one subject, often teaching in teams. Each student takes responsibility for two hours of *pro bono* work per week, either out in the community or within the school. Some work in the cafeteria, others in the library, others help deliver food to needy folks in the neighborhood.

A spirit of thoughtfulness prevails. The Central Park East

Secondary School has a credo called "The Promise," which swears to develop the students' minds. Students are to learn to ask and answer four key questions in each and every subject matter:

1. From whose viewpoint are we seeing or reading or hearing? From what angle or perspective?
2. How do we know what we know? What's the evidence, and how reliable is it?
3. How are things, events, or people connected to each other? What is the cause and what the effect? How do they "fit" together?
4. So what? Why does it matter? What does it all mean? Who cares?

Central Park East does not rest at the end of a sumptuous suburban lane amidst graceful elms. It sits in the center of a tough urban neighborhood plagued by drugs, poverty, and the usual array of urban ills. So how does it fare? In this vexed setting, attendance is routinely 90 percent and the drop-out rate almost zero. Remarkable! Obviously, the students have decided the payoffs are right: The gains are worth the costs. The hot cognitive economy is alive and well at Central Park East.

Another example of school restructuring is the Comer model, initiated by James P. Comer of Yale Medical School and the Child Study Center at Yale. Comer, a black psychiatrist, developed an acute sensitivity to the dilemmas of disadvantaged students attempting to survive and learn in the alien world of conventional schools. Their plight both resembled and differed from his own as a child. Growing up in poverty, he nevertheless benefited from the support of his mother and adults who were, as he put it, "locked into a conspiracy to see that I grew up a responsible person."

How could schools help disadvantaged children receive the support Comer had enjoyed at home. Comer conceived and put into practice a school structure that reached out to individual students. Its first premise is community involvement. The principal leads a governing council of teachers, counselors, and parents to set directions for the school. Attention goes first where it seems to be most needed—replacing boarded-up windows with glass, making the playground safe. Comer schools encourage parents to be a presence in the classroom as assistants, tutors, or aids. Social events help to bond teachers, parents, and youngsters.

An especially distinctive feature of Comer schools is a "mental health" team consisting of guidance counselors, school psychologists, special-education teachers, nurses, and classroom teachers. The team serves as a safety net for youngsters that might drop out or get expelled in conventional schools. One of their main jobs: case-by-case analysis of any child having difficulty, working over a period of time to help the child thrive.

In his recent book *Smart Schools, Smart Kids,* Edward Fiske relates the story of a first grader he calls Robert at Columbia Park Elementary School in Landover, Maryland. An authentic cutup, Robert had a repertoire that included sticking pencils in other children's ears and pouring chocolate milk on his cafeteria mashed potatoes. Trouble with Robert was constant.

The guidance counselor and Robert's teacher helped Robert's mother to evolve an explicit plan of rewards and punishments that might lure Robert away from his mischief. Robert's behavior improved some, but not enough.

The mental health team met to consider Robert's difficulties. In the midst of a long interview, Robert told them one thing he wanted—more time with a favorite teacher. It was arranged. They also worked with Robert's mother, guiding her to administer rewards and punishments as she had to but always to make her love clear and unconditional. They set up an information hotline for Robert's mother: When Robert behaved well, someone would call home to say so. Robert would be welcomed home with praise.

Eventually, all these efforts took hold. Robert went half a day, then a day, then three days without trouble. School counselor John Haslinger says:

> On the fourth day in a row, I'll never forget it, he came up to me and shouted, "I am going to go for fifty days, then a hundred days." His arm was raised in the air like a champion. And he did it! He became a good kid, a success story. It's very gratifying.

Comer schools illustrate the idea that one key to a hotter cognitive economy among students is a hotter cognitive economy among adults linked to the school. In all too many urban settings, teachers and administrators sleepwalk through their responsibilities, dulled and discouraged by the endless pressures and problems. Comer schools broaden the constituency by emphatically including parents in the thought and work of the school, and they revitalize everyone's interest by asking all to be thoughtful and responsible, not just for the school in a general sense but for each individual child.

There are, of course, many other models for restructuring schools. But restructuring does not come easy. There are endless roadblocks in the form of entrenched attitudes and expectations, limited textbooks, commando-style leaders, and so on. Often, schools find themselves trapped like insects in an ancient amber of outdated regulations and accountability. Perhaps no mechanism figures here more dominantly than conventional assessment, to which we turn.

TEACHING TO THE WRONG TEST

The inherent conflict-of-interest dilemma of the teacher in the typical classroom has not gone unnoticed. Indeed, there is a familiar solution to it: external testing. By this I mean that some sort of test is declared the official gauge of student performance at a key point in the students' schooling—say, the end of elementary school. The teacher does not make up the test, although the teacher may grade it if this can be done objectively. To advance, students must pass the test.

It's easy to see how this dissolves teachers' conflict of interest. With the external test in place, the teacher no longer is in a position to strike compromises, demanding less "cognitive coin" from the students to ensure that most of them will pass. Students must work to achieve well on the external tests, and teachers must help them to make sure that most do.

Of course, neither students nor teachers always welcome the pressure imposed by an external testing system. Moreover, the installation of such a system can certainly occur in clumsy, high-handed ways. Finally, occasional external testing does not take the place of the much more frequent testing a teacher needs to do to keep in touch with students' progress. Nonetheless, it's important to recognize how some external testing *liberates* teachers to pursue instruction in closer partnership with their students.

So, by this scheme, both students and teachers think carefully about what the external test demands, and the teacher tries to teach to it. "Aha, teaching to the test," someone will say. "That's a bad thing."

Not necessarily. There is nothing wrong at all with teaching to a test *provided the test tests the outcomes you really want.*

The trouble with the external testing maneuver is that typically the test is a reductive one, reflecting a trivial pursuit conception of education, emphasizing knowledge retention through a multiple-choice or fill-in-the-blank format (with its tendency to cultivate inert knowledge) and the execution of algorithms. When teachers teach to such tests, students generally get better at them but not better at the complex cognition we're looking for.

Test bashing has become one of the most popular sports in the educational arena. The tests are awful, the story goes. The tests drive the system. If the tests were not so awful, that might be acceptable. But how could they be so awful?

Besides designing better tests (see the next section), we have to understand why tests are as awful as they are. It is not accident or obtuseness that makes tests awful, but factors in the cognitive economy. First of all, money is one part of the cognitive economy, and more cognitively demanding, open-ended tests can be more costly to administer and grade.

But there are less obvious and more pernicious factors at work, too. First of all, installing external tests as gatekeepers to credentialing does not really remove the conflict of interest teachers face. It only "promotes" that conflict of interest up the hierarchy of education to the school-system level or the state level. Now it is the school system or state which decides what tests to use and what thresholds count as passing. So now it is they who receive pressure toward straightforward, simple testing from teachers, parents, school boards, and government leaders, who all want to see successful students.

Of course, such pressure does not take the form of a direct

request to "be lenient." But a test system that looks esoteric, that does not resonate with popular attitudes about the importance of spelling, that asks fancy questions that parents cannot understand, and that does not yield "reasonable" numbers of passes may be deemed unfair, racist, and ill chosen. Those who established it may get fired or lose elections.

This is not to say that school-system- or state-mandated external tests are a bad idea. Levels of the hierarchy above that of the individual classroom teacher are probably better able to hold the line. So moving the conflict of interest upward from the classroom level serves education well. But we should not deceive ourselves into thinking that the conflict of interest has vanished.

Besides the conflict-of-interest problem, there is another one with external tests. Cognitively demanding tests introduce a complication. When the testing is straightforward—facts and routines—teachers know quite a bit about how to teach to the test. They can enter into fairly effective partnerships with their students to help them toward mastery and over the hurdle of the test. Moreover, texts feed into the process nicely with their heaps of facts and piles of problems at the ends of the chapters.

However, when the test demands complex cognitive performances, teachers do not on the whole know how to teach for it. Nor should they, since neither their preservice educations nor the texts they are using give much information about complex performances like, for example, the understanding performances discussed in chapter 4 or some of the kinds of thinking discussed in chapter 5.

Consequently, installing a test that demands complex cognition without revamped instruction is a recipe for disaster. While the simple, reductive, external test will effectively drive the system, the cognitively demanding test will not, because the system is not able to respond. Widespread failure can result, impugning the competence of those administrators at the school system or state level responsible for putting the test in place.

None of this is meant as an argument for knuckling under and making do with reductive tests. But it is meant as an appeal to recognize that, in the cognitive economy of classrooms, school systems, and state education systems, reductive tests thrive not because people are starkly unenlightened but because they are responding to the cost in risk and cost in resources of cognitively demanding tests.

TEACHING TO THE RIGHT TEST: THE IDEA OF AUTHENTIC ASSESSMENT

If teaching to the wrong test does so much mischief, what is the right test to teach to? Over the past several years, a vision of and a name for such a test has emerged. The name is authentic assessment.

Well chosen as a term, authentic assessment implies that the test in question tests students by engaging them in examples of the very target performances we really want. An authentic test of writing stories asks students to write stories and gauges their response on the basis of the richness of the stories they write. Authentic assessment of mathematical attainments engages youngsters in working through open-ended problems that require mathematical reasoning and appraises how well students do and in what ways.

Concretely, what do such questions look like? Mathematics is a good area to pick for some examples, since mathematics testing so commonly takes a simple figure-out-an-answer form. One useful source is a booklet called *Assessment Alternatives in Mathematics,* produced by the Lawrence Hall of Science, Berkeley, California. One problem in gist goes like this:

> *A tape recorder is just beginning to play a tape. The tape passes over the head of the tape recorder at a constant speed. The challenge: Draw a qualitative graph showing how the length of the tape on the uptake reel changes with time; and draw another showing how the radius of the tape on the uptake reel changes with time; and yet another showing how the radius of the tape on the feed reel changes with time, with an explanation of why.*

Notice that such a problem calls for no numbers. It is a qualitative problem that gives no opportunity to turn the crank of some routine. Rather, it requires the learner to reason about what would happen and represent it by using graphs and giving a verbal explanation.

Another kind of problem challenges students to *compose* conventional problems rather than solve them; for example, "Write a word problem that would probably involve multiplying 59 times 12 for its solution." Yet another asks students to make up a lesson plan to teach younger students what multiplication is all about, using whatever materials they want from such resources as blocks, beans, balance scales, tiles, graph paper, calculator, and so on.

To reach elsewhere for examples, one popular category of activities is called "Fermi problems" after the Nobel Prize–winning physicist Enrico Fermi, who offered such problems for fun. A typical Fermi problem is "Estimate the number of pencils in Chicago."

Outrageous, isn't it! The problem is deliberately ill defined. Plainly, no more than an estimate can be derived. That estimate in turn is going to depend on other estimates, such as pencils per home or pencils per person. But after a little thought, the problem does not seem so impossible after all. Population figures can be obtained from almanacs, encouraging use of library resources. Pencils-per-person or pencils-per-home estimates can be obtained from home surveys done by students themselves. Students may seek to refine estimates by taking into account institutions other than homes. Would stationery and other stores that sell pencils add appreciably to the estimate? Would schools in Chicago add appreciably to the estimate?

As these examples suggest, items for authentic assessment have a number of salient characteristics:

- They are open-ended rather than one-right-answer problems.
- They are not solvable by applying a routine method.
- They require substantive understanding of meaning (in the case of mathematics, of arithmetic operations and other mathematical knowledge).
- They demand considerably more time than conventional problems; accordingly, an assessment might only involve one or a very few authentic assessment problems.
- They call for pulling together a number of different ideas from the subject matter.
- They often involve writing as well as formal manipulations such as computation.

- They usually have a complex product: an essay, a lesson plan, a problem set for others to solve.

   Note that there is a fringe benefit to authentic assessment. Because of all these characteristics, doing an authentic assessment problem tends to be very much a learning as well as a testing experience. Authentic assessment problems stretch the learner even as they create an occasion for a learner to display mastery and understanding. Inherently, they test for, and therefore press for, transfer and understanding, two principal concerns of the metacurriculum. Indeed, in classrooms that emphasize authentic assessment, little distinction appears between assessment and other activities. Youngsters are simply assessed in terms of the rich thinking and learning activities underway. Teaching, learning, and assessment merge into one seamless enterprise.

   Besides the kind of problem posed, there are also variations in the form of the product and the time scale. An assessment may be based on a test administered over a few hours, or on a portfolio where students keep what they judge to be their own best problem write-ups, or on notebooks that students keep for an entire semester. Small-group projects can be used, and the projects may endure for a day, a week, or longer. As mentioned earlier, the Coalition of Essential Schools calls for "exhibitions" from students, demonstrating their academic prowess to qualify for graduation. The possibilities are endless.

THE COGNITIVE ECONOMY MEETS THE MONEY ECONOMY

So why don't we do it everywhere tomorrow? Because there are counterforces. Let us look back to the cognitive economy of the classroom and some of the dilemmas posed by so greatly enlarged a conception of assessment. The gain of authentic assessment is, of course, to create a system where complex cognition carries much greater value. Authentic assessment upgrades performances requiring persistence, understanding, problem-solving abilities, and ready use of resources at the expense of more routine problems. Remember, in the normal classroom, complex cognition costs more in time, effort, and risk but typically is not rewarded more. By attaching greater value to complex cognition, one makes it a more fallible commodity.

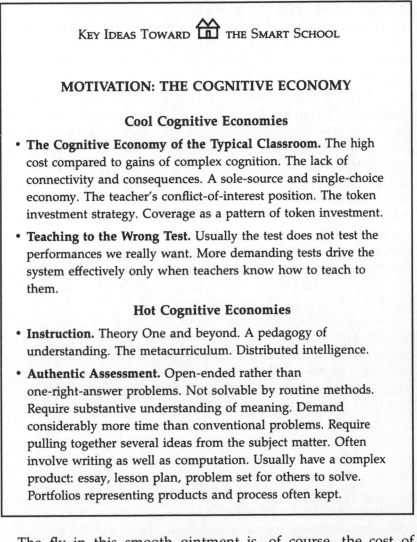

KEY IDEAS TOWARD THE SMART SCHOOL

MOTIVATION: THE COGNITIVE ECONOMY

Cool Cognitive Economies

- **The Cognitive Economy of the Typical Classroom.** The high cost compared to gains of complex cognition. The lack of connectivity and consequences. A sole-source and single-choice economy. The teacher's conflict-of-interest position. The token investment strategy. Coverage as a pattern of token investment.

- **Teaching to the Wrong Test.** Usually the test does not test the performances we really want. More demanding tests drive the system effectively only when teachers know how to teach to them.

Hot Cognitive Economies

- **Instruction.** Theory One and beyond. A pedagogy of understanding. The metacurriculum. Distributed intelligence.

- **Authentic Assessment.** Open-ended rather than one-right-answer problems. Not solvable by routine methods. Require substantive understanding of meaning. Demand considerably more time than conventional problems. Require pulling together several ideas from the subject matter. Often involve writing as well as computation. Usually have a complex product: essay, lesson plan, problem set for others to solve. Portfolios representing products and process often kept.

The fly in this smooth ointment is, of course, the cost of authentic assessment within the cognitive economy of the classroom, the school system, and the state. As mentioned already, such assessments are more costly, in time, effort, and money, to compose and grade. And they are more costly in quite a different sense: the risks of a backlash when you demand more of students. And, to guard against that backlash, they are more costly in putting into place instructional innovations that adequately prepare students for higher cognitive complexity. It's an expensive proposition all around.

Thus it is that authentic assessment sounds wonderful on paper but tends not to market well in the actual cognitive economy of classrooms, school systems, and states. What is the solution to this dilemma?

There is no *magic* solution. We simply have to face up to the problems inherent in a cognitive economy. One initial hindrance but long-term help is that much of the cost is a front-end investment, as noted earlier. Ongoing work to illustrate and systematize approaches to authentic assessment, work such as that distilled in *Assessment Alternatives in Mathematics*, mentioned above, helps make authentic assessment less costly not only in dollars but in teachers' and students' uncertainties and anxieties. Ongoing work toward better instruction—for instance, via a pedagogy of understanding, the metacurriculum, and better distributed cognition—helps make the kind of instruction that can prepare students for authentic assessment more economical in all the senses of the cognitive economy.

The current enthusiasm for school choice reflects a recognition of economic conundrums. In conventional settings, the local public school is a virtual monopoly. Apart from costly private schools, it is the sole source of educational services and thus largely protected from the consequences of any shortfalls.

School choice says that, under one plan or another, children and their parents get to pick the school they attend within some region. School-choice plans assume that, like consumers everywhere, children and parents want a good deal: in this case, an effective education. Schools that perform poorly will fail to draw students. They will find ways to do better or go out of business.

School choice is a complex and volatile issue. Will children and parents have good information to make choices? Often no, not even if local schools provide information. Will children and parents opt for better education? Not always. The convenience of the school next door commonly outdraws the glitter of the school across town.

And does school choice guarantee a push toward what I have called the smart school? Assuredly not. Many parents and

children in disadvantaged settings aspire more to better performance on conventional tests than to a genuinely thoughtful
education. To them, the smart school can all too easily look like
an upper-middle-class luxury or even a boondoggle. While I have
argued that the simple goals of retention, understanding, and the
active use of knowledge *require* the smart school, such lines of
reasoning and evidence are hardly known in the ghetto and if
known, would be viewed skeptically.

Despite all that, school choice certainly creates a press for
better education in general and sometimes for the smart school.
Moreover, we have evidence that it does what it is supposed to
do: push schools toward more responsive and responsible conduct. For about a decade, the school system in Cambridge,
Massachusetts, has followed a limited school-choice plan, where
parents and children signal preferences and get their choice
when it is consistent with desegregation requirements. Ninety
percent of Cambridge children choose public over private
schools, up from 70 percent a few years ago. Standardized test
scores have risen, whatever their flaws. Racial minorities can no
longer be distinguished from the mainstream by lower test scores
in the Cambridge system, although social class still makes a
difference.

In New York City's District 4, where a school-choice plan has
operated since 1982/3, two schools closed for lack of students,
and new schools and schools within schools, sharing the same
building, have thrived. District 4 now draws over 1,000 students
from other areas of New York City. District 4 includes the Central
Park East Secondary School, discussed earlier.

So there is motion. The best hope for accelerating the pace and
achieving the aim may be the fact that the cognitive economy of
classrooms is yoked to the money economy of the nation. As
discussed toward the end of chapter 2, a number of countries in
the world have made this connection work for them through
assessment and credentialing systems that virtually require considerable general and specialized educational achievement in
order to enter the job market, even at the blue-collar level. These
systems include safety nets to catch those who have trouble. In
the United States, as companies cut back on upper management
to save money, they must ask employees at the lower end to make
more decisions, to respond to greater cognitive demands. Tradi-

tionally less-skilled or less-educated employees need to think and learn on the job now, more so than a few years ago, if the money economy is to thrive. The spiraling economic problems in the United States are a powerful motivator in the money economy toward getting our act together in the cognitive economy.

AN EXAMPLE OF PROGRESS TOWARD A HOT COGNITIVE ECONOMY

How hot is hot? What does a hot cognitive economy look like? And who would be so bold as to try to set one up on a wide scale?

We do not have to grope for examples because the state of Vermont has launched just such an endeavor. Already on a pilot basis and soon statewide, Vermont teachers in the fourth and eighth grades will assess their students in writing and mathematics in a new way.

The program relies on "portfolio assessment." In writing and mathematics, students accumulate portfolios of works during the school year. The works represent a variety of open-ended problems and tasks. They reflect the students' efforts not only in English and mathematics classes but in other subject matters that invite written statement or mathematical analysis. While a portfolio represents a student's work as a whole, students also select for special scrutiny pieces they and their teachers view as their best accomplishments.

A fine picture. But what actually goes into these portfolios? In the case of writing, the pilot initiative developed a profile of important portfolio elements. It's suggested that a portfolio include at least these:

1. Table of contents.
2. A dated "best piece," chosen with the teacher's help.
3. A dated letter from the students to the reviewers, explaining the choice of the "best piece" and the process of its composition.
4. A dated poem, short story, play, or personal narration.
5. A dated personal response to a cultural, media, or sports exhibit or event or to a book, current issue, math problem, or scientific phenomenon.

6. *Fourth grade:* A dated prose piece from any curriculum area that is not English or Language Arts. *Eighth grade:* Three dated prose pieces from any curriculum areas that are not English or Language Arts.

For sure, a rich array of products, and students can go well beyond this. As to the assessment itself, teachers evaluate the portfolios on a scale from 1 (not so good) to 4 (outstanding), paying heed to five important characteristics: clear purpose in the piece; coherence of organization; detail used to support the main theme; voice and tone established; and finally, spelling, punctuation, and related matters.

What about the risks of subjectivity? It's worth remembering that assessments of writing are typically subjective once we get beyond spelling and punctuation. If anything, the five criteria make the process more systematic than usual. But the Vermont process takes the question of subjectivity seriously, providing training and, at the end of the year, gathering teachers together with a sample of their students' portfolios to score one another's portfolios, look for discrepancies, detect teachers who seem not as well calibrated with the others, and provide further guidance.

The tale in mathematics is much the same—an emphasis on open-ended problems that may take days to pursue, the building of a portfolio, criteria that look for mathematical insight across a variety of problems and settings, and a four-level rating scheme.

Of course, this program of authentic assessment aims to magnetize the process of teaching and learning in a new direction, toward new poles. All would be for naught if classrooms remain stuck to the all-too-common "What I did this summer" essays and battalions of routine arithmetic problems. But since students have to build portfolios full of their responses to invitingly open-ended tasks, teachers find themselves in a wonderful position: motivated to teach as most have always been wanting to.

So what happens in classrooms? Ann Rainey, an eighth-grade mathematics teacher in Shelburne, asks her students questions like this:

You and a friend read in the newspaper that 7 percent of all Americans eat at McDonald's each day. Your friend says that this is impossible. You know that there are approximately 250,000,000 Americans and approximately 9,000 McDonald's restaurants in the United States. Convince your friend (in writing) that the statistic is possible.

Tough? Yes, if you're a student who's not used to it. You'll have to make estimates. You'll have to plan computations to knit them all together. You'll have to wrap it all up in a written argument that mixes math and essay form. But it's doable. Indeed, it's not so different from the Fermi problem discussed earlier, estimating the number of pencils in Chicago.

And whatever you do with the problem, into your portfolio it goes. Maybe it will be one of your best pieces.

From a state policy stance on assessment to Rainey's particular question about how many Americans eat at McDonald's is quite a stretch. But that is exactly what we need to sustain a hot cognitive economy. Only the most courageous and even outrageous teachers can build hot cognitive economies in classrooms that sit within schools, school systems, and states timid in their aspirations and comfortable with cool cognitive economies. But when up and down the administrative ladder of education the voices sound in chorus, demanding authentic intellectual performance of youngsters, then the smart school with its high positive energies can thrive.

SCHOOLS

CHAPTER 8

VICTORY GARDENS FOR REVITALIZED EDUCATION

The first time I ever heard of a victory garden was on public television. One of the popular programs in the Boston area for a number of years was *Crockett's Victory Garden*. For thirty minutes every week, Jim Crockett took the audience out into his garden and demonstrated how ample knowledge along with tender loving care could do remarkable things with a little land.

I also learned why victory gardens were called victory gardens. The concept developed during World War II, when the citizenry was encouraged to help out the war economy during rationing by provisioning themselves insofar as they could. So in odd back lots, small gardens sprang up, lovingly tended, yielding carrots, broccoli, cabbage, lettuce, and other fine vegetables, along with a feeling of unity with the nation's effort.

The spirit and substance of a victory garden can be summed up by this little *Victory Garden* poem of mine:

With plenty of savvy
And T.L.C.,
You can do a lot
On a small plot.

Which brings us back to the dilemmas of education.

The previous chapters of this book have tried to deal with the "plenty of savvy" mentioned above. They have offered several ways of thinking about better education—ensuring that we teach at least as well as Theory One prescribes, building a pedagogy of understanding, attending to the metacurriculum, arranging better-distributed cognition in the classroom, and cultivating hot cognitive economies, all toward the smart school.

It's fair to wonder how to get these notions off the printed page and put them to work in behalf of better education. One answer is that they can serve as lively tools for evaluating educational settings and designing new ones. This chapter puts the "savvy" in order in three steps: (1) a brief review of the principles behind the smart school; (2) a series of classroom examples that show the principles in action; (3) a discussion of what's special about these principles, how they go not only beyond ordinary instruction but beyond what many innovations attempt.

But there's more to the story. Besides savvy about teaching and learning, a vision of enhanced education needs a way to cope with what we might call the "small plot" problem. There are in fact many successes in education. There are innumerable tales to be told about the wonderful results that occur in one teacher's classroom or sometimes in an entire school. A deservedly popular example is the achievement of Jaime Escalante in developing high school kids' mathematics abilities, celebrated in the film *Stand and Deliver*. These successes teach us a lot.

But they almost always occur on "small plots." They are victory gardens, where unusual savvy and unusual tender loving care have cultivated fine results. How do we think about scaling up, then? What kinds of results can we hope for in most schools for most students—not just meticulous victory gardens but the amber waves of grain we would like to see as our educational crop? That question is the topic of the chapter after this.

BETTER TEACHING AND LEARNING IN REVIEW

The mainspring of this book is a fundamental principle about learning underscored in the introduction. Simple to state, its message continues through chapter after chapter, rewriting the way we should proceed with matters educational: Learning is a consequence of thinking.

The principle implies a different conception of educational practice than we usually find in the classroom down the street. It calls for educational settings where students learn by way of thinking about and with what they are learning, no matter what the subject matter is—history, mathematics, English, science, geography, you name it. Thoughtful learning in turn requires informed and energetic schools, settings where teachers and administrators know a lot about both learning and working together and have time to learn themselves and where the management style, schedules, and forms of assessment create positive energy in everyone. Thus, the smart school—informed, energetic, and thoughtful.

One might dismiss the smart school as something of a luxury, okay for especially able students and for wealthier communities but nothing so very essential for the larger part of our population. This would be a great mistake. While educational goals make for an endless debate, almost everyone could agree on at least three: retention, understanding, and the active use of knowledge. Because without these three, what students learn in school would not be very useful to them. But given them, the evidence presented in the last seven chapters argues that we need smart schools. We need to put to work the principle that learning is a consequence of thinking. If we do not, we simply will not get the amount or kind of learning that we want.

What we get instead was surveyed in chapter 2. Students acquire fragile knowledge, often inert (not remembered in open-ended situations that invite its use), naive (reflecting stubborn misconceptions and stereotypes), or ritualized (reflecting classroom routines but no real understanding). And students show poor thinking in many ways—inadequate reasoning from texts they read, bafflement in the face of story problems in mathematics, and so on. Behind these shortfalls lie two tacit theories that pervade our education and our culture more broadly. The Trivial

Pursuit theory of learning says that learning is a matter of accumulating facts and routines, not a consequence of thinking. The Ability-Counts-Most theory says that ability influences achievement far more than anything else, when in fact effort counts at least as much.

So what do we do? Besides battling these shortfalls and the tacit theories underlying them, we can seek to remake education along five dimensions familiar from the preceding chapters. Here they are:

1. *Theory One* says that we need instruction that emphasizes clear information, reflective practice, informative feedback, and intrinsic and extrinsic motivation. Teachers can draw on didactic, coaching, and Socratic teaching styles in applying Theory One. And they can explore methods beyond Theory One. Given methods at least as good as Theory One, our most important choice is what we try to teach.

2. *A pedagogy of understanding* highlights students' engagement in understanding performances (explaining, finding examples, generalizing). Powerful representations can help build up students' mental images and equip them for understanding performances. Instruction needs to give attention to higher levels of understanding, capturing how in different subject matters we solve problems, explain and justify, and inquire. And we need to organize instruction around generative topics that connect in rich ways within the subject matter, to other subject matters, and to life beyond the classroom.

3. *The metacurriculum* urges us to include attention to higher-order knowledge in several senses: levels of understanding (as above); languages of thinking (terms and concepts like hypothesis and evidence; graphic organizers); intellectual passions; integrative mental images (that knit a large topic or subject matter together); learning to learn; and teaching for transfer.

4. *Distributed intelligence* calls for a shift from a person-solo to a person-plus organization of classroom activities. Physical resources such as writing materials and computers should support thinking and learning. Thinking and learning should be socially shared as in cooperative learning, peer collaboration, peer tutoring, Socratic interaction, and like relationships.

And diverse symbol systems (language, graphic organizers, improvisations) should figure in thinking and learning.

5. *The cognitive economy* underscores the need to build hot rather than cool cognitive economies, where the extra financial and psychological cost of complex cognition makes sense to students and teachers because of the gains. Dimensions 1–4 above profile a culture of complex cognition and authentic assessment that can help sustain that culture.

Victory Gardens and How They Grow

With these five dimensions toward better education freshly in mind, we can get an even better sense of them by looking at some classroom-sized examples—some small-scale victory gardens, where what we want to see happening *is* happening.

Victory gardens are to be cherished for many reasons. One reason is that at least on a small plot of the educational turf, something immensely fruitful occurs. Another is that they teach us what is possible. To be sure, what is possible in individual classrooms or even individual schools may not be so on a larger scale, that of those amber waves of grain addressed in the next chapter. Nonetheless, seeing what can happen on a small scale helps us to recalibrate our sense of how much youngsters can learn and how deeply and wisely they can learn it.

EXAMPLE 1. EXPERT TUTORING

The smallest of small plots, the most intimate of victory gardens, is the individual tutorial relationship—one tutor and one learner. Here is your ultimate teacher/student ratio, profoundly different from the one-to-twenty or one-to-thirty found in most schools. Although not the sort of relationship that one readily replicates in classrooms, the individual tutorial situation teaches us something enormously important about how much better youngsters can do.

Benjamin Bloom of the University of Chicago is the noted formulator of Bloom's taxonomy and the notion of mastery learning. Several years ago, Bloom described "the two sigma problem" in an article called "The Search for Methods of Group Instruction As Effective as One-to-One Tutoring." The Greek letter sigma by convention refers to the standard deviation of a statistical distribution: If we are talking about a bell-shaped curve, how fat is the curve? The two sigma problem Bloom discussed in the article concerned the impact of good tutorial instruction on students. In a variety of cases, good tutoring had advanced a student starting at the *average* of his or her peers to two standard deviations beyond the average.

How much is that? A lot! For a better sense of the two sigmas, we can talk in percentile terms. An average student falls in the fiftieth percentile: Half the students are scoring worse and half better. Assuming a normal distribution (the bell-shaped curve), a boost two standard deviations beyond the mean puts a learner in the ninety-eighth percentile: 98 percent of students are scoring worse, 2 percent better. This is not only impressive, it is quite amazing. Who would have thought that an average student had that much potential?

Studies of expert tutoring conducted by Stanford psychologist Mark Lepper have helped to illuminate just what it is that expert tutors do to advance learners so much. One very important aspect of their art is letting the learner undertake most of the work. Expert tutors often do not help very much. They hang back, letting the student manage as much as possible. And when things go awry, rather than help directly, they raise questions: "Could you explain that step again?" "How did you get the 7?" "I notice that on this earlier problem you said 8. How was this case different?"

Another interesting characteristic is very little direct praise. Expert tutors commonly emphasize beforehand how tough a problem is, rather than praising the learner's ability afterward. The front-end emphasis on difficulty is an artful move: If the student succeeds with the problem, it's self-rewarding because the student has surmounted an impressive obstacle. If not, well, the problem has been framed as quite difficult—it's only reasonable to look at some more tractable ones before reattempting the tough one.

Applying the Five Dimensions

Our five dimensions of better teaching and learning help to explain why expert tutoring has such an impact. In terms of

Theory One, the tutor is in a position to offer clear information, lead the student in reflective practice (the reflection generated by the tutor's probing questions), provide informative feedback (the tutor's questions help the student to generate his or her own feedback), and tap the strong intrinsic motivation of task mastery (hence the tough-problem ploy).

In terms of a pedagogy of understanding, the tutor's emphasis on "How do you get that?" "Why is this different?" and such matters presses for understanding performances; in particular, explanation. This in turn helps build the learner's higher-order reflective knowledge of how to do things—knowledge at the problem solving and epistemic levels in the scheme discussed in chapter 4.

By engaging students in such discourse, tutors encourage a language of thinking, where students give conjectures, reasons, and plans. By pressing students to explain things for themselves, tutors encourage learning to learn. Tutors mediate transfer by bringing in problems different enough to challenge the learner to bridge a gap. In other words, the metacurriculum is well represented.

As to distributed cognition, the tutorial relationship presents an obvious example of cognitive partnership, with the tutor supporting the student as much as needed . . . and no more! Thus the tutor strives to leave with the student as much executive control of the task as the student can handle. As to a hot cognitive economy, the intimate and artfully sustained relationship between tutor and tutored creates enormous valuing of progress and mastery while supporting the learner's efforts in ways that reduce cognitive cost: the cognitive effort and risk of failure that discourage so many youngsters.

EXAMPLE 2. BIOLOGY FOR YOUNG INQUIRERS

If the tutorial relationship can be so powerful, it is natural to wonder whether anything as rich can be mounted even at classroom scale. The answer is clearly yes. One interesting case in point is a provocative experimental classroom maintained by University of California at Berkeley researchers Ann Brown and Joseph Campione. Their goal was to bring together a number of innovations into a very mindful experience of learning biology.

A number of contrasts distinguish the experience of youngsters in this classroom from youngsters studying biology in more conventional ways. One is that much of the work occurs by way of cooperative learning. In "research groups," students explore a variety of materials relating to a component of the larger topic being studied by the class. Then they form "learning groups," which consist of one member from each of the research groups. The "expert" on each subtopic assumes responsibility for teaching the other learning group members about it (this is a version of the jigsaw method discussed in chapter 6).

Another contrast is the amount of control students have in determining their curriculum. In the research groups, students make decisions about what is important information and what can be sidelined. They then write their own textbooks—booklets revised and published with the help of computers and used to teach other members of the learning groups about that subtopic.

Another contrast is that great emphasis falls on the why of things: What makes for interdependence in nature? Why do disturbances in one part of the system create problems in another? What causes some animals to survive while others die out?

Researchers that they are, Brown and Campione not only created this educational setting in the midst of an ordinary school but took pains to formally investigate youngsters' response to it. The findings are impressive. In addition to gains on tests of biological knowledge, results showed students' achievements in more global skills. Although reading, writing, and computer use were not taught as such—they were simply very important to the highly interactive conduct of the biology instruction—the participating students showed improvement on standardized measures of all three.

Perhaps more importantly, class discussions revealed that students' thinking processes became increasingly sophisticated and complex. Over time, students began to explain phenomena more precisely and coherently. They used evidence more skillfully to support conclusions, systematically compared and critiqued different viewpoints, and engaged spontaneously in developing and exploring hypothetical situations.

Applying the Five Dimensions

In Theory One terms, this setting makes the students responsible for clear information by putting them in charge of teaching one another, thus also assuring reflective practice as students prepare information for others. How informative feedback comes in is not clear. But the approach to the subject matter and intriguing topics within it as well as the cooperative-learning instruction style ensure plenty of intrinsic motivation.

In terms of a pedagogy of understanding, understanding performances—especially explanation—and good representations figure prominently in the Brown/Campione setting, along with some very generative topics within biology, such as camouflage.

In terms of the metacurriculum, the setting creates enormous emphasis on learning to learn, and the emphasis on communication among the students cultivates languages of thinking. There is considerable attention to transfer of concepts from one context to another.

As to distributed cognition, we have cooperative learning. As to the physical distribution of cognition, computers are used as a medium for students' publishing lessons for one another. As to executive functioning, the whole setting encourages considerable student autonomy. The sum of it all is a rich cognitive economy driven by the students' responsibility for one another's performances, the intrinsic interest of the themes, social connectedness, and related motivators.

EXAMPLE 3. HISTORY FOR THINKERS

Who fired the shot heard 'round the world—the first shot of the American revolution—on April 19, 1775, in Lexington, Massachusetts? All sources agree that someone fired that shot, but did a British soldier or a rebellious colonist trigger this turning point in history?

The historical evidence leaves the matter in doubt. A number of years ago, Peter Bennett, capitalizing on the uncertainties, developed an instructional unit entitled *What Happened at Lexington Green?* The unit teaches history and aspects of evidence and argument at the same time. Bennett provided students with original-source testimonials, some American and some British, about the first shot. What do the testimonials suggest? Students are invited to puzzle over the evidence and reach conclusions.

As the lesson unfolds, students learn more about not just the testimonials but the circumstances behind them. One testimonial was offered by a colonist over fifty years after the event. Another, averring that the British fired the first shot, was given by a British soldier—but while in American captivity! Thus simultaneously, students learn something about the first moments of the American Revolution, the dilemmas of historians in interpreting evidence, and the process of evidential reasoning.

Kevin O'Reilly, a high school teacher at the Hamilton-Wenham Regional High School in Massachusetts, has for a number of years taught history in the style and spirit represented by Bennett's materials. His aim is at one and the same time to build in his students a deeper understanding of history and to cultivate their critical-thinking abilities. He avers that it's not enough to teach history in a thoughtful way. History instruction should include point-blank attention to relevant principles of evidence and argument.

A favorite O'Reilly artifice involves five students role-playing a theft. Other students watch. After all return to the classroom, the observers have to ask questions to try to determine what really happened. At first, O'Reilly notes, the questions disclose little. Gradually, some information comes to light. O'Reilly uses this as an occasion to talk about evidence. Evidence only yields information, it's stressed, when the source becomes clear, so that we can assess its reliability. Activities like this help O'Reilly's students recognize the hazards of evidence—how perceptions differ, and how difficult it is moments later, never mind years or centuries later, to nail down what happened.

As the course unfolds, O'Reilly laces his teaching of history with discussions of argument and evidence. He uses the acronym PROP to remind students that good sources prop up the evidence for a conclusion. PROP stands for Primary versus secondary (not an eyewitness) source, Reasons the source may have to distort the evidence, Other witnesses or kinds of evidence that corroborate, and Private versus public statement, the former more reliable because said in confidence. PROP is just one element in a fairly elaborate conceptualization of evidence and argument O'Reilly employs.

O'Reilly has developed his own materials to accompany the teaching of American history in a project he calls Critical Thinking in American History. In a number of ways, these materials challenge students to think through historical episodes and struggle with questions of evidence and argument. For one example, a version of the Lexington Green activity appears. For another, students are challenged by multiple interpretations of the Salem witch trials. What actually happened? Was witchcraft practiced by any of the victims? For yet another, why was the Constitution written and ratified? Students need to examine and assess two very different views, one averring that wealthy landowners shaped the document to ensure that majority rights did not override property rights, another challenging this monolithic motive.

In working with his classes, O'Reilly used essays to gauge the success of the approach. He found that students in his class wrote analyses of historical situations that appeared considerably richer than those written by students from another class.

Applying the Five Dimensions

It is easy to see Theory One characteristics in O'Reilly's approach: plenty of information from multiple sources, ample reflective practice in working through historical events from different perspectives, the intrinsic motivation of O'Reilly's lively style.

There is of course enormous emphasis on a pedagogy of understanding and in particular what was called the epistemic level of understanding: how we know what we know (and do we really know it?). As to the metacurriculum, the language of critical thinking employed in O'Reilly's setting is a straightforward example of languages of thinking. Moreover, the bringing in of immediate experiences and events, such as the staged theft, should cultivate generalization and transfer of ideas.

It's not clear that there are any unusual moves toward distributed cognition. But a hot cognitive economy is apparent: an emphasis on understanding, thinking, working out perspectives,

authentic tasks, and so on that engages students in learning as a
meaning-making rather than a fact-amassing process.

EXAMPLE 4. A TEXTBOOK FROM THE PAST

As I write this, I have beside me a high school textbook published
by Allyn and Bacon in 1971 called *The People Make a Nation*. Not a
surprising name for a history text, but what is found inside would
surprise you. It's worth remembering that the 1960s included a
number of vigorous efforts to deepen education. This text was
one of the outcomes. The classic example would be the famous
Man: A Course of Study, developed by psychologist/educator
Jerome Bruner and a committed and ingenious group of colleagues. But much has been written about *Man: A Course of Study*,
which also hews a path well away from conventional social
studies content. *The People Make a Nation* is worth a look in part
because it cleaves fairly closely to conventional content with
section titles such as "Founders and Forefathers," "Government
by the People," "Slavery and Segregation," and the like.

But the book's style and method are surprising. I open at
random to a page about "Methods of Persuasion." In fact, it is a
four-page spread with color photographs illustrating the paraphernalia of political campaigns. We see crowds of people at a
rally, campaign buttons, newspaper headlines, baloons with
slogans.

We are also faced with a set of questions. The learner is
challenged to identify as many methods of persuasion as possible
in the illustrations. Then the learner is sent back to an earlier
page to list persuasion techniques from an early presidential
campaign. The account of the election is not your typical
watered-down text; it was adapted from an historical analysis of
the Andrew Jackson campaign of 1828 written by Robert Remini.

And that is not the end of it. Students are asked to search
magazines for advertisements that use the same persuasion
techniques. And the final part of the activity: "Think up some
methods of persuasion and apply them to a particular situation."

Impressive! Yes, I may have hit on a particularly lucky page.
But throughout this text, emphasis falls on the use of original
source materials, artful use of graphics, and challenging learning
activities.

Applying the Five Dimensions

Although a textbook is only a part of a complete educational intervention, we see several of our five dimensions clearly at work in *The People Make a Nation*. Front and center appears a pedagogy of understanding, where students are urged to understand the political process through such understanding performances as identifying tactics of persuasion. There is a significant presence of the metacurriculum through building students' critical awareness of persuasion techniques and provoking transfer to contemporary situations (magazine advertisements) and the students' own lives (the request to apply methods of persuasion).

We also find writing, scrapbook, and other activities that download cognition onto paper more so than is typical, a move in the direction of person-plus. The entire book, in the expectations it projects, fuels a more vigorous cognitive economy fostering complex cognition. At the same time, all this is packaged in the conventional wrappings of a textbook designed for mass distribution.

Regrettably, textbooks like this are rarely found in schools today. This copy was given to me by Sandra Parks, an individual who has worked with many school systems on approaches to teaching thinking. Sandra Parks has encouraged teachers to make use of such texts and explains the problems that the teachers encounter. The youngsters have difficulty reading the original source materials in the text. In addition, they have little experience with the critical-thinking skills the text activities require. One has to go slowly. The teachers do not always know how to support the youngsters in their learning process. Neither do they always adhere to the same view of the discipline as the text's. Perhaps in-service was needed here more than the publishers expected. For reasons such as these, texts of this caliber did not succeed in the marketplace.

Indeed, that was the era when the problems of instruction that attempted complex cognition were just being discovered. Today we realize that materials requiring complex cognition demand, from teachers and the materials themselves, much scaffolding of thinking and learning processes. This means that teachers, in turn, need opportunities to learn how to offer such scaffolding. We also realize that thinking and learning processes require explicit articulation—they need to be looked at and talked about as objects, in the spirit of the metacurriculum. Moreover, we understand much more today about the complex challenge of establishing stable, long-term innovations in school settings, as discussed in the following chapter.

Whatever the shortcomings such texts and materials possessed, their weakest point was perhaps their place in the cognitive economy of classrooms, school systems, and states. As the analysis in chapter 7 suggested, they created risks for the teachers that taught with them and the principals that approved them. So much safer to go with less challenging materials! And it was just such materials that wrested the market from them. Today, with a greater feeling of urgency about remaking education, texts in this ambitious style should emerge again and compete in the educational marketplace.

EXAMPLE 5. A METACOURSE FOR COMPUTER PROGRAMMING

I would like to describe briefly a project that my colleague Steve Schwartz of the University of Massachusetts, Boston, and I directed as part of the work of the Educational Technology Center at the Harvard Graduate School of Education.

Working with graduate students and participating teachers, we evolved what we termed a "metacourse" for enhancing students' understanding of computer programming and programming abilities. As the name implies, our intervention was a point-blank effort to provide a metacurriculum for programming instruction. In keeping with the idea of the metacurriculum, the aim was not necessarily to displace the usual curriculum of basic content and procedures. It was presumed that the teacher would provide programming instruction in something like his or her usual manner, using a text, class notes, or other means.

Concretely, our metacourse took the form of a dozen or so lessons. These lessons were not to be taught all at once but interspersed with the regular instruction, once every week or two. Additionally, there were guidelines helping the teacher to infuse the ideas in the lessons throughout the normal instruction.

In chapter 5, I mentioned the overarching image of the "data factory"; we used it as a conceptual integrator in this metacourse. The data factory image consists in a conceptual (rather than hardware) map of the computer: a place for programs to be stored, a scratchpad for doing arithmetic, a memory area, a keyboard area for input, a screen area for output, and other features. In the data factory lives a worker called NAB. It's NAB that gets things done. Students are encouraged to tell the story of the execution of a program in terms of actions taken by NAB. For instance, NAB looks at the first instruction in the program storage area. Perhaps it says to place the number 41 in the "bin" of a variable called X in the memory area. So NAB picks up the number and puts it in the bin.

Telling the story this way gives learners a way of envisioning what the computer does. Moreover, we also developed a computer animation in which students actually see NAB running around the data factory, undertaking such jobs.

And what about the name? Well, of course NAB nabs data and manipulates it. But really NAB is an acronym for Not Awfully Bright. Students are told this and why. Many people (research shows) think that computers are intelligent and "understand" what a program is supposed to do. A number of typical programming errors stem from this tacit assumption on the part of students. NAB's name is a way of reminding students that the computer understands nothing. It just does what it is told. Thus, NAB's name is part of the overall enterprise of giving students a strong, clear mental image of the capacities and functioning of the computer.

The metacourse also provided students with several learning and problem-solving strategies targeted on the particular problems of programming. For example, a learning strategy urged the students to pay attention to three key characteristics of a new command: its purpose, or typical applications; its syntax, or how to tell the computer to execute that command; and its action, exactly what happened in the data factory during execution of the command. Thus, purpose, syntax, action become a key phrase that the teachers and students were urged to use throughout the programming course. To keep the data factory imagery and the learning and problem-solving strategies on teachers' and students' minds, large posters went up on the walls of the

classrooms, actually showing the data factory and bulleting out
the strategies.

Applying the Five Dimensions

In a number of ways, the programming metacourse exhibits
features sought in our five dimensions. The thinking and learning
strategies offered by the metacourse work against inert knowledge and poor thinking, constituting a metacurriculum for
programming. The overarching mental image of the data factory
and the purpose/syntax/action learning strategy contribute to a
pedagogy of understanding. The posters, as well as the emphasis
on envisioning what happens during program execution with
use of the data factory posters, help distribute cognition. The
entire spirit of the metacourse fosters a cognitive economy that
demands more complex cognition.

The materials went through three rounds of testing. The last
round was testing at a distance, with very little contact between
the development team and the participating teachers and classrooms: only one brief kickoff meeting, an occasional newsletter
giving tips during the semester, and a few telephone consultations.

A programming test with several different types of problems
was used to compare the classes using the metacourse with
control classes. The test disclosed a considerable edge for the
metacourse groups: about half a standard deviation. This is, of
course, far less than Benjamin Bloom's two standard deviations
for expert tutoring. But half a standard deviation is considered a
good solid gain for an educational intervention. Also, our
metacourse was by design a minimalist intervention; not a whole
new course but a few added lessons and practices. Now under
development are metacourses for algebra and Euclidean geometry, although formal findings are still some time in the future.

EXAMPLE 6. ESCALANTE HIMSELF

The introduction to the notion of victory gardens mentioned a
classic case: Jaime Escalante's teaching of mathematics and
especially advanced placement calculus in Garfield High School
in East Los Angeles. This stroll through several victory gardens

could hardly be complete without a look at his singular achievement.

When Jaime Escalante arrived at Garfield High School and took the first steps along a path that would lead to national recognition, the setting was anything but conducive. The school's enrollment was largely Latino, more than 95 percent, and came from low-income families with poorly educated parents. The drop-out rate was high. Academic success was rare. It is hard to imagine a less likely arena for building a program that would send nearly as many students to the advanced placement exam in calculus as the famous Bronx High School of Science.

How did Jaime Escalante effect this magic? Perhaps the first thing to be said is that nothing requiring so much dedication could be called magic. Escalante's teaching of mathematics became for him an obsessive twenty-four-hour-a-day endeavor. He would meet with students before school and after school. In the evening, he would visit the parents of students who demanded that they hold jobs that interfered with their studies. A committed and strong-willed individual, Escalante argued, cajoled, and threatened administrators, parents, and, of course, students, all for the sake of inculcating the spirit, understanding, and skill of mathematics.

Could students respond with indifference in the face of his outspoken enthusiasm? Of course, many of them could. Indifference in Garfield High School was a natural state of mind. But Escalante brought more than commitment to the mathematics classroom; he also brought an armamenarium of artful tactics for motivating students. One of the most basic and conspicuous was a motto hung prominently in the classroom:

Calculus need not be made easy;
it is easy already.

Escalante would not let his students think of calculus as hard.

At the same time, he would not let them take an indolent approach to the subject matter. Early in the term, Escalante made friends with his students, clowning around, devising pet names for the many students whose names he found it difficult to remember. Then the guilt trips began. Completing homework on time was a must. Have you got your homework today? No? Off to the office then. Out of this class. We don't want you here! Students could negotiate their way back in, but only with promises of reform.

Quizzes were frequent, but help was ample. As mentioned earlier, Escalante made himself available before and after school. He would routinely demand the presence of students who needed special attention.

Escalante's skills as a communicator were as peerless as his arts as a motivator. He would frame calculus concepts in several different vivid ways, often using sports metaphors to get the ideas across and make them memorable. Discussing the concept of a limit, he spoke of a pitched baseball approaching the catcher's glove and interacted with youngsters to get them to keep naming the key elements in the metaphor—pitcher, catcher, fastball, curveball. He introduced the concept of absolute value by analogy with the "give and go" in basketball. Miming the give and go with his back to an imaginary basket, he passed to a guard crossing on his right or left. He explained how the absolute value is like that: There are two possibilities. If the absolute value of x is such and such, maybe x is greater than zero. Or maybe x is less than zero.

The solid measure of Escalante's success in mobilizing his students' efforts and intellects is the advanced placement exam administered by the College Board. Grading of the exam occurs on a five-point scale, 1 to 5, and anyone scoring 3 or more has shown a college level of competence in the subject matter. In the most famous incident associated with Escalante, eighteen students from Escalante's AP calculus took the exam in May of 1982. While four passed outright, the scorers raised the concern that fourteen may have copied answers from some common source on one question. An enormous controversy ensued, resolved by giving the fourteen the opportunity to take another version of the exam at the end of August. With only a few days to prepare, twelve students did so, and all passed.

Although this was a very special moment for Escalante and his dedicated students, none of the events of 1982 were a fluke. Escalante and fellow teacher Benjamin Jimenez expanded the program of calculus instruction. In 1986, 84 percent of 93 students passed the exam. In 1987, the figure was 66 percent of 129. Escalante found this disappointing although it was close to the national average of 71 percent. He blamed himself for letting class size grow too large.

Applying the Five Dimensions

Escalante's teaching style is a model of Theory One, with clear, vivid explanations, abundant practice and feedback, and a mountain of motivation. The pedagogy of understanding appears most clearly in Escalante's use of vivid, concrete representations to make calculus concepts immediate for his students and thereby help them build lucid mental images.

As to the metacurriculum, Escalante's approach does not appear to be very "meta." His teaching seems to focus doggedly on the craft of calculus, with little philosophizing about it or efforts to connect it with other subject matters. Some of his language amounts to problem-solving heuristics of a sort, but certainly his approach to the teaching of mathematics does not seem as heuristics-centered as many.

However, as to distributed cognition, Escalante is a master of the use of imagery and social networking. And in the cognitive economy we find Escalante's forte. He establishes in his classrooms a cognitive economy with powerful, multiple rewards for investing effort in the complex cognition demanded by calculus —and sharp rebukes for slackers.

A SMART SCHOOL IS SOMETHING RATHER SPECIAL

In offering these six classroom-sized examples, it is important to stress that they are unusual, yet not unusual. Percentagewise, they stand out. It is seldom that one finds the energy, the ingenuity, the social pattern, the emphasis on understanding to sustain these victory gardens, precious enclaves of effective teaching and learning that they are.

However, by count rather than percentage, they are not so rare. There are hundreds of such success stories that could be told. Those above have been singled out because they exemplify their kind, not necessarily because they are the best of their kind. They show what can be done when the multiple factors that impact on learning are configured in more potent ways in the local arena of a classroom, text, or set of materials.

But let's think bigger: What is the smart school that this book envisions? How does it go beyond what we occasionally find in ambitious classrooms? How does it go beyond what we occasionally find in a whole school's worth of such classrooms? Is a smart school, in the present sense, any more than a school where teaching and learning proceed in a rather thoughtful way?

A fair question. Here is an answer.

Extended.   First of all, a smart school is of course a school. A whole school. Or more, a school system. A smart school does not stop at the end of a text or the end of a class. The informed, energetic, and thoughtful culture of the smart school impregnates all subject matters and activities. Ideally, it does not even stop at the end of the school day but filters in subtle ways into the lives of students outside of school.

Inclusive.   Second, a smart school includes systematically a number of features that both research and educational practice have found to be important to thoughtful learning. I have tried to organize these features into five dimensions: Theory One, a pedagogy of understanding, the metacurriculum, distributed intelligence, and the cognitive economy. The next chapter will add a sixth, concerning effective change.

All six dimensions are important. But many generally worthwhile innovations in education pay no particular heed to one or another. Perhaps they fail to harness the power of distributed intelligence. Or they neglect the metacurriculum. Or they do not do enough to establish a hot cognitive economy.

Explicit.   The dimensions seek to make explicit and articulate what goes into thoughtful teaching and learning. In the past, many fruitful educational innovations have rested on the good intuitions of their originators. But for wide-scale fundamental change in education, an educational green thumb will not do. We need explicit models of thoughtful learning.

Elaborated.   Perhaps the easiest way for a generally thoughtful approach to teaching and learning to fall short is through a Swiss-cheese version of the principles laid out here—tasty but full of large holes. For example, in many classrooms students write potentially rich, open-ended essays. This serves well a pedagogy of understanding. But if there is no regular mechanism of informative feedback (not necessarily from the teacher but perhaps from peers), Theory One principles are violated. In many classrooms students reason out problems and debate issues, creating a generally thoughtful classroom. But if there is no explicit metacurriculum, where students have a chance to learn concepts and strategies that support thinking and learning, students will not gain as much as they might through the immersion in thoughtfulness.

In other words, a smart school in the fullest sense is more than a place where teachers and students work in a generally thoughtful way. It requires more than a bundle of tactics that lean toward thoughtfulness—open-ended assignments, peer collaboration, discussion and debate, and the like. These are all steps in the right direction, but they do not necessarily reach the destination. A smart school in the fullest sense is an intricate social mechanism, where multiple factors—in the present rubric, Theory One, a pedagogy of understanding, a metacurriculum, distributed intelligence, a hot cognitive economy, and (in the next chapter) attention to the dynamics of change—all mesh to support informed, energetic, and thoughtful teaching and learning.

To get systematic about all this, Appendix A includes a checklist of questions for each of the six dimensions to help gauge how far a school—or a classroom or text or unit of instruction—has moved. Teachers and school administrators are in the best position to put this checklist to work. They can assess where they stand and ponder directions for innovation. But I am also hoping that parents will look over these questions and ask themselves what kind of an education their children are receiving. I am hoping that school board members will survey the checklist and ponder how education works in the school they serve. I am hoping that educational planners at the state level will pay heed to the checklist and ask how state procedures and policies can encourage the smart school. In the mosaic of principles represented by the six dimensions, we find a demanding vision of what education could be.

sm**A**rt

SCHOOLS

CHAPTER 9

THE CHALLENGE OF WIDE-SCALE CHANGE

The Escalante syndrome works like this. Media attention gets attracted to a conspicuously successful educational setting; for example, Jaime Escalante's inspired teaching of his calculus students. Celebration follows. Characteristics of the efficacious setting are bruited far and wide. "There," we all say. "See. It's possible. It's great. Let's get on with it." And then comes the last stage of the syndrome: Nothing happens.

Jaime Escalante's admirable achievements can only be applauded, but the Escalante syndrome is another matter. It keeps recurring, such is the hunger for solutions to the educational binds that beset our culture. And it does harm. People gradually learn that none of this seems really to work. Oh, it works for Jaime Escalante, but it does not work for us. So hopelessness begins to set in.

The Escalante syndrome comes from our not thinking carefully enough about our victory gardens and what they really teach us. Enthusiasm for their warm, intimate fermentations of learning leads us to want more of the same everywhere. We do not think hard enough about how special many of those victory garden settings are, how they depend on special people like Jaime Escalante and special conditions like tolerance for experimentation in a given setting.

We have victory gardens, many of them. But what we need is "amber waves of grain." What we need is innovations that work on a wide scale, in the school down the street and the one across the river, in the automotive and human gridlock of the inner city and out on the long reach of the prairie.

The past twenty years have seen an unprecedented amount of research scrutinizing the process of change—how an innovation takes hold or falters, how it persists or withers away. The single greatest moral to be drawn from these thousands of experiences and studies is a profoundly discouraging one: Almost all educational innovations fail in the long term. Even those that get a good start typically fall back into business as usual five years later.

It's easy to blame the peculiarities of the educational malaise in the United States for this history of setbacks. Inner-city poverty and violence sap students' energy and will. Cultural diversity makes it hard for texts and teachers to strike resonant notes across a range of students. Agendas in tension—from fundamentalist backlash to multiculturalism—make a deep and challenging curriculum difficult to sustain.

All this is true and truly part of the problem. At the same time, I remain determined to look to the fundamentals of teaching and learning for understanding the shortfalls of education. While dilemmas of inner-city poverty and violence, cultural diversity, and agendas in tension exacerbate the difficulties of innovation and deserve the ample treatment they receive in pages other than these, in my view they do not constitute the essence of the challenge. That essence is structural in character. It has to do not with the oddities of American circumstance but with principles unconfined by setting or society.

There seem to be three fundamental challenges to far-reaching educational innovation:

- *Facing the necessities of scale.* Many innovations workable on a small scale in settings favored in one way or another are simply not suitable for wider-scale use.
- *Making change work.* The process of implementing home-grown or "imported" innovations is crucial. Without artful implementation, innovations viable in principle will generally fail.
- *Advancing thoughtful professionalism.* Teacher development, both in-service and preservice, is essential if challenging innovations are to be taken in stride.

The moral: For smart schools on a wide scale, we must understand all three of these challenges and pay heed to their nature. Indeed, with Theory One, a pedagogy of understanding, the metacurriculum, distributed intelligence, and the cognitive economy as five crucial dimensions toward schooling minds, effective wide-scale change can be seen as a sixth. If we want every school to be a smart school, we must listen carefully to new understandings of school change.

FACING THE NECESSITIES OF SCALE

We can cure the Escalante syndrome. We can escape the cycles of discouragement that plague education. We can have powerful innovations not just on the small victory-garden scale but for the amber waves of grain.

But not all innovations. Crucial to the enterprise of educational change is recognizing this reality: Some innovations can work on a wide scale, but many others contain the seeds of their own failure. They have virtually no chance of thriving widely, even though they may have great impact under hothouse conditions.

What are the realities of scale that we must face if we are to see far-reaching change in education? They are part and parcel of the cognitive economy discussed in chapter 7. Many innovations simply ask more in the way of effort and other resources than many teachers and students are willing to pay. Innovations often develop in special circumstances where social, administrative, financial, and other supports make the cognitive economy favorable. But out in the wide world of educational realities, they can't survive.

So here are some survival conditions.

A wide-scale innovation should not escalate teacher workload. Many small-scale innovations ask for effort way beyond the call of duty. Jaime Escalante himself, for example, pursued his educational agenda with all the zeal of a missionary. On a wide scale this is simply unrealistic. An innovation cannot add substantially to teachers' already overburdened schedules. It should make things easier, or at least not much harder. Innovations that are conspicuously demanding of time need to come with a plan to lighten other loads. One that dramatically escalates the total time required of teachers will simply fail.

A wide-scale innovation should allow teachers a creative role. The opposite sin to making an excessive workload is making hardly any demands at all—providing a package that teachers can execute point by point. The trouble is that, quite understandably, teachers won't do it. They balk. And they should. An effective wide-scale innovation should not be a paint-by-numbers kit. It needs to be respectful of, and take advantage of, teachers' ingenuity in adjusting to their circumstances and making distinctive contributions.

A wide-scale innovation should avoid extreme demands on teachers' skills and talents. Many small-scale innovations call for very sophisticated performances from teachers. The expert tutoring discussed in chapter 8 is quite an art. Remember the biology class organized by Ann Brown and Joseph Campione, with its emphasis on cooperative learning and students writing texts for one another? Choreographing such a setting requires consummate skill.

From such victory-garden settings we can learn principles to put to work on a wider scale. But we cannot expect most teachers to undertake them with skill and confidence. At the least, substantial teacher development would be required, far more than normal in-service provides. Moreover, some small-scale innovations call for extraordinary levels of skill in Socratic interaction or other teaching styles that many people will have trouble mastering.

In summary, innovations can certainly ask for a solid level of professional skill, but those that require virtuosic performance from teachers, especially without ample time and support to learn the technique, are doomed.

A wide-scale innovation should include strong materials support. In many quarters these days, textbooks, worksheets, posters, and the other physical paraphernalia of teaching get bad press. And not without reason, because they often convey distorted and simple-minded content in boring ways. Moreover, ample experience with innovation shows that materials alone are not the solution.

However, let me suggest that for effective wide-scale change, strong materials support is an essential. First of all, materials do not have to be bad. Materials such as the textbook reviewed in the previous chapter or the metacourse for helping students to understand programming afford stimulation, challenge, and insight. In the second place, teachers cannot always be reinventing every spoke of the wheel of education. Education requires too much time and ingenuity as it is. Third, good materials are enormously supportive. They give a path to follow and milestones along the way. Although the creative teacher will not follow that path blindly, its presence helps keep things oriented.

A wide-scale innovation should not boost costs a lot. Obvious though this seems, the fact of the matter is that many educational innovations developed in university or government centers end up, when ready for dissemination, costing far more per student than conventional budget items such as textbooks. Who is going to pay?

On a wide scale, no one. Maybe people will shell out a little more for something special. But they can't dig deeply into pockets that are mostly empty. High per-student costs are anathema if we aim to remake education.

A wide-scale innovation should fulfill many conventional educational objectives at least as well as conventional instruction. Consider again some of the innovations discussed in the previous chapter. The metacourse for computer programming improves student performance on programming quizzes. The biology curriculum of Brown and Campione instills plenty of biological knowledge. Yes, these interventions and others seek more thoughtful learning and deeper student understanding. But they serve some more conventional objectives at the same time. It is not difficult to craft an innovation that does at least as well as typical instruction.

The Paradoxes of Scale

Readers will notice some oddities about the needs of scale spelled out above. Oddity number one is that they are by and large obvious. Naturally, innovations that cost a lot more or demand enormous effort will fail. The paradox is that, although obvious, such concerns get short shrift in much educational development work. So the message has to be pounded home again and again.

Oddity number two is that many of these characteristics stand in some tension with one another. For instance, we do not want to add to teachers' workloads, but we want room for teacher creativity, which requires time. We desire innovation, but we want conventional objectives served well, too. All this is paradoxical. Can we really have our cake and eat it, too?

Yes, we can. With clever design of programs and approaches. An instructional approach that asks teachers to invest creative time can come imbedded within a larger framework of school restructuring that frees the needed time. Many instructional approaches that build students' understanding of mathematics or science also enhance performance on conventional problem-solving tests, as well as yield more insightful responses to authentic assessments that probe understanding more deeply. Still and all, it has to be recognized that the demands of scale pull against one another somewhat. Artful balances need to be struck.

Oddity number three is that an innovation is sensitive to any one of these conditions. You might think that an innovation which scores well on half or two thirds of them would do fine. But it's not as easy as that. Individually, these conditions are not niceties but necessities. For instance, almost apart from its other merits, an innovation will not see wide usage if it costs a lot more than normal instruction. It will not see wide usage if it demands a great deal of additional teacher time and effort. It will not see wide usage if it makes extreme cognitive demands on teachers. It only takes one hole to sink the ship.

So simple a point should not need such emphasis. But experience teaches otherwise. Over the years, innumerable innovations, ambitiously crafted for wide-scale impact, have had virtually no chance because of one or another of the flaws listed earlier. Not that everything has to be perfect. But we do well to remember that almost all of a number of conditions have to be met for an innovation to do wide-scale service.

Indeed, one problem with contemporary research and development in education is a dogged victory-garden bias. Almost everyone tries to set up an optimal educational experience next door where everything wonderful happens. Hardly anyone worries about designing for wide impact. This is not a criticism of any individual, because, as emphasized before, we learn a great deal from what can be done in hothouse settings. But it is a criticism of persistent tunnel vision in the research community.

Educators and developers must recognize a simple truth: Wonderful as victory gardens are and as much as we learn from them, not all victory-garden innovations are suitable for wide-scale impact. Attention to the factors that make for wide-scale viability is imperative. Only then can we build toward educational change that works not just next door, where we can administer tender loving care, but down the block, on the next block, and in the next community as well.

MAKING CHANGE WORK

Educational innovation is one of the gristly challenges of contemporary society. Most innovations do not succeed. If they get beyond the gleam-in-the-eye stage, they generally falter and fail during implementation. If they thrive for a couple of years, they generally fall into disuse when the special circumstances that launched them shift: government funds cease, enthusiastic personnel move away, newer, more trendy priorities emerge.

Yet amidst these worries, something remarkable has happened over the past several years. Educators and scholars concerned with school change have looked hard at the innumerable practical experiments with change carried out in thousands of classrooms and schools nationwide. They have found the fossils of failure in school records and teachers' and administrators' memories. But they have discovered occasional successes. And they have made sturdy progress toward teasing out the conditions for change.

While the previous section dealt with some necessary features of innovations viable on a wide scale, the process of change itself got little attention. Moreover, the story of successful change is understandably complex, certainly beyond the scope of these few pages to treat in detail. Nonetheless a book committed to the smart school can hardly settle for articulating the vision without any words on how to get there.

So how might progress toward a smart school occur? For a comprehensive sourcebook of information on change, one can hardly do better than Michael Fullan's recent *The New Meaning of Educational Change.* Drawing on ideas synthesized there, especially from chapters 5 and 6, let us by way of illustration formulate a particular story of change.

Initiation

Constancia Sanchez, principal of Magellan High School, is on edge. Her vigorous efforts to rally her teachers to improve student performance on SATs and like yardsticks have yielded some incremental gains, but students still score significantly below the state average. And anyway, Constancia, like many educators, finds herself skeptical of the significance of SAT scores, although she is bound by the political milieu to pay some heed to them.

So Constancia Sanchez has pressed her faculty for ideas. "I'm open to your suggestions. Although there's a lot we may not be able to do, I'm ready for some imagination," she says. When two teachers of science, Jeff Orono and Rudy Baker, come to her with a fresh angle and a request for some resources to buy new materials, she pays close attention.

Jeff and Rudy want to build toward a smart school. Familiar with the basic idea of a pedagogy of understanding (perhaps from reading this book), they want to put such a pedagogy in motion in Magellan High's science program. They especially like the idea of understanding performances ("Let's get students *thinking* science—real inquiry, not canned labs.") and the idea of higher levels of understanding ("Youngsters have got to see and talk about and think about how the game of science is played— how you solve problems, how you justify things—if they're going to understand what science is all about.").

For a framework that highlights understanding, Jeff and Rudy decide to use "knowledge as design," discussed in the example that closes chapter 5. At the heart of knowledge as design lies a key understanding performance: Students think about the purposes of things and how the parts and features of the thing work to fulfill those purposes. ("We can have our students analyze a microscope from top to bottom, for instance—optics, wheels and gears, weight on the bottom for stability. A microscope bundles together half a dozen ideas from physics. And you know, our students can also look at something abstract in terms of parts and purposes, like Newton's law of gravity. Newton made it up for a purpose—explaining why the planets moved as they did. And our students ought to be able to tell us, with a little help, how every part of the law contributes to that purpose.")

Jeff and Rudy also have some ideas about materials they need—some booklets, some lab equipment. Constancia could tap a $2,000 gift from an alumnus to seed a program. Should it be this one? Constancia thinks it over.

"Start small, think big," she says. "It's fine to get started this way. But let's work toward bringing in some other subject matters. Not just science, but some math. Maybe some history. What do you think?"

Jeff and Rudy agree. They will get started themselves and as soon as possible—maybe even from the beginning—marshal involvement from a few others.

This is one story of what many researchers call "initiation," the first stage of innovation where decisions get made to attempt change. Magellan High is off to a good start because of some propitious conditions:

- **Clear need** recognized by the principal and the two teachers.
- **Strong advocacy,** in this case from Jeff and Rudy.
- **Clarity.** Jeff and Rudy have at this point a sufficient sense of the innovation's philosophy and approach. As they get more involved, they will constantly need to work for clarity.
- **Practicality.** Jeff and Rudy have done their homework. They see how in broad stroke a pedagogy of understanding can be made to work in their situation. Again, as they and others advance, they will need to think further to sustain a practical vision.

- **Resources.** Constancia is ready to supply the modest resources needed.

The initiation stage, like all the stages of change, is peppered with hazards. So far, Constancia, Jeff, Rudy, and the others they draw in have avoided some major pitfalls.

- **Don't be too simple.** Research also suggests that more challenging changes (so long as they are reasonable to attempt) stand a better chance of success than meeker goals. Thus, Constancia ups the ante a bit, suggesting a broader initial effort involving more teachers and subject matters.
- **Pressure and support.** Although pressure has a bad name, the evidence is that successful innovation requires both pressure and support from administrators. Without support, innovation loses momentum. Without some pressure, it tends to sprawl and lose direction. Thus, Constancia presses her faculty for ideas and offers both support and a certain amount of direction. Significant at this early stage, pressure and support will continue to be important throughout the change process.

Implementation

Jeff Orono and Rudy Baker do their best with a persuasive pitch to a number of other faculty members. Despite approval from Constancia, they run into some discouragement: "I already do pretty much what you're talking about, and I don't have time to rethink it next fall." "I'm already starting this other new thing, and that's all I can handle." "I've decided I really need to help my students build up some basic skills; this is too esoteric for them."

But they secure some interest from Sara Greenbaum in mathematics and, in history, Barbara Finelli and Leland Parks. "Is that enough?" they ask Constancia later.

"Plenty," she says. "Start small, think big! If you try to involve folks who aren't that interested early on, it's just going to bog things down. Give it room to grow."

Over the summer, the five teachers meet a couple of times to plan. They decide to try a number of strategies in their classrooms during the Fall term. They articulate understanding goals for their students and spell out understanding performances their students will engage in to build those understandings. With knowledge as design in mind, they figure out what objects and concepts they want their students to look at as designs. They begin to map out higher levels of understanding in their subject matters. (See chapter 4.)

Also, to help think all this through and begin to draw other teachers in, they decide to spend some of their money for a consultant to do a workshop or two. They contact Rosa Ferris, a local free-lance consultant with a good reputation. But Rosa has a concern about their plan. "I think it's a great thing you're getting into," she says. "And I don't want you to think I'm selling myself. But a couple of workshops isn't going to help much."

Rosa goes on to explain that she finds a series of small-scale orientation meetings with those who will be most involved much more effective. "Even then, don't depend on me," she urges. "You need to develop 'internal consultants,' people within the school system who help others and keep up momentum." Also, Rosa urges, there needs to be a program of peer observation and collaboration.

Is Rosa just selling them a bigger package? "Maybe," history teacher Barbara Finelli says. "But she's right anyway. What will Constancia say?"

Constancia hears their arguments and okays spending a little more for Rosa's regular involvement.

Implementation, the launch period for an innovative program, typically takes two to three years. During this time, teachers learn about the approach or develop it themselves, most often a mix of the two. They try the approach in practical classroom contexts, discover its problems, and strive to solve them.

Many innovations sputter out during this period. Potential participants prove resistant, plans look impractical, competing agendas appear, support from consultants inside or outside the school system turns out to be weak or misguided, and enthusiasm wanes. But Jeff, Rudy, Sara, Barbara, and Leland have avoided the worst hazards.

- **Start small, think big.** Research suggests that often big starts are a mistake. When too many people get involved early on, the initiative drowns in its own social complexity and the marginal commitment of some participants. Thus, it's fine with Constancia that only a few more teachers get involved.

- **Continuing sound counsel.** One-shot workshops or consultations almost never have a lasting impact. As teachers actually try to work through innovations in the classroom, they encounter innumerable problems and need counsel along the way. Rosa's suggestion for continuing contact is crucial.
- **Internal expertise.** Also apt is Rosa's emphasis on building internal expertise that can in time come to fill her role. However much of Rosa's time the school can buy, it will not in the long run be enough. If the pedagogy of understanding innovation (or any other) is to last, it must be because of strong internal commitments and understanding, not continuing outside help.

More Implementation

During the fall term, science teachers Jeff Orono and Rudy Baker, who initiated the understanding project in the first place, prove aggressive in trying things out in their classrooms. A rich conversation evolves among them, the other three teachers, and Rosa Ferris.

For the first several weeks of the term, the three teachers Jeff and Rudy recruited find themselves strangely reluctant to take the plunge.

History teacher Leland Parks says, "I already teach this lesson where students play historical roles and improvise what figures might say. They do this Boston Tea Party skit where they're the plotters, arguing about what to try and how to get away with it. Now that would be an 'understanding performance' wouldn't it?"

The rest agree. "So I'll do that again," Leland says, "and maybe emphasize it a little more, give it more time."

This makes sense to everyone. But after a while, it becomes obvious that Leland, his colleague in history Barbara Finelli, and Sara Greenbaum in math are plugging in their best lessons without really attempting much new.

"Frankly," Sara Greenbaum says, "I think that I'm doing a lot of this already. And I don't completely get the idea of 'higher-order understanding.' I mean, I get the general idea. But just what kinds of explanations or examples count as higher order? And how do you know that the students aren't going through the motions?"

"You know," says Leland, "we were talking about that same question a week ago. And the week before. We keep coming back to it and I'm not sure we're getting anywhere."

"Maybe," says Sara, almost reversing her previous stance, "well, maybe we just have to bite the bullet and try out some new things. See how it plays."

They talk this over with Rosa, who not only agrees but adds, "I'm glad you came to this, because it was on my mind too. Sometimes the only way to make sense of a new approach is to get in there and try it and see what happens."

Rosa is right. Indeed, there is almost a paradoxical role reversal of action and reflection in educational change.

- **Action, then understanding.** Teachers often want to be completely clear about an innovation before trying it. But research and experience suggest that understanding develops gradually as teachers try things, not by talking everything through in advance.
- **The hazard of action without understanding.** On the other hand, if the approach highlights straight cultivation of teaching skills without reflection, teachers can develop classroom routines that play well superficially but soon wither for lack of commitment. Fortunately, the five are persistently reflective about what they are trying to do.
- **Commitment and ownership evolve.** Sara, the math teacher, is somewhat skeptical in the familiar "I already do this" mold. No doubt she does do much of it. And skepticism is fine so long as participants are interested enough to keep at it. Commitment and ownership evolve gradually. They need not exist from the first, and thinking that they must tends to stall efforts at change.

And Yet More Implementation

Sara, initially wary of the innovation, becomes in the spring term an ardent champion of it with other teachers, who begin to get cautiously interested. She finds that she has a knack for putting it into words that make sense to teachers from different disciplines. "If you can move in this direction in math, you can do it *anywhere!*" she says. And she tells a tale from her classroom about eleventh graders who "finally caught on to fractions."

At Sara's urging, the five plan an interest-building workshop with Rosa Ferris for all interested teachers. But the announcement of the workshop several weeks in advance triggers a backlash. It turns out that several teachers of English and social studies have been talking informally about Mortimer Adler's *Paideia Proposal*. "This is really the same idea," they say. "So couldn't we have a Paideia expert come?" It turns out that they made a budget request of Constancia several weeks before and, hard pressed on the budget, Constancia said no.

"We want you to do this workshop," Jeff says to consultant Rosa. "But how can we handle it diplomatically? Any ideas?"

"This is an opportunity, not a problem," says Rosa. "I know a good Paideia person. If your colleagues don't have a connection already, let's suggest him. It's not quite the same thing as the pedagogy of understanding perspective, but it's close enough. Why not invite him to come, and we'll do a joint session. I'll split the fee. Maybe you can form a coalition with the English teachers."

Again, the group at Magellan High have dodged some problems.

- **Vision building.** A philosophy plus technique isn't enough to make most innovations work. One needs visionaries that can paint pictures of what the school would be like. Sara, unexpectedly even to herself, finds a calling there.
- **Power sharing.** When an individual or group attempts to maintain tight control over an innovation, others understandably shy away from it. Here, Jeff and Rudy, who initiated the process, are quite happy to see Sara becoming its most conspicuous spokesperson. And all five are willing to share resources with the Paideia interest group.

> • **Evolutionary planning and problem solving.** One can't plan
> innovations down to a T. All successful innovations have
> problems that, as they arise, need to be solved through ingenious
> and committed efforts, with plans revised accordingly. In this
> spirit, the five are ready to change their workshop plans and
> explore an alliance with the Paideia group. Rosa projects the
> right spirit when she says, "This is an opportunity, not a
> problem."

Continuation

Two years go by. The Pedagogy of Understanding group indeed
merges with the Paideia group. By now, some twenty teachers
are consistently involved, with several others around the fringes.
SAT scores have nudged just above the state average, although
the teachers have not been paying a lot of attention to exam
cramming.

At the end of that year, some hazards threaten. Jeff and Rudy,
who launched the pedagogy of understanding group, and Sara,
who became its chief missionary, all leave for other positions. It's
sheer chance, but so it happens. Also, the seed money Constancia had used to support the innovation runs out. Will the
program falter? Jeff, Rudy, and Sara are all a little embarrassed at
leaving and more than a bit worried.

"Don't fuss," says history teacher Leland Parks. "Remember
where things are. There are five of us now who do the internal
consulting thing. And as to the seed money, we haven't used any
of it for a semester. In fact, Constancia warned us to taper off,
remember."

Viewed whole, the tale of a few teachers at Magellan High
School affords a panorama of fundamental principles of school

> "Continuation" or "institutionalization" is what scholars of school
> change call the next phase of an innovative program. It's nothing to
> take for granted. Constancia has kept her eye on the project. She
> knew something about the likely fate of innovations, even vigorous
> ones. She felt confident that this one would be with Magellan High
> for quite a while longer.

- **Dollar sensitive.** Successful innovations often falter when special funds disappear. This innovation was never lavishly supported, and Constancia warned its devotees to shrink their expectations. When an innovation does need continuing special resources, its survival often depends on administrators' building them routinely into the budget rather than always treating them as a special request.
- **People sensitive.** Successful innovations often end when key people move away. Here, many people have become involved with shared leadership and expertise. So the innovation is not brittle.

Of course, in a way "continuation" or "institutionalization" paints the wrong picture. Both words suggest persistence of a pattern. However, innovations almost inevitably evolve. They turn in unexpected directions, adopt new strategies, discover new grails to seek.

Indeed, more important than any particular innovation is a culture of innovation in a school setting with a cadre of teachers ready to move it forward. And along the way, figuring out what "forward" means.

---

change and the lessons of several decades' worth of research and practical experience. Change is seen outfitted for a long and trying trek. From the early recognition of clear need, through "start small, think big," on to the idea that action ordinarily precedes understanding, and further still to the people and dollar sensitivity of innovations, we find that lasting change demands a complex art and craft.

Today's teachers, administrators, and university-based developers are coming to a new awareness of the demands of change, and none too soon. The enthusiasm for deeper learning in better schools will not sustain itself against an endless parade of partial measures and faltering forays. We have to make it *work*.

ADVANCING THOUGHTFUL PROFESSIONALISM

It is time now to turn to the third leg of wide-scale change in education: the role of teachers. The story of Magellan High School can be put to work once more to make a basic point:

Smart schools need to be places of thoughtful learning not only for students but for teachers too.

Notice how the teachers at Magellan High face problems of learning with understanding quite akin to those of their students. While their students puzzle over Boyle's law or the Boxer Rebellion, they puzzle over what a pedagogy of understanding means. While their students engage in understanding performances to build understandings, the teachers need to try different teaching approaches—the teachers' understanding performances—to build an understanding of how a pedagogy of understanding translates into practice. While the teachers build students' understanding through mental images, they themselves benefit from Sara's anecdotes, which help the teachers form good mental images of a pedagogy of understanding.

All this has to do with a pedagogy of understanding. But the teachers at Magellan High School benefit from other dimensions of a smart school, too. Take distributed intelligence, for instance. The success of their innovation depends crucially on the socially distributed know-how they establish among many teachers in different disciplines. Or consider learning to learn. Their long-term momentum depends on a kind of learning to learn—learning to manage the process of change.

The inherent thoughtfulness of the teaching process shines through in the Magellan example: Teaching at its best involves active reasoning about the myriad aspects of practice. Stanford University scholar Lee Shulman speaks out directly about the centrality of what he calls pedagogical reasoning to the art and craft of teaching:

> As we have come to view teaching, it begins with an act of reason, continues with a process of reasoning, culminates in performances of imparting, eliciting, involving, or enticing, and is then thought about some more until the process can begin again.

Shulman sees teaching as an interweaving of pedagogical reason and action, in which teachers build their understandings of their discipline and the purposes of instruction, develop ways of representing ideas to students, carry out instruction, monitor results, and reflect critically on what they have done, to begin a new cycle.

In sum, a school in the midst of innovation is a setting of fundamental learning for teachers as well as students. And not just routine learning either, the mechanical kind that yields inert, naive, and ritualized knowledge. The same principle applies to both students and teachers: Learning is a consequence of thinking. A smart school, or a school on its way to becoming one, cannot just feature thoughtful learning for students. It has to be an informed and energetic setting for teachers' thoughtful learning, too.

A Home for the Mind

What are the payoffs of such schools? In an essay called "The School as a Home for the Mind," Arthur Costa warns of the costs of a negative school climate:

> When . . . a dismal school climate exists, teachers understandably become depressed. Their vivid imagination, altruism, creativity, and intellectual prowess may soon succumb to the humdrum dailiness of unruly students, irrelevant curriculum, impersonal surroundings, and equally disinterested co-workers.

However, Costa adds, a few sentences later:

> When the conditions in which teachers work signal, promote, and facilitate their intellectual growth, they will gradually align their classrooms and instruction to promote students' intellectual growth as well.

A thoughtful climate, or what I have called earlier a culture of thoughtfulness, makes all the difference.

Roland Barth, first director and one of the founders of the

Principals' Center at the Harvard Graduate School of Education, sees the plight of teachers in the frenetic character of schools. In *Improving Schools from Within,* he likens the professional life of a teacher to a "tennis shoe in a laundry dryer."

What is the key to a more orderly and enlightened profession? Of many factors, Barth underscores collegiality. Collegiality means something different from congeniality, Barth emphasizes. It's not just good manners and telling jokes in the teacher's room. Collegiality means working together in a mutually supportive and thoughtful way at the business of education. Barth borrows a four-way characterization of collegiality from Judith Warren Little. In a collegial atmosphere, teachers talk about practice, observe each other, work on curriculum together, and teach each other. The school that serves as a home for teachers' minds is much more likely to become one for students' minds as well.

A collegial climate of mutual learning cannot be plugged in like a new dishwasher, Barth acknowledges. While cautious of categorizing people, he finds it broadly useful to think about teacher development in terms of three kinds of teachers. Group One teachers resist scrutiny and counsel from others and show little tendency to reflect on their own practice. They go through the motions. Group Two teachers—the most numerous, in Barth's view—rethink their own practice according to their classroom experiences. But they do not welcome the eyes, minds, and mouths of outsiders, even outsiders who teach across the hall. Group Three teachers not only pursue self-examination but throw the door open to collegial interaction around their teaching.

All this reveals a path of development toward the smart school: teachers progressing from Group One to Group Two and Group Two to Group Three. Regrettably, Barth notes that school pressures typically trigger just the opposite effect. Critical parents, competitiveness among teachers, rituals of authoritative feedback from principals, and pressures to comply with mandated teaching practices all work to make teachers closet their endeavors more and more, ultimately even from themselves. They settle inward toward the "humdrum dailiness" of which Costa writes.

What can make a difference? Turning to his personal experience as a principal, Barth reports that formal workshops and direct advice had modest impact. What helped more was responsiveness to questions and suggestions from teachers. He learned to listen hard. Did a teacher want a thousand tongue depressors? Perhaps he could do something about it. Would this new angle on fractions arithmetic be worth trying? Why not. And would there be some way he could help? Barth observed that encouraging teachers in their own initiatives rekindled guttering enthusiasm. And the diversity cultivated in different classrooms by teachers of different visions promoted general thoughtfulness: Teachers began to ponder over and talk about what they were variously doing and why.

From such clues as these we recognize once again the risks of a conventional, command-style leadership in educational institutions. It undermines a culture of thoughtfulness at the faculty level and, through ripple effects, at the student level too. Sara Lawrence Lightfoot, professor at the Harvard Graduate School of Education, writes harshly of the plight of teachers not treated with the respect due them:

> In the worst schools, teachers are demeaned and infantilized by administrators who view them as custodians, guardians, or uninspired technicians. In less grotesque settings, teachers are left alone with little adult interaction and minimal attention is given to their needs for support, reward, and criticism.

The smart school, in contrast, honors the ingenuity, commitment, and centrality of teachers and provides time, resources, and encouragement toward the expansion and refinement of their craft.

The Asian Example

Roland Barth and many other principals have found some strategies to open the way toward the smart school. But these are more victory gardens—small plots of progress in a generally dusty plain. What would a wide-scale culture of thoughtfulness in teaching be like? Is such a thing possible?

An illustration comes from halfway around the world: the pattern of professional teaching practices in China and Japan. In a recent article, University of Chicago psychologist James Stigler and University of Michigan developmentalist Harold Stevenson offer a bird's-eye view of teachers and teaching in the Asian setting. They underscore how supportive and thoughtful an environment exists in China and Japan for the professional development of teachers and the promotion of potent teaching practices.

To be sure, comparisons with the Asian model have bombarded the American public to the point of irritation. In backlash, critics complain that the United States and other settings are too culturally diverse for the Asian model to work. Maybe. Let us first look over the Asian model and then return to the question of how it might speak to settings marked by great diversity.

Time to Think.   One of the most notable features of the Asian model is the time teachers have to think about their craft, separately and together. Anyone familiar with the U.S. educational scene recognizes the racehorse pace that teachers must sustain. This was the central point in Theodore Sizer's book *Horace's Compromise*, touched on more than once in previous pages. Sizer and many others have documented how little time dedicated teachers have to give to lesson planning, paper grading, and other important elements of the teaching profession because they must spend so much time standing at the front of the class or cruising up and down the aisles.

In the Asian context, we find a different and liberating pattern. Teacher/student ratios are much the same as in the United States. But, paradoxically, class sizes are larger. By teaching larger classes, teachers have more time during the school day outside of the classroom for other responsibilities, including the building of their craft. In Beijing, as Stigler and Stevenson report, teachers work in class only three to four hours per day. This does not mean a shorter workday for teachers; on the contrary, they generally spend more hours at the school building than do U.S. teachers. But they invest their time differently.

The Asian pattern invites an immediate objection: those large class sizes. Do not large class sizes lead to poorer learning? That large classes inevitably reduce learning is one of the entrenched myths of education, though challenged by abundant research and experience. Most pertinent to the present context is the marked success of the Asian model and the fact that in such subjects as mathematics it yields students who understand concepts and solve problems far better than U.S. students. More broadly, numerous studies of class size and student learning have shown no effective relationship between the two with class sizes of around twenty or more. In summary, concerns about class size are a poor reason to reject the Asian model. Buying more time to think at the cost of larger class sizes (but with the same teacher/student ratio, which means the same attention per student on assignments and exams) is a good trade that serves teachers and learners well.

A Shared Culture of the Craft of Teaching.   Asian teachers have time to think. But what do they think about? According to Stigler and Stevenson, much of the time they think about the lessons they teach. They plan lessons, share plans with one another, get critiques, attend workshops, observe other teachers teaching, watch videotapes of teaching practices.

Here, an entrenched attitude says that teachers are born and not made. This is the teacher's version of the Ability-Counts-Most theory criticized in chapter 2. Just as we think that ability counts most for youngsters and thus do not recognize how much effort contributes to performance, so we think that ability counts most for teachers and so do not support a culture of learning for teachers. In contrast, the Asian model is effort centered for teachers as well as students. Through organized time and commitment, teachers can learn to teach much better than native ingenuity alone could allow.

Another entrenched attitude says that we are not copycats: Teachers should develop their own lessons. In contrast, the Asian model urges that teachers have much to learn from one another. They routinely share lesson plans. Teachers strive to emulate others they see as displaying potent practices. A lack of creativity? Not according to Stigler and Stevenson. They say that Asian teachers do not blindly copy but adapt and extend. They make an analogy with different performers of a piece of music: They play the same piece, but they each put their own stamp upon it.

Stigler and Stevenson note that the Asian culture of shared professional development gets sustenance from the very physical structure of educational institutions themselves. Whereas teachers here typically remain isolated in their classrooms, teachers in Asian schools are provided with desks in a large area where they can interact and share their craft. While not actually teaching, teachers work in this common space rather than in their classrooms.

An Apprenticeship Model of Teacher Development.   Part and parcel of this culture of the craft of teaching is the treatment of novice teachers. The U.S. model is more or less sink or swim. New teachers get assigned classrooms where they must do their best with scant support from older and more experienced colleagues.

The Asian model takes a different approach. It's not assumed that preservice education equips teachers for the trials of managing classrooms and delivering lessons. For at least a year, beginning teachers pair with older ones. Extensive in-service is expected: for beginning teachers in Japan, twenty days per year by law—far more than almost any U.S. teacher enjoys. Master teachers receive leaves for a year to tour other teachers' classrooms, spreading ideas and critiquing lessons.

But What About Cultural Diversity?   This brings us back to the backlash. Stigler and Stevenson underscore how commonly the complaint is heard: "All well and good for the Japanese or the Chinese with their uniform cultures. But it's not so easy in America, the great melting pot."

Stigler and Stevenson show little sympathy for this argument. They acknowledge that our culture (and, of course, many other cultures around the world) contains great diversity. But most of that diversity, they urge, appears not within individual classrooms but across classrooms and school systems, between, for example, urban and suburban schools. Within a classroom, where the teaching and learning happen, students are no more diverse here than in Asian classrooms.

Stigler and Stevenson conclude—and so do I—that much can be learned from the Asian exemplar. We make a bad tradeoff when we insist on smaller class sizes and keep our teachers busy all day. We would do better to adopt the larger class sizes that allow teachers time to refine their craft. We adopt a mistaken vision of human nature when we treat teachers as born and not made. We would do better to get away from the ability-counts-most model and invest in developing teachers' craft. We serve teachers and students poorly when we toss novice teachers into classrooms and hope they will perform. More networking with experienced teachers seems essential. We undermine the essence of human cultural advance—passing knowledge along—when in the name of creativity we expect teachers always to invent their own lessons instead of passing around well-designed ones. A culture of thoughtful sharing and refinement of lessons would strengthen every teachers' repertoire.

All in all, there is no need to grope about for a vision of a thoughtful culture of teaching. We have examples in Asia. While we cannot clone the Asian model here, some of its basic structural principles would seem to serve a thoughtful culture of teaching in the United States or anywhere else. Schools that are informed and energetic settings of thoughtful learning for teachers as well as students stand within reach.

WHAT WE KNOW CAN MAKE A DIFFERENCE

The last quarter century has seen an Odyssey of educational experimentation and an Alps of experience and research findings. Comparison with ways of schooling in other countries has only been one element. Our understanding of education has advanced on many fronts, from the details of the learning process in the individual human mind and brain to the broad structural and long-range factors that influence the viability of an innovation on a wide scale.

Some points confirmed by the new science of teaching and learning are hardly news. Figures such as John Dewey, William James, or, for that matter, Aristotle or Plato anticipated them. Those points we know more freshly and firmly and in more detail. Others really do stake out new terrain—for example, emerging conceptions of intelligence, understanding, and the process of wide-scale change.

To revisit ideas from this and previous chapters, let me list some insights toward the smart school that we can tap today.

- Research on school and teacher change has alerted us to typical pitfalls and helps us organize processes of change likely to take hold and last.
- Comparison with other cultures has provided yardsticks by which to gauge more objectively how well we are doing.
- Comparison with other cultures has also revealed wide-scale models of thoughtful instruction and the thoughtful development of professional practice.
- Research on the nature of knowledge and understanding has underscored the importance of mental images (or as many psychologists would say, mental models) in building understanding.
- Such conceptions of human understanding as the understanding-performance perspective discussed in chapter 4 have begun to inform instruction more widely.
- Research and diverse educational experiments on human thinking have shown that instruction can elevate students' abilities to think and learn and have revealed much about the design of such instruction.
- Such new conceptions of intelligence as the notion of distributed intelligence explored in chapter 6 have emerged to picture intelligence as a more malleable and accessible commodity than many have heretofore held.
- Studies of transfer of learning have reidentified transfer as a serious roadblock to educational impact but also have disclosed how we can teach for transfer effectively.
- Techniques of cooperative learning have been widely researched and implemented, providing the know-how for successful classroom use.
- Different ways of harnessing social relations for learning—cooperative learning, peer collaboration, peer tutoring, and Socratic interaction, to name a few—have been distinguished, investigated, and put to work more widely and systematically.

- Innovators have designed and investigated learning environments where computers or videodisc/computer systems provide an engaging and supportive setting for thoughtful learning activities.
- Vigorous exploration of alternative means of assessment (those that get beyond a "facts and algorithms" mentality) has begun to yield useable methods.

This list does not purport to itemize all the recent knowledge gains in education, not even those underscored in this book. But perhaps it serves to make the case that we know a lot more now than the "last time around"—the 1960s and early 1970s—about how to work for smart schools. And today, in the essential schools movement launched by Theodore Sizer, in Mortimer Adler's Paideia schools, and in other initiatives across the American landscape, we see students, teachers, administrators, university people, and others working toward more thoughtful patterns of education and drawing upon this accumulated savvy.

With all these signs of a new spring in educational practice, we should recognize that it's still *early* spring. Many of the initiatives underway today certainly serve to make schools more thoughtful places. But they do not often enough take full advantage of what we know about thinking and learning. They generally do not have a point-blank metacurriculum. While striving to teach for understanding, they do not usually do so against the backdrop of a model of what understanding is. Very often, caught up in the momentum of innovation and the shine of new ideas, they can neglect fundamental facets of learning underscored in Theory One.

This book, then, points toward quite a special star in the educational firmament. The smart school finds its motivation in the three hard-to-argue-with educational goals of retention, understanding, and active use of knowledge. The smart school makes a commitment to informed, energetic, and thoughtful teaching and learning. The smart school finds its foundation in a rich and evolving set of principles about human thinking and learning. The smart school in its fullest sense will take us beyond even the ingenious educational innovations now to be found. Smart schools were an ambition and an endeavor a quarter-century ago and at other points in history before that. Today they are within reach.

Thinking back to the first pages of chapter 2, I am reminded that Edgar Alan Poe in "The Bells" wrote not only of alarm bells but of other bells with brighter tones, sleigh bells and wedding bells. He never mentioned school bells at all.

I have often wondered why. Perhaps they were too ambiguous in character.

However, Poe does spread out a palette of sounds from which we can choose. Among the options are "the moaning and the groaning of the bells." That is what we are trying to get away from. Another sonority Poe offers I like better: "the tintinnabulation" of the bells. That's what the spirit of a school ought to sound like.

Just as Poe contrived his phrase and his poem to sound the way he wanted, so will we have to make up our schools for the spirit and substance we want them to express. With commitment, effort, and intelligence, we can look forward to an era when schooling will be an upbeat and effective enterprise day in, day out:

> Keeping time, time, time,
> In a sort of Runic rhyme,
> To the tintinnabulation that so musically wells
> From the bells, bells, bells, bells,
> Bells, bells, bells—
> From the jingling and the tinkling of the bells.

smART

SCHOOLS

APPENDIX

A CHECKLIST FOR CHANGE

This checklist can help anyone to appraise how far a unit, classroom, curriculum, text, or whole school has moved toward the spirit of the smart school—informed, energetic, and thoughtful. The checklist moves systematically through major features of the five dimensions discussed earlier: Theory One, a pedagogy of understanding, the metacurriculum, distributed intelligence, and the hot cognitive economy. And it adds a sixth, conditions for change. Of course, an innovation need not score well on all these dimensions and subcategories to be worthwhile. Few innovations could reasonably undertake all these agendas at once in a full-blown way.

DIMENSION 1. THEORY ONE AND BEYOND

1. Does the instruction offer clear information about topics and processes (for instance, through modeling) that students are to learn?
2. Does the instruction provide for reflective practice, where students practice the very performances they are supposed to achieve and ponder how their learning is going and how they might manage it better?
3. Does the instruction offer informative feedback, helpful to students in improving their performance?

231

4. Does the instruction use extrinsic and/or intrinsic motivation to ensure students' interest and commitment?
5. Does the instruction take advantage of good didactic teaching when students need information?
6. Does the instruction take advantage of coaching when students are practicing challenging performances?
7. Does the instruction take advantage of Socratic instruction when the students engage in complex inquiry?
8. Does the instruction take advantage of teaching and learning methods beyond Theory One; for example, a constructivist or developmental perspective, cooperative learning, emphasis on intrinsic motivation, honoring multiple intelligences, situated learning?

DIMENSION 2. A PEDAGOGY OF UNDERSTANDING

1. Does the instruction engage students in understanding performances as a major part of the learning experience (explaining, finding new examples, generalizing, making analogies)?
2. Does the instruction pay heed to students' existing mental images and try to build mental images that represent well the target concepts?
3. Does the instruction use powerful representations to help create needed mental images?
4. Does the instruction pay direct attention not only to content knowledge but to the problem-solving level of understanding: how problems are solved in the subject matter, including problem-solving strategies?
5. Does the instruction pay direct attention to the epistemic level of understanding: how justification and explanation are handled in the subject matter?
6. Does the instruction pay direct attention to the inquiry level of understanding: what makes good questions and how they are approached in the subject matter?
7. Is the instruction organized around generative topics, which are central to the discipline, accessible to teachers and students, and rich in their ramifications and implications?

DIMENSION 3. THE METACURRICULUM

1. Does the instruction pay direct attention to the problem-solving, epistemic, and inquiry levels of understanding? (Same as under Dimension 2, here for completeness.)
2. Does the instruction explicitly use languages of thinking (terms like reason, evidence, hypothesis, strategy; graphic organizers; efforts to cultivate a culture of thinking in the classroom)?
3. Does the instruction model and encourage intellectual passions (intellectual persistence, curiosity, concern with truth and fairness)?
4. Does the instruction employ integrative mental images to knit together large topics or entire subject matters?

5. Does the instruction explicitly involve learning to learn, in which students learn learning strategies and reflect upon their own learning processes?

6. Does the instruction involve teaching for transfer, where connections beyond the immediate topic to other topics in the subject matter, other subject matters, and outside of school are explored?

DIMENSION 4. DISTRIBUTED INTELLIGENCE

1. Does the instruction take advantage of the physical distribution of intelligence through "thinking on paper" or on computer or other graphic and writing devices?

2. Does the instruction take advantage of the social distribution of intelligence through cooperative learning, tutoring relationships, and other social mechanisms?

3. Does the instruction take advantage of the symbolic distribution of intelligence through varied symbolic vehicles such as concept maps, diagrams, improvisations, and prose?

4. Does the instruction avoid the trap of the "fingertip effect," not assuming that students will simply catch on to the opportunities brought by distributed intelligence but coaching students in good ways to proceed?

5. Does the instruction take care that the executive function (which decides what the task is and how to manage it), if it does not stay with the students, at least returns to them toward the end of the episode of learning so that they have experience with managing their thinking and learning?

DIMENSION 5. THE COGNITIVE ECONOMY

1. Does the instruction demand complex cognition (understanding performances, higher levels of understanding, use of languages of thinking) of the students?

2. Does the instruction make plain the gains of the complex cognition through highlighting enjoyment and making connections to other matters in and out of school?

3. Does the instruction minimize the costs of the complex cognition through supporting students in their efforts?

4. Does the instruction make sense to the teacher in terms of cost in effort and other factors?

5. Does the instruction minimize conflict of interest for the teacher through use of external testing at least sometimes?

6. Does the instruction decrease the pressure on teachers toward the token investment strategy through a small number of clear topics and priorities?

7. Does the instruction employ authentic assessment (testing students

with open-ended tasks that tap the very performances one wants them to develop) to allow the teacher to teach to the test legitimately and fruitfully?

DIMENSION 6. CONDITIONS FOR CHANGE

Some Conditions for the Wide-Scale Viability of an Innovation

An innovation viable on a wide scale:
1. Does not escalate overall teacher workload.
2. Allows teachers a creative role.
3. Avoids extreme demands on teachers' skills and talents.
4. Includes strong materials support.
5. Does not boost costs a lot.
6. Fulfills many conventional educational objects at least as well as conventional instruction.

Some Conditions for an Effective Process of Change

During initiation (and beyond), an effective process of change:
1. Rests on a clear need discernible by the participants.
2. Enjoys strong advocacy within the institution.
3. Brings clarity of philosophy and approach.
4. Is practical to pursue in the context.
5. Includes the needed financial, human, and other resources.
6. Involves challenge, rather than being very simple to do.
7. Includes both some pressure and good support from administrators.

During implementation, an effective process of change:
8. Starts small but thinks big, aiming to include many people and change much.
9. Benefits from regular counsel from outside the institution, counsel that continues for some time.
10. Develops internal experts responsible for orienting new participants, training, and other functions.
11. Moves toward action without expecting everyone to understand everything or buy into everything at first.
12. Avoids unreflective mechanical implementation.
13. Recognizes that commitment and ownership will evolve gradually for many participants.
14. Includes visionaries who paint pictures of what the school could be like.
15. Shares power, avoiding situations where a few try to control the innovation tightly.
16. Recognizes that opportunities and problems will come up along the way and will need to be dealt with as they arise.

Moving toward continuation, an effective program of change:

17. Avoids overdependence on external funds, which may sink the program when they disappear.
18. Avoids overdependence on one or two key people, instead distributing expertise over several.

Some Conditions for Advancing Thoughtful Professionalism

1. A smart school needs to be an informed and energetic setting of thoughtful learning for teachers and administrators, not just for students. This involves most of the features discussed: emphasis on understanding, attention to thinking (the metacurriculum), distributed intelligence (cooperative and collaborative work), and the rest.
2. Collegiality, including talk about practice, observing one another teach, working on the curriculum together, and teaching one another.
3. An administrative style that is responsive to teachers' ideas and not too directive.
4. Time to think rather than constant teaching.
5. A shared culture of the craft of teaching.
6. Apprenticing of beginning teachers to more experienced ones.

NOTES

CHAPTER 1 SMART SCHOOLS

Goals: Toward Generative Knowledge (pp. 4–6)
Lawrence Cremin on the multiple agendas of education: Cremin (1990).
Mortimer Adler's *Paideia Proposal:* Adler (1982).

Means: Thoughtful Learning (pp. 6–8)
Students cannot identify the date of the Civil War within a half century: Ravitch and Finn (1987).
Fundamental science misconceptions: See, for example, Clement (1982, 1983); McCloskey (1983); Novak (1987); Perkins and Simmons (1988).
Rexford Brown's study: Brown (1991).
Quote from William James on memory: James (1983), p. 87.

Precedents: Swings of the Pendulum (pp. 8–11)
Quote from John Dewey on intellectual learning: Archambault (1964), p. 249.
Progressivism and life adjustment education: Toch (1991), pp. 44–55.
On *Man: A Course of Study:* Dow (1991).
On *Project Physics:* Holton, Rutherford, and Watson (1970).
"Back to the basics:" Toch (1991), p. 64.
Paideia Proposal: Adler (1982).
Essential schools: Sizer (1984).
Whole language: Edelsky, Altwerger, and Flores (1991).
New standards for the learning of mathematics: National Council of Teachers of Mathematics (1989).

Mission: Smart Schools (pp. 16–18)
Quote from Jerome Bruner on psychology: Bruner (1973a), p. 478.

CHAPTER 2 THE ALARM BELLS

Lawrence Cremin on the cacophony of teaching: Cremin (1990).

A Shortfall: Fragile Knowledge (pp. 21–27)
Statistics about what students don't know: Ravitch and Finn (1987).
The research of John Bransford and colleagues on inert knowledge: Bransford, Franks, Vye, and Sherwood (1989).

Inert knowledge in computer programming: Perkins and Martin (1986).
Children's belief in a flat earth: Neussbaum (1985).
The film *A Private Universe:* Schneps (1989).
Misconceptions in science and mathematics in general: for example, Clement (1982, 1983); McCloskey (1983); Novak (1987); Perkins and Simmons (1988).
Howard Gardner's idea of stereotypes: Gardner (1991).
Ritual knowledge—the girl with the clever word-problem strategy: Taba and Elzey (1964).
Fragile knowledge in general: Perkins and Martin (1986).

A Shortfall: Poor Thinking (pp. 27–31)
Students' difficulties with story problems in mathematics: see, for instance, Schoenfeld (1985); Nesher (1988); Bebout (1990).
Quote from the National Assessment: National Assessment of Educational Progress (1981).
The knowledge-telling strategy for writing: Bereiter and Scardamalia (1985).
The importance of active thinking in memorization: for example, Baddeley (1982); Higbee (1977).
Quote from Rexford Brown on students' ability to reason about what they are involved with: Brown (1991), p. 187–188.
Lauren Resnick's remark about higher-order thinking: made at the Council of Chief State School Officers Summer Institute, Mystic, Connecticut, July 29–August 1, 1990.

A Deep Cause: The Trivial Pursuit Theory (pp. 31–34)
Quote from Vito Perrone on the trivial pursuit character of teaching and learning: Perrone (1991b), p. 2.
Goodlad's information on classroom events: Goodlad (1984).
Boyer's information on classroom events: Boyer (1983).
Lack of the language of thinking in education: Astington and Olson, 1990.
The school administrator's story: this was from Carolee Matsumoto, now at the Educational Development Corporation. Thank you, Carolee.
The idea of cultural literacy, with a list of concepts to be familiar with: Hirsch (1987).

A Deep Cause: The Ability-Counts-Most Theory (pp. 34–37)
Japanese versus U.S. attitudes toward effort in learning: White (1987).
Quote from Rexford Brown on the intelligence required by a literacy of thoughtfulness: Brown (1991), p. 240.
The critical role of effort as the key variable in learning is, for instance, well documented in studies of mastery learning: see Bloom (1984). Another set of sources is the voluminous work on "time on task," for instance Denham and Lieberman (1980).
Dweck and colleagues' work on incremental and entity learners: Dweck and Bempechat (1980); Dweck and Licht (1980); Cain and Dweck (1989).

On the Rosenthal effect: Rosenthal and Jacobson (1968).

A Consequence: Economic Erosion (pp. 37–42)
Marc Tucker on education and the economy: Tucker (1990).

CHAPTER 3 TEACHING AND LEARNING: THEORY ONE AND BEYOND

The Devastating Critique Levied by Theory One (pp. 46–53)
Research in "direct explanation": see Roehler, Duffy, Putnam, Wesselman, Sivan, Rackliffe, Book, Meloth, and Vavrus (1987); Duffy, Roehler, Meloth, and Vavrus (1986).
Other innovative approaches to teaching history: See, for instance, the insightful booklet by Tom Holt (1990).
E. D. Hirsch's cultural literacy (also discussed in chapter 2): Hirsch (1987).
Computational achievements in mathematics are not so bad, but word problems present many difficulties: National Council of Teachers of Mathematics (1989).
On the importance of explicit modeling of thinking processes in mathematics: Schoenfeld (1979, 1980).
Quote from Lee Shulman: Shulman (1983), p. 497.
Horace's Compromise: Sizer (1984), quote from p. 20.

Three Ways to Put Theory One to Work (pp. 53–58)
The Paideia Proposal: Adler (1982).
Gaea Leinhardt's research on teaching: Leinhardt (1989).
For a further perspective on coaching, see Collins, Brown, and Newman (1989).
Allan Collins on Socratic teaching: Collins and Gentner (1982); Collins (1988); Collins (1987); Collins and Stevens (1983).

The Bogeyman of Behaviorism (pp. 58–60)
"On 'Having' a Poem:" Skinner (1972).

Beyond Theory One (pp. 60–69)
Constructivism in education: For a very recent assembly of viewpoints, see Duffy and Jonassen (1991). Also see Liben (1987).
Regarding Piaget, see, for instance, Piaget (1954); Inhelder and Piaget (1958).
Bruner's thesis that any subject can be taught at any age: Bruner (1973c).
Problems with Piaget's theory: See, for example, Brainerd (1983); Case (1984, 1985); Piaget (1972).
Cooperative learning: See Damon (1984); Slavin (1980); Glasser (1986); Johnson, and Johnson, Holvbec-Johnson (1986).
On collaborative versus cooperative learning: Damon and Phelps (1989).
Intrinsic motivation: See Lepper and Green (1978).

Teresa Amabile's experiment with student writers: Amabile (1983), pp. 153–157.
Multiple intelligences: Gardner (1983).
Situated learning: e.g., Brown, Collins, and Duguid (1989).

CHAPTER 4 CONTENT: TOWARD A PEDAGOGY OF UNDERSTANDING

What Is Understanding? (pp. 75–79)—The Role of Understanding Performances
"Going beyond the information given:" Bruner (1973b).
The idea of understanding performances: See also Perkins (1988; 1991).

Understanding and Mental Images (pp. 79–83)
The idea of mental images or, more commonly in psychological writings, mental models: See, for example, Gentner and Stevens (1983); Johnson-Laird (1983).
Note: Often in psychology, "mental image" is taken to mean a visualization that people create in their "mind's eye." The present use of mental image is broader than that.

Levels of Understanding (pp. 83–87)
"If you can't solve it in ten minutes . . .": Schoenfeld (1985).
Dan Chazen's investigations of geometry learning: Chazen (1989).
Levels of understanding: Perkins and Simmons (1988).
Strategies at the problem-solving level: For example, see Perkins (1990); Polya (1954, 1957).
Epistemic level reasoning: For example, see Perkins (1989); Perkins, Farady, and Bushey (1991); Toulmin (1958).
Inquiry level: For example, see Duckworth (1987); Perkins (1986).
The epistemic and inquiry levels correspond roughly to what Joseph Schwab a number of years ago termed the "syntactic structure" of a discipline: Schwab (1978).

Powerful Representations (pp. 87–92)
The Sufi tale: paraphrased from Shah (1970), p. 193.
The rocket trajectory task: McCloskey (1983).
Thinker Tools: White (1984); White and Horwitz (1987).
Richard Mayer's work on conceptual models: Mayer (1989).
On concrete, stripped, constructed analogs: Perkins and Unger (1989).

CHAPTER 5 CURRICULUM: CREATING THE METACURRICULUM

The Idea of the Metacurriculum (pp. 101–104)
Four levels of metacognition: Swartz and Perkins (1989).
High School: Boyer (1983).

Project 2061: *Science for All Americans* (1989).
Recommendations of the National Council of Teachers of Mathematics (1989).

Levels of Understanding (pp. 104–107)
Good problem management and problem-solving strategies: Schoenfeld (1982); Schoenfeld and Herrmann (1982).
Conceptual ecology: Posner, Strike, Hewson, and Gertzog (1982).
The Geometric Supposer: Schwartz and Yerushalmy (1987).
Does the table push back on the book? Clement (1991).
Lesson on Truman and the atomic bomb: from Swartz and Parks (1992).

Languages of Thinking (pp. 107–114)
The everyday language of thinking and its absence from textbooks: Astington and Olson (1990); Olson and Astington (1990).
Speaking "Cogitare": From the article "Do You Speak Cogitare?" in Costa (1991), quotes from pp. 111, 113, and 114.
Project Intelligence and its testing: Herrnstein, Nickerson, Sanchez, and Swets (1986).
The Teaching of Thinking: Nickerson, Perkins, and Smith (1985).
Concept mapping: Novak and Gowin (1984).
Pictorial formats for thinking: Clarke (1990); Jones, Pierce, and Hunter (1988–89); McTighe and Lyman (1988); for Sandra Parks, Black and Black (1990).
Whole language: Edelsky, Altwerger, and Flores (1991).
The thoughtful classroom: Newman (1990a,b).
Quote from Sara Lawrence Lightfoot: Lightfoot (1983), p. 365.

Intellectual Passions (pp. 114–117)
Quote from Arthur Costa on aesthetics: Costa (1991), p. 17.
Quotes from *In the Name of Excellence:* Toch (1991), p. 235.
Dewey's three attitudes of open-mindedness, whole-heartedness, and responsibility: Archambault (1964).
The cognitive emotions: Scheffler (1991).
Strong sense critical thinking: Paul (1990).
Dispositions: Ennis (1986).
A dispositional model of good thinking: Perkins, Jay, and Tishman (in press).

Integrative Mental Images (pp. 117–119)
A metacourse for programming: Perkins, Schwartz, and Simmons (1988); Schwartz, Perkins, Estey, Kruidenier, and Simmons (1989).
Rissland's concepts, examples, and results: Rissland (1978).
Concept maps: Novak and Gowin (1984).

Learning to Learn (pp. 119–122)
Entity versus incremental learners: Dweck and Bempechat (1980); Dweck and Licht (1980); Cain and Dweck (1989).

Attention monitoring: Miller (1985).

Research on learning from examples: Chi and Bassok (1989).

Learning electrical and economic principles from computer environments: Schauble, Glaser, Raghavan, and Reiner (1991).

Review of metacognitive reading strategy results: Haller, Child, and Walberg (1988).

Helping college students to become better academic performers: Bloom and Broder (1950).

Guided design: Wales and Stager (1977).

Findings on guided design at West Virginia University: Wales (1979).

Teaching for Transfer (pp. 122–128)

Early studies of transfer: Thorndike (1923); Thorndike and Woodworth (1901).

Studies of transfer from programming: Clements (1985); Clements and Gullo (1984); Salomon and Perkins (1987).

Findings on Philosophy for Children: Lipman, Sharp, and Oscanyan (1980), appendix B.

The Reading Partner findings: Salomon (1988).

The low road–high road theory of transfer: Salomon and Perkins (1989).

Ann Brown and colleagues' research on transfer: Brown (1989).

Hugging and bridging in teaching for transfer: Fogarty, Perkins, and Barell (1991); Perkins and Salomon (1988).

An Example of Teaching the Metacurriculum (pp. 128–130)

Knowledge as design: Perkins (1986).

CHAPTER 6 CLASSROOMS: THE ROLE OF DISTRIBUTED INTELLIGENCE

The Idea of Distributed Intelligence (pp. 133–135)

The concept of distributed intelligence: Pea (in press); Perkins (in press); Salomon (in press).

Effects with and of technology: Salomon, Perkins, and Globerson (1991).

Distributing Cognition in the Classroom (pp. 135–144)

John Barell's journal-keeping approach and example: Barell (1991), p. 3.

Assessment by portfolios: Valencia (1990); Wiggins (1989); Wolf (1989); Baron (1990).

Processfolios and Arts PROPEL: Zessoules and Gardner (1991); Howard (1990); Wolf (1989); Gardner (1989).

The computer language Logo: Papert (1980).

Idit Harel's design experience around factions: Harel (1991).

King Tut's Chronicle activity: Fiske (1991), pp. 157–8.

Brown and Palinscar's review of cooperative learning: Brown and Palincsar (1989).

On cooperative learning generally: Johnson, Johnson, and Holubec-Johnson (1986); Glasser (1986); Damon (1984); Slavin (1980).
On peer learning (peer tutoring, cooperative learning, and collaborative learning): Damon and Phelps (1989).
On pair problem solving: Whimbey and Lochhead (1982); Lochhead (1985).

The Fingertip Effect (pp. 144–148)
On the fingertip effect: Perkins (1985).
Students' response to word processors: Daiute (1985).
Problems with cooperative learning: See the above references on cooperative learning.
Computer support environments for writing: Daiute and Morse (in press); Salomon (1991).

CHAPTER 7 MOTIVATION: THE COGNITIVE ECONOMY OF SCHOOLING

The fourth grader's questions about fractions are drawn from the same study mentioned at the beginning of chapter 5. Thanks again to colleagues Heidi Goodrich, Jill Mirman, and Shari Tishman.

The Idea of a Cognitive Economy (pp. 156–159)
Quote on teachers' reasons for rejecting innovations: Fullan (1991), p. 130.
Teachers' spontaneous criteria about worthwhile changes: Fullan (1991), pp. 127–128.
Herbert Simon's notion of limited rationality: Simon (1957).
The concept of "giving reason": Duckworth (1987).

The Cool Cognitive Economy of the Typical Classroom (pp. 159–164)
Problems with textbooks: Toch (1991), pp. 225–226.
Watered-down courses in Florida: Toch (1991), p. 104.
Horace's Compromise: Sizer (1984).

Creating a Hot Cognitive Economy (pp. 164–167)
The New Meaning of Educational Change: Fullan (1991).

School Restructuring: A Cognitive Economic Revolution (pp. 167–171)
Theodore Sizer's "nine points": Sizer (1984), pp. 225–227.
Central Park East Secondary School: Toch (1991), various mentions pp. 260–270.
"The Promise," credo of Central Park East: Quoted from Perrone (1991b), pp. 13–14.
James Comer and Comer Schools: Fiske (1991), 205–220.
"Locked into a conspiracy" quote from Comer: quoted from Fiske (1991), p. 206.

The story of Robert: Fiske (1991), pp. 212–215.
Quote from John Haslinger: Fiske (1991), p. 215.

Teaching to the Right Test: The Idea of Authentic Assessment (pp. 174–176)
About authentic assessment: Gifford and O'Connor (1991); Perrone (1991a); Schwartz and Viator (1990).
Assessment Alternatives in Mathematics: Stenmark (1989).

The Cognitive Economy Meets the Money Economy (pp. 176–180)
School choice: see Fiske (1991), chapter 7; Toch (1991), pp. 246–263.
Impact of choice in the Cambridge school system: Fiske (1991), pp. 178–179.
Impact of choice in New York District 4: Toch (1991), pp. 256–257.
Countries with a good relationship between money and cognitive economies: Besides the latter part of chapter 2, see Tucker (1990).

An Example of Progress Toward a Hot Cognitive Economy (pp. 180–182)
The Vermont authentic assessment program: Fiske (1991), pp. 132–138; Writing Assessment: The Pilot Year (1990).
The contents of a writing portfolio: a direct quote from Vermont Writing Assessment: The Pilot Year (1990).
Ann Rainey's mathematics problem: Fiske (1991), p. 134.

CHAPTER 8   VICTORY GARDENS FOR REVITALIZED EDUCATION

Example 1. Expert Tutoring (pp. 187–189)
The two-sigma effect: Bloom (1984).
Research on expert tutoring: Lepper, Aspinwell, Mumme, and Chabay (1990).

Example 2. Biology for Young Inquirers (pp. 189–191)
Ann Brown's and Joseph Campione's biology course: Brown and Campione (1990).

Example 3. History for Thinkers (pp. 191–194)
Critical thinking and the shot heard 'round the world: Bennett (1970).
Kevin O'Reilly's approach to critical thinking in American history: O'Reilly (1991).
Materials developed by O'Reilly: O'Reilly (1990).

Example 4. A Textbook from the Past (pp. 194–196)
Man: A Course of Study: Dow (1991).
The People Make a Nation: Sandler, Rozwenc, and Martin (1971).

Example 5. A Metacourse for Computer Programming (pp. 196–198)
A metacourse for programming: Perkins, Schwartz, and Simmons (1988);
  Schwartz, Perkins, Estey, Kruidenier, and Simmons (1989).

Example 6. Escalante Himself (pp. 198–201)
On Jaime Escalante: Matthews (1988).

CHAPTER 9   THE CHALLENGE OF WIDE-SCALE CHANGE

Making Change Work (pp. 210–219)
The New Meaning of Educational Change: Fullan (1991).
Knowledge as design: Perkins (1986).
For some other perspectives on teaching for understanding, see Gardner
  (1991); Mayer (1989); Perkins (1991); Perkins and Simmons (1988);
  Rissland-Michener (1978).
The Paideia Proposal: Adler (1982).

Advancing Thoughtful Professionalism (pp. 219–227)
Quote from Lee Shulman: Shulman (1987), p. 13.
Quotes from Arthur Costa: Costa (1991), p. 3.
Improving Schools from Within: Barth (1991).
"Tennis shoe in a laundry dryer": Barth (1991), p. 1.
Collegiality: Barth (1991), chapter 3.
Judith Warren Little on collegiality: Little (1981).
Three kinds of teachers: Barth (1991), chapter 5.
Quote from Sara Lawrence Lightfoot: Lightfoot (1983), p. 334.
Teacher development in Japan: Stigler and Stevenson (1991).

REFERENCES

Adler, M. 1982. *The paideia proposal: An educational manifesto*. New York: Macmillan.

Amabile, T. M. 1983. *The social psychology of creativity*. New York: Springer-Verlag.

Archambault, R., ed. 1964. *John Dewey on education: Selected writings*. New York: Modern Library.

Astington, J. W., and Olson, D. R. 1990. Metacognitive and metalinguistic language: Learning to talk about thought. *Applied Psychology: An International Review, 39* (1), 77–87.

Baddeley, Alan. 1982. *Your memory: A user's guide*. New York: Macmillan.

Barell, J. 1991. *Teaching for thoughtfulness: Classroom strategies to enhance intellectual development*. New York: Longman.

Baron, J. 1990. Performance assessment: Blurring the edges among assessment, curriculum, and instruction. In A. Champagne, B. Lovetts, and B. Calinger, eds., *This year in school science: Assessment in the service of instruction*. Washington, DC: American Association for the Advancement of Science.

Barth, R. S. 1991. *Improving schools from within: Teachers, parents, and principals can make a difference*. San Francisco: Jossey-Bass.

Bebout, H. 1990. Children's symbolic representation of addition and subtraction word problems. *Journal for Research in Mathematics Education, 21* (2), 123–131.

Bennett, P. 1970. *What happened at Lexington Green?* Menlo Park, CA: Addison-Wesley.

Bereiter, C., and Scardamalia, M. 1985. Cognitive coping strategies and the problem of inert knowledge. In S. S. Chipman, J. W. Segal, and R. Glazer, eds., *Thinking and learning skills, vol. 2: Current research and open questions*, pp. 65–80. Hillsdale, NJ: Erlbaum.

Black, H., and Black, S. 1990. *Organizing thinking*. Pacific Grove, CA: Midwest Publications Critical Thinking Press and Software.

Bloom, B. S. 1984. The search for methods of group instruction as effective as one-to-one tutoring. *Educational Leadership, 41*(8), 4–17.

Bloom, B. S., and Broder, L. 1950. *Problem-solving process of college students*. Chicago: University of Chicago Press.

Boyer, E. 1983. *High school: A report on secondary education in America*. New York: Harper & Row.

Brainerd, C. J. 1983. Working-memory systems and cognitive development. In C. J. Brainerd, ed., *Recent advances in cognitive-developmental theory:*

Progress in cognitive development research, pp. 167–236. New York: Springer-Verlag.

Bransford, J. D., Franks, J. J., Vye, N. J., and Sherwood, R. D. 1989. New approaches to instruction: Because wisdom can't be told. In S. Vosniadou and A. Ortony, eds., *Similarity and analogical reasoning*, pp. 470–497. New York: Cambridge University Press.

Brown, A. L. 1989. Analogical learning and transfer: What develops? In S. Vosniadou and A. Ortony, eds., *Similarity and analogical reasoning*, pp. 369–412. New York: Cambridge University Press.

Brown, A. L., and Campione, J. C. 1990. Communities of learning and thinking, or a context by any other name. In D. Kuhn, ed., *Developmental perspectives on teaching and learning thinking skills* (special issue). *Contributions to Human Development*, 21, 108–126.

Brown, A. L., and Palinscar, A. S. 1989. Guided, cooperative learning and individual knowledge acquisition. In L. Resnick, ed., *Knowing, learning and instruction*, pp. 393–452. Hillsdale, NJ: Lawrence Erlbaum Associates.

Brown, J. S., Collins, A., and Duguid, P. 1989. Situated cognition and the culture of learning. *Educational Researcher, 18* (1).

Brown, R. G. 1991. *Schools of thought: How the politics of literacy shape thinking in the classroom*. San Francisco: Josey-Bass.

Bruner, J. S. 1973a. Education and social invention. In J. Anglin, ed., *Beyond the information given*, pp. 468–479. New York: Norton.

———. 1973b. Going beyond the information given. In J. Anglin, *Beyond the information given* pp. 218–238. New York: Norton.

———. 1973c. Readiness for learning. In J. Anglin, ed., *Beyond the information given*, pp. 413–425. New York: Norton.

Cain, K., and Dweck, C. 1989. The development of children's conception of intelligence: A theoretical framework. In R. Sternberg, ed., *Advances in the psychology of human intelligence, vol. 5*, pp. 47–82. Hillsdale, NJ: Lawrence Erlbaum Associates.

Case, R. 1984. The process of stage transition: A neo-Piagetian viewpoint. In R. J. Sternberg, ed., *Mechanisms of cognitive development*, pp. 19–44. New York: W. H. Freeman and Company.

———. 1985. *Intellectual development: Birth to adulthood*. New York: Academic Press.

Chazen, D. 1989. *Ways of knowing: High school students' conceptions of mathematical proof*. Unpublished doctoral dissertation, Harvard Graduate School of Education, Cambridge, MA.

Chi, M., and Bassok, M. 1989. Learning from examples via self-explanations. In L. Resnick, ed., *Knowing, learning and instruction*, pp. 251–282. Hillsdale, NJ: Lawrence Erlbaum Associates.

Clarke, J. H. 1990. *Patterns of thinking: Integrating learning skills in content teaching*. Boston, MA: Allyn and Bacon.

Clement, J. 1982. Students' preconceptions in introductory mechanics. *American Journal of Physics, 50*, 66–71.

———. 1983. A conceptual model discussed by Galileo and used intuitively by physics students. In D. Gentner and A. L. Stevens, eds., *Mental models*. Hillsdale, NJ: Erlbaum.

————. 1991. Nonformal reasoning in experts and in science students: The use of analogies, extreme case and physical intuition. In J. Voss, D.N. Perkins, and J. Segal, eds., *Informal Reasoning and Education*, 345–362. Hillsdale, NJ: Lawrence Erlbaum Associates.

Clements, D. H. 1985b. Research on Logo in education: Is the turtle slow but steady, or not even in the race? *Computers in the Schools*, 2(2/3), 55–71.

Clements, D. H., and Gullo, D. F. 1984. Effects of computer programming on young children's cognition. *Journal of Educational Psychology*, 76(6), 1051–1058.

Collins, A. 1987. A sample dialogue based on a theory of inquiry teaching. In C.M. Reigeluth, ed., *Instruction theories in action: Lessons illustrating selected theories and models*, pp. 181–199. Hillsdale, NJ: Lawrence Erlbaum Associates.

————. 1988. Different goals of inquiry teaching. *Questioning Exchange*, 2, 39–45.

Collins, A., Brown, J. S., and Newman, S. F. 1989. Cognitive apprenticeship: Teaching the craft of reading, writing, and mathematics. In L. B. Resnick, ed., *Knowing, learning, and instruction: Essays in honor of Robert Glaser*, pp. 453–494. Hillsdale, New Jersey: Erlbaum.

Collins, A., and Gentner, D. 1982. *Constructing runnable mental models. Proceedings of the Fourth Annual Conference of the Cognitive Science Society*. Hillsdale, NJ: Lawrence Erlbaum Associates.

Collins, A., and Stevens, A. L. 1983. A cognitive theory of inquiry teaching. In C.M. Reigeluth, ed., *Instructional design theories and models: An overview*, 247–278. Hillsdale, NJ: Lawrence Erlbaum Associates.

Costa, A. 1991. *The school as a home for the mind*. Palatine, IL: Skylight Publishing.

Cremin, L. A. 1990. Popular education and its discontents. New York: Harper & Row.

Daiute, C. 1985. *Writing and computers*. Reading, MA: Addison-Wesley.

Daiute, C., and Morse, F. In press. Access to knowledge and expression: Multi-media writing tools for children with diverse needs and strengths. *Journal of Special Education Technology*.

Damon, W. 1984. Peer education: The untapped potential. *Journal of Applied Developmental Psychology*, 5, 331–343.

Damon, W., and Phelps, E. 1989. Critical distinctions among three approaches to peer education. *International Journal of Educational Research*, 13 (1), 9–19.

Denham, C., and Lieberman, A., eds. May 1980. *Time to learn*. Washington, D.C.: National Institute of Education.

Dow, P. 1991. *Schoolhouse politics: Lessons from the Sputnik era*. Cambridge, MA: Harvard University Press.

Duckworth, E. 1987. *The having of wonderful ideas and other essays on teaching and learning*. New York: Teachers College Press.

Duffy, G., Roehler, L., Meloth, M., and Vavrus, L. July 1986. *The curricular and instructional conceptions undergirding the teacher explanation project.* Lansing, MI: Institute for Research on Teaching, Michigan State University.

Duffy, T. M., and Jonassen, D. H., eds., May 1991. Theme issue on constructivism. *Educational Technology, 31* (5), 18–23.

Dweck, C. S., and Bempechat, J. 1980. Children's theories of intelligence: Consequences for learning. In S. G. Paris, G. M. Olson, and H. W. Stevenson, eds., *Learning and motivation in the classroom*, pp. 239–256. Hillsdale, NJ: Lawrence Erlbaum Associates.

Dweck, C. S., and Licht, B. G. 1980. Learned helplessness and intellectual achievement. In J. Garbar and M. Seligman, eds., *Human helplessness.* New York: Academic Press.

Edelsky, C., Altwerger, B., and Flores, B. 1991. *Whole language: What's the difference?* Portsmouth, NH: Heinemann.

Ennis, R. H. 1986. A taxonomy of critical thinking dispositions and abilities. In J. B. Baron and R. S. Sternberg, eds. *Teaching thinking skills: Theory and practice*, pp. 9–26. New York: W. H. Freeman.

Fiske, E. B. 1991. *Smart schools, smart kids.* New York: Simon & Schuster.

Fogarty, R., Perkins, D. N., and Barell, J. 1991. *How to teach for transfer.* Palatine, IL: Skylight Publishing.

Fullan, M. G. 1991. *The new meaning of educational change.* New York: Teachers College Press.

Gardner, H. 1983. *Frames of mind.* New York: Basic Books.

———. 1989. Zero-based arts education: An introduction to Arts PROPEL. *Studies in Art Education: A Journal of Issues and Research, 30* (2), 71–83.

———. 1991. *The unschooled mind: How children think and how schools should teach.* New York: Basic Books.

Gentner, D., and Stevens, A. L., eds. (1983). *Mental models.* Hillsdale, New Jersey: Lawrence Erlbaum Associates.

Gifford, B. R., and O'Connor, M. C., eds. (1991). *Changing assessments: Alternative views of aptitude, achievement and instruction.* Norwood, MA: Kluwer Publishers.

Glasser, W. 1986. *Control theory in the classroom.* New York: Harper & Row.

Goodlad, J. 1984. *A place called school: prospects for the future.* New York: McGraw-Hill.

Haller, E. P., Child, D. A., and Walberg, H. J. 1988. Can comprehension be taught? A quantitative synthesis of "metacognitive" studies. *Educational Researcher, 17*(5), 5–8.

Harel, I. 1991. *Children designers.* Norwood, NJ: Ablex.

Herrnstein, R. J., Nickerson, R. S., Sanchez, M., and Swets, J. A. 1986. Teaching thinking skills. *American Psychologist, 41*, 1279–1289.

Higbee, K. L. 1977. *Your memory: How it works and how to improve it.* Englewood Cliffs, NJ: Prentice-Hall.

Hirsch, E. D. 1987. *Cultural literacy: What every American needs to know.* Boston: Houghton Mifflin.

Holt, T. 1990. *Thinking historically: Narrative, imagination, and understanding.* New York: College Entrance Examination Board.

Holton, G., Rutherford, J., and Watson, F., eds. 1970. *Project physics.* New York: Holt, Rinehart and Winston.

Howard, K. Spring 1990. Making the writing portfolio real. *The Quarterly for the National Writing Project & The Center for the Study of Writing, 12* (2), 4–7.

Inhelder, B., and Piaget, J. 1958. *The growth of logical thinking from childhood to adolescence.* New York: Basic Books.

James, W. 1983. *Talks to teachers on psychology.* Cambridge, MA: Harvard University Press.

Johnson, D., Johnson, R., and Holubec-Johnson, E. 1986. *Circles of learning.* Edina, MN: Interaction Book Company.

Johnson-Laird, P. N. 1983. *Mental models.* Cambridge, Massachusetts: Harvard University Press.

Jones, B. F., Pierce, J., & Hunter, B. 1988–89. Teaching students to construct graphic representations. *Educational Leadership, 46*(4), 20–25.

Leinhardt, G. 1989. Development of an expert explanation: An analysis of a sequence of subtraction lessons. In L. Resnick, ed., *Knowing, learning and instruction: Essays in honor of Robert Glaser,* pp. 67–124. Hillsdale, NJ: Lawrence Erlbaum Associates.

Lepper, M., Aspinwall, L., Mumme, D., and Chabay, R. 1990. Self-perception and social perception processes in tutoring: Subtle social control strategies of expert tutors. In J.M. Olson and M.P. Zanna, eds., *Self-inference processes: The Ontario symposium, vol. 6.* Hillsdale, NJ: Lawrence Erlbaum Associates.

Lepper, M., and Green, D. 1978. Overjustification research and beyond: Toward a means-ends analysis of intrinsic and extrinsic motivation. In M. Lepper and D. Green, eds., *The hidden costs of reward: New perspectives on the psychology of human motivation,* pp. 109–148. Hillsdale, NJ: Lawrence Erlbaum Associates.

Liben, L., ed. (1987). *Development and learning: Conflict or congruence?* Hillsdale, NJ: Lawrence Erlbaum Associates.

Lightfoot, S. L. 1983. *The good high school: Portraits of character and culture.* New York: Basic Books.

Lipman, M., Sharp, A. M., and Oscanyan, F. 1980. *Philosophy in the classroom.* Philadelphia: Temple University Press.

Little, J. W. 1981. *School success and staff development in urban desegregated schools: A summary of recently completed research.* Boulder, CO: Center for Action Research.

Lochhead, J. 1985. Teaching analytic reasoning skills through pair problem solving. In J. Segal, S. Chipman, and R. Glaser, eds., *Thinking and learning skills, vol. 1: Relating instruction to research,* pp. 109–132. Hillsdale, NJ: Lawrence Erlbaum Associates.

Matthews, J. 1988. *Escalante: The best teacher in America.* New York: Holt and Company.

Mayer, R. E. 1989. Models for understanding. *Review of Educational Research,* 59, 43–64.

McCloskey, M. 1983. Naive theories of motion. In D. Gentner and A. L. Stevens, eds., *Mental models,* pp. 299–324. Hillsdale, NJ: Lawrence Erlbaum Associates.

McTighe, J., and Lyman, F. T. 1988. Cueing thinking in the classroom: The promise of theory embedded tools. *Educational Leadership,* 45(7), 18–24.

Miller, P. 1985. Metacognition and attention. In D. Forrest-Pressley, G. MacKinnon, and T. Walker, eds., *Metacognition, cognition and human performance,* pp. 181–222. Orlando, FL: Academic Press.

National Assessment of Educational Progress. 1981. *Reading, thinking, and writing.* Princeton, NJ: Educational Testing Service.

National Council of Teachers of Mathematics. 1989. *Curriculum and evaluation standards for school mathematics.* Reston, VA: National Council of Teachers of Mathematics.

Nesher, P. 1988. Multiplicative school word problems: Theoretical approaches and empirical findings. In M. Behr and J. Hiebert, eds., *Number concepts and operations in the middle grades, vol. 2,* pp. 19–40. Hillsdale, NJ: Lawrence Erlbaum Associates.

Neussbaum, J. 1985. The earth cosmic boy. In R. Driver, E. Guesne, and A. Tiberghien, eds., *Childrens' ideas in science.* Philadelphia: Open University Press.

Newmann, F. 1990a. Higher order thinking in teaching social studies: A rationale for the assessment of classroom thoughtfulness. *Journal of Curriculum Studies,* 22 (1), 41–56.

———. 1990b. Qualities of thoughtful social studies classes: An empirical profile. *Journal of Curriculum Studies,* 22 (3), 353–275.

Nickerson, R., Perkins, D. N., and Smith, E. 1985. *The teaching of thinking.* Hillsdale, NJ: Lawrence Erlbaum Associates.

Novak, J. D., ed. 1987. *The proceedings of the second misconceptions in science and mathematics conference.* Ithaca, NY: Cornell University.

Novak, J. D., and Gowin, D. B. 1984. *Learning how to learn.* New York: Cambridge University Press.

Olson, D. R., and Astington, J.W. 1990. Talking about text: How literacy contributes to thought. *Journal of Pragmatics,* 14 (15), 557–573.

O'Reilly, K. 1990. *Evaluating viewpoints: Critical thinking in United States history series.* Pacific Grove, CA: Midwest Publications.

———. 1991. Informal reasoning in high school history. In J. F. Voss, D. N. Perkins, and J. W. Segal, eds., *Informal reasoning and education,* pp. 363–379. Hillsdale, NJ: Lawrence Erlbaum Associates.

Papert, S. 1980. *Mindstorms: Children, computers, and powerful ideas.* New York: Basic Books.

Paul, R. 1990. *Critical thinking: What every person needs to survive in a rapidly changing world.* Rohnert Park, CA: Center for Critical Thinking and Moral Critique, Sonoma State University.

Pea, R. In press. Practices of distributed intelligence and designs for education. In G. Salomon, ed., *Distributed cognitions.* New York: Cambridge University Press.

Perkins, D. N. 1985. The fingertip effect: How information-processing technology changes thinking. *Educational Researcher, 14*(7), 11–17.

———. 1986. *Knowledge as design.* Hillsdale, NJ: Lawrence Erlbaum Associates.

———. 1988. Art as understanding. *The Journal of Aesthetic Education, Special Issue: Art, Mind, and Education, 22*(1), 1988, 111–131. And in H. Gardner and D. Perkins, eds., *Art, mind, and education.* Urbana-Champaign and Chicago: University of Illinois Press, 1989, 111–131.

———. 1989. Reasoning as it is and could be. In D. Topping, D. Crowell, and V. Kobayashi, eds., *Thinking: The third international conference,* pp. 175–194. Hillsdale, NJ: Lawrence Erlbaum Associates.

———. 1990. Problem theory. In V. A. Howard, ed., *Varieties of thinking,* pp. 15–46. New York: Routledge.

———. 1991. Educating for insight. *Educational Leadership, 49*(2), 4–8.

———. In press. Person plus: A distributed view of thinking and learning. In G. Salomon, ed., *Distributed cognitions.* New York: Cambridge University Press.

Perkins, D. N., and Martin, F. 1986. Fragile knowledge and neglected strategies in novice programmers. In E. Soloway and S. Iyengar, eds., *Empirical studies of programmers,* pp. 213–229. Norwood, NJ: Ablex.

Perkins, D. N., and Salomon, G. 1988. Teaching for transfer. *Educational Leadership, 46*(1), 22–32.

Perkins, D. N., and Simmons, R. (1988). Patterns of misunderstanding: An integrative model of misconceptions in science, mathematics, and programming. *Review of Educational Research, 58*(3), 303–326.

Perkins, D. N., and Unger, C. June 1989. *The new look in representations for mathematics and science learning.* Paper presented at the Social Science Research Council conference "Computers and Learning," Tortola, British Virgin Islands, June 26–July 2, 1989.

Perkins, D. N., Jay, E., and Tishman, S. In press. Beyond abilities: A dispositional theory of thinking. *The Merrill-Palmer Quarterly.*

Perkins, D. N., Schwartz, S., and Simmons, R. 1988. Instructional strategies for the problems of novice programmers. In R. Mayer, ed., *Teaching and learning computer programming: Multiple research perspectives,* pp. 153–178. Hillsdale, NJ: Lawrence Erlbaum Associates.

Perkins, D. N., Farady, M., and Bushey, B. 1991. Everyday reasoning and the roots of intelligence In J. Voss, D.N. Perkins, and J. Segal, eds., *Informal reasoning and education,* pp. 83–106. Hillsdale, NJ: Lawrence Erlbaum Associates.

Perrone, V., ed. 1991a. *Expanding student assessment.* Alexandria, VA: Association for Supervision and Curriculum Development.

———. 1991b. *A letter to teachers: Reflections on schooling and the art of teaching.* San Francisco: Jossey-Bass.

Piaget, J. 1954. *The construction of reality in the child.* New York: Basic Books.

————. 1972. Intellectual evolution from adolescence to adulthood. *Human Development 15*, 1–12.

Polya, G. 1954. *Mathematics and plausible reasoning.* 2 vols. Princeton, NJ: Princeton University Press.

————. 1957. *How to solve it: A new aspect of mathematical method.* 2nd ed. Garden City, NY: Doubleday.

Posner, G. J., Strike, K. A., Hewson, P. W., and Gertzog, W. A. 1982. Accommodation of a scientific conception: Toward a theory of conceptual change. *Science Education, 66*(2), 211–227.

Ravitch, D., and Finn, C. 1987. *What do our 17-year-olds know?: A report on the first national assessment of history and literature.* New York: Harper & Row.

Rissland-Michener, E. 1978. Understanding understanding mathematics. *Cognitive Science 2*, 361–383.

Roehler, L., Duffy, G., Putnam, J., Wesselman, R., Sivan, E., Rackliffe, G., Book, C., Meloth, M., and Vavrus, L. March 1987. *The effect of direct explanation of reading strategies on low-group third graders' awareness and achievement: A technical report of the 1984–85 study.* Lansing, MI: Institute for Research on Teaching, Michigan State University.

Rosenthal, R., and Jacobson, L. 1968. *Pygmalion in the classroom.* New York: Holt, Rinehart, & Winston.

Salomon, G. 1988. AI in reverse: Computer tools that turn cognitive. *Journal of Educational Computer Research, 4*, 123–139.

————. In press. No distribution without individuals' cognition: A dynamic interactional view. In G. Salomon, ed., *Distributed cognitions.* New York: Cambridge University Press.

Salomon, G., and Perkins, D. N. 1987. Transfer of cognitive skills from programming: When and how? *Journal of Educational Computing Research, 3*, 149–169.

————. 1989. Rocky roads to transfer: Rethinking mechanisms of a neglected phenomenon. *Educational Psychologist, 24*(2), 113–142.

Salomon, G., Perkins, D.N., and Globerson, T. 1991. Partners in cognition: Extending human intelligence with intelligent technologies. *Educational Researcher, 20*, 2–9.

Sandler, M. W., Rozwenc, E. C., and Martin, E. C. 1971. *The people make a nation.* Boston: Allyn and Bacon.

Schauble L., Glaser R., Rahavan K., and Reiner M. 1991. Causal models and experimentation strategies in scientific reasoning. *Journal of Learning Sciences, 1* (2), 201–238.

Scheffler, I. 1991. In praise of cognitive emotions. In I. Scheffler, ed., *In praise of cognitive emotions*, pp. 3–17. New York: Routledge.

Schneps, M. H. 1989. *A private universe.* Santa Monica, CA: Pyramid Film & Video.

Schoenfeld, A. H. 1979. Explicit heuristic training as a variable in problem solving performance. *Journal for Research in Mathematics Education, 10*(3), 173–187.

————. 1980. Teaching problem-solving skills. *American Mathematical Monthly, 87*, 794–805.

————. 1982. Measures of problem-solving performance and of problem-solving instruction. *Journal for Research in Mathematics Education, 13*(1), 31–49.

————. 1985. *Mathematical problem solving.* New York: Academic Press.

Schoenfeld, A. H., and Herrmann, D. J. 1982. Problem perception and knowledge structure in expert and novice mathematical problem solvers. *Journal of Experimental Psychology: Learning, Memory, and Cognition, 8,* 484–494.

Shulman, L. S. (1983. Autonomy and obligation: The remote control of teaching. In L. S. Shulman and G. Sykes, eds., *Handbook of teaching and policy* (pp. 484–504). New York: Longman.

————. (1987). Knowledge and teaching: Foundations of the new reform. *Harvard Educational Review, 57* (1), 1–22.

Schwab, J. 1978. *Science, curriculum, and liberal education: Selected essays.* I. Westbury and N. J. Wilkof, eds. Chicago: University of Chicago Press.

Schwartz, J. L., and Viator, K. A., eds. 1990. *The prices of secrecy: The social, intellectual, and psychological costs of current assessment practice.* Cambridge, MA, Harvard Graduate School of Education: Educational Technology Center.

Schwartz, J. L., and Yerushalmy, M. (1987). The geometric supposer: Using microcomputers to restore invention to the learning of mathematics. In D. N. Perkins, J. Lochhead, and J. Bishop, eds., *Thinking: Proceedings of the second international conference* (pp. 525–536). Hillsdale, NJ: Lawrence Erlbaum Associates.

Schwartz, S. H., Perkins, D. N., Estey, G., Kruidenier, J., and Simmons, R. 1989. A metacourse for BASIC: Assessing a new model for enhancing instruction. *Journal of Educational Computing Research, 5*(3), 263–297.

Science for all Americans: A project 2061 report on literacy goals in science, mathematics and technology. 1989. Washington, D.C.: American Association for the Advancement of Science.

Shah, I. 1970. *Tales of the dervishes: Teaching stories of the Sufi masters over the past thousand years.* New York: E. P. Dutton.

Simon, H. 1957. *Models of man: Social and rational.* New York: Wiley.

Sizer, T. B. 1984. *Horace's compromise: The dilemma of the American high school today.* Boston: Houghton Mifflin.

Skinner, B. F. 1972. A lecture on "having" a poem. In *Cumulative record: A selection of papers.* 3rd ed., pp. 345–355. New York: Meredith Corporation.

Slavin, R. 1980. Cooperative learning. *Review of Educational Research, 50* (2), 315–342.

Stenmark, J. K. 1989. *Assessment alternatives in mathematics.* EQUALS and the California Mathematics Council Campaign for Mathematics, Lawrence Hall of Science, University of California.

Stigler, J. W., and Stevenson, H. W. 1991. How Asian teachers polish each lesson to perfection. *American Educator, 15*(1), 12–20, 43–47.

Swartz, R., and Parks, S. 1992. *Infusing critical and creative thinking into content instruction: A handbook for secondary school teachers.* Pacific Grove, CA: Midwest Publications.

Swartz, R. J., and Perkins, D. N. 1989. *Teaching thinking: Issues and approaches.* Pacific Grove, CA: Midwest Publications.

Taba, H., and Elzey, F. 1964. Teaching strategies and thought processes. *Teachers College Record, 65,* 524–34.

Thorndike, E. L. 1923. The influence of first-year Latin upon the ability to read English. *School Sociology, 17,* 165–168.

Thorndike, E. L., and Woodworth, R. S. 1901. The influence of improvement in one mental function upon the efficiency of other functions. *Psychological Review, 8,* 247–261.

Toch, T. 1991. *In the name of excellence: The struggle to reform the nation's schools, why it's failing, and what should be done.* New York: Oxford University Press.

Toulmin, S. E. 1958. *The uses of argument.* Cambridge, UK: Cambridge University Press.

Tucker, M. 1990. *America's choice: High skills or low wages! The report of the Commission on the Skills of the American Workforce.* Rochester, NY: National Center on Education and the Economy.

Valencia, S. 1990. A portfolio approach to classroom reading assessment: The whys, whats, and hows. *The Reading Teacher,* pp. 338–340.

Wales, C. E. 1979. Does how you teach make a difference? *Engineering Education, 69* (5).

Wales, C. E., and Stager, R. A. 1977. *Guided design.* Morgantown, WV: West Virginia University, Center for Guided Design.

Whimbey, A., and Lochhead, J. 1982. *Problem solving and comprehension.* Hillsdale, NJ: Lawrence Erlbaum Associates.

White, B. 1984. Designing computer games to help physics students understand Newton's laws of motion. *Cognition and Instruction, 1,* 69–108.

White, B., and Horwitz, P. 1987. *ThinkerTools: Enabling children to understand physical laws* (BBN Inc. Report No. 6470). Cambridge, MA: BBN Laboratories Inc.

White, M. 1987. *The Japanese educational challenge.* New York: Free Press.

Wiggins, G. May 1989. A true test: Toward more authentic and equitable assessment. *Phi Delta Kappan, 70,* 703–713.

Wolf, D. January 1988. Opening up assessment. *Educational Leadership, 45* (4), 24–29.

———. April 1989. Portfolio assessment: Sampling student work. *Educational Leadership, 46* (7), 35–40.

Writing Assessment: The Pilot Year. 1990. Part of a package on the authentic assessment program of Vermont. Montpelier, VT: Department of Education.

Zellermayer, M., Salomon, G., Globerson, T., and Givon, H. Summer 1991. Enhancing writing-related metacognitions through a computerized writing partner. *American Educational Research Journal, 28* (2), 373–391.

Zessoules, R., and Gardner, H. 1991. Authentic assessment: Beyond the buzzword and into the classroom. In V. Perrone, ed., *Expanding student assessment*. Alexandria, VA: Association for Supervision and Curriculum Development.

INDEX